LINCOLNSHIRE NATIVES AND OTHERS

Volume III in the LINCOLNSHIRE PEOPLE series

**Compiled by
John R. Ketteringham
MBE, PhD**

***

Dedicated to all those who have contributed
to the heritage of 'the Forgotten County'.

***

Here's Volume Three about those who appear
At some time in their lives in fair Lincolnshire.
St. Botolph came first, to give Boston a name.
And Guthlac, a hermit, brought Crowland its fame.
There are Churchmen in plenty, some high and some low,
And Thomas de Aston, Archdeacon of Stow.
Poets and Painters and Authors abound,
And Pick, who built railways under the ground.
Aeronaut, Astronaut, Actors galore,
Astronomer, Air Marshal and many more.
Henry Law James, good at ringing a bell,
And Pitman the shorthand inventor as well.
An Anarchist, poor at obeying the rule,
And Sutton the founder of Charterhouse School.
Headmaster, good at using his cranium,
And Folkard who bred a hardy geranium.
Designers, broadcasters, woodcarver and nurse;
I think it is time to give pause to this verse.
With so many people to view in the book,
No doubt you are keen to start having a look.

Jill Rundle

Published by John R. Ketteringham
2002

First published in 2002 by the author.

Copyright : John R. Ketteringham 2002.

All rights reserved. No part of this book may be reproduced in any form without prior permission in writing from the publisher.

Typeset by John R. Ketteringham and printed by Elpeeko Ltd., Lincoln.

ISBN 0 9512738 7 6

British Library Cataloguing in Publication Data.
A catalogue record for this book is available from the British Library.

Books by John R. Ketteringham

The Church That Moved (1983)

Lincoln Cathedral : A History of the Bells, Bellringers and Bellringing
(First published 1987; Second Edition 2000)

A Lincolnshire Hotchpotch (1989)

A Second Lincolnshire Hotchpotch (1990)

Lincolnshire People (1995)

James Arundel of Locksley Hall, North Somercotes (1995)

A Cathedral Miscellany (1997)

Lincolnshire Women (1998)

A Third Lincolnshire Hotchpotch (1999)

Lincolnshire Bells and Bellfounders (2000)

Participants in the Lincolnshire Rising of 1536 and some inscriptions on Lincolnshire Church Bells as Sources for Genealogists (2001)

CONTENTS

Photographs and engravings		vi
Drawings by David Freeman		viii
Foreword by Lt Col. John Dymoke		ix
Preface and Acknowledgements		x
Index		165

ALDERTON, John	(1940 -)	Actor	1
ALLWOOD, Montagu	(1879 - 1958)	Nurseryman.	2
ANDERSON, Edmund	(1530 - 1605)	Lord Chief Justice	3
ANGELL, Norman	(1872 - 1967)	Winner of Nobel Peace Prize	4
ARUNDEL, James	(1875 - 1947)	Lighthouse builder and artist	5
ASTON, Thomas de	(c1325 - 1401)	Archdeacon of Stow	6
BAKER F. T.	(1911 - 1998)	Archaeologist and Local Historian	7
BARLEY, Maurice W.	(1909 - 1991)	Professor of Archaeology and History	9
BOHEME, George	(1628 - 1711)	Commonwealth Vicar of Sleaford	11
BOOTH, Webster	(1902 - 1984)	Singer	12
BOTOLPH	(7th cent)	Saint	13
BRADLEY, Edward	(1827 - 1889)	Author 'Cuthbert Bede'	13
BRANDON, Charles	(c1484 - 1545)	Duke of Suffolk	15
BROADBENT, Jim	(1949 -)	Actor	17
BROWN, Joe	(1945 -)	Singer	19
BROWN, Peter	(1945 -)	Journalist	21
CALEB, Theophilus	(1878 - 1959)	Indian vicar of Huttoft	22
CARNLEY, Sidney B.	(1861 - 1947)	Solicitor	24
CLAYTON, Nathaniel	(1811 - 1890)	Industrialist	25
COLEMAN, Ernest	(1943 -)	Arctic explorer	26
COLLIER, Brett	(1920 -)	Rambler	29
COTTON, John	(1585 - 1652)	Puritan minister	32
DADLEY, William	(died 1839)	Murdered by poachers	33
DAVIDSON, Harold F.	(1875 - 1937)	Eccentric clergyman	35
DEXTER, Colin	(1930 -)	Author	36
DICKINSON, Margaret	(1942 -)	Novelist	37
DOBSON, Fred	(1913 - 1993)	Dialect expert	39
DREWRY, Arthur	(1891 - 1961)	President, International Football Federation	40
DYER, H.J.H.	(1902 - 1993)	Grammar School Headmaster	41

EDWARDES, George	(1855 - 1915)	Theatre owner and manager	44
ELSEY, William E.	(1855 - 1922)	Race horse trainer	44
EUSDEN, Laurence	(1688 - 1730)	Poet laureate and clergyman	45
FAIERS, Roy	(1927 -)	Founder and editor of *Lincolnshire Life*	46
FLOWERS, Field	(1830 - 1843)	Schoolboy	49
FOALE, C. Michael	(1957 -)	Astronaut	50
FOLKARD, Oliver G.	(1941 -)	Clergyman and plant breeder	51
FORDYCE, Keith	(1928 -)	Broadcaster	52
FRINTON, Freddie	(1925 - 1968)	Actor	54
GALITZINE, Yuri	(1919 -)	Russian prince	55
GLEW, Montague F.	(1893 - 1969)	Aviator	57
GODFREY, Robert	(1876 - 1953)	Clerk of Works at Lincoln Cathedral	59
GOOD, Jabez	(1831 - 1911)	Woodcarver	60
GOODRICH, Philip H. E.	(1929 - 2001)	Bishop	61
GOULDING, Richard W.	(1868 - 1929)	Librarian, Naturalist and Antiquary	63
GUTHLAC	(died 714)	Saint	64
HADFIELD, Geoffrey	(1904 – 2001)	Seaborne Observer and Local Historian	65
HAMMOND, Richard	(1829 - 1901)	Inventor	66
HASSALL, John	(1868 - 1948)	Artist	67
HAWKE, Martin B.	(1860 - 1938)	Cricketer	68
HEATH, Winifred	(1892 - 1988)	Missionary, nurse and naturalist	69
HENSHAW, Alexander A.	(1912 -)	Test pilot	70
HOLLES, Gervase	(1606 - 1674)	Historian	72
HOOLEY, Ernest Terah	(1859 - 1947)	Speculator	73
HUDSON, Charles	(died 1865)	Clergyman and mountaineer	76
HURT, John	(1940 -)	Actor	77
HUSSEY, John	(1466 - 1537)	Lord Lieutenant	80
JACKLIN, Tony	(1944 -)	Golfer	81
JAMES, G. W.	(1858 - 1923)	Travel writer	82
JAMES, Henry Law	(1868 - 1932)	Clergyman and bellringer	83
JENNINGS, Elizabeth	(1926 – 2001)	Poet	86
JOHNSON, Maurice	(1688 - 1755)	Antiquarian	88
JOLLAND, Wolley	(1745 - 1831)	Eccentric Vicar of Louth	89
KERRIGAN, Jonathan	(1972 -)	Actor	90
KNOLLYS, Hansard	(1598 - 1691)	Baptist minister	93

LAWRENCE, Thomas E.	(1888 - 1935)	'Lawrence of Arabia'	94
LEACH, Terence R.	(1937 - 1994)	Local Historian	96
LEE, Austin	(1905 - 1965)	Clergyman and author	98
LUCAN, Arthur	(1887 - 1954)	Actor	99
LUNN, Henry S.	(1859 - 1934)	Holiday travel pioneer and preacher	101
MACKINDER, Halford J.	(1861 - 1947)	Geographer	103
MACKWORTH, John	(Died 1451)	Dean of Lincoln	104
MAGEE, John G.	(1922 - 1941)	Airman poet	106
MALONEY, Michael	(1950 -)	Newspaper photographer	107
MARSHALL, Philip	(1921 -)	Cathedral organist and choirmaster	110
MAYS, Raymond	(1899 - 1980)	Motor racing driver	112
MERRYWEATHER, John	(1768 - 1861)	Governor of Lincoln Prison	114
MITCHELL, Austin V.	(1934 -)	MP, broadcaster and author	115
MONOLULU. Ras, Prince	(c1880 - 1964)	Racing tipster	117
MOSSMAN, Thomas W.	(1826 - 1885)	Clergyman	119
NOTTINGHAM, Max	(1933 -)	Serial letter writer and broadcaster	120
PADLEY, James S.	(1792 - 1881)	Cartographer and surveyor	121
PAGE, Russell	(1906 - 1985)	Garden designer	123
PARSONS, Nicholas	(1928 -)	Broadcaster, actor and comedian	125
PICK, Frank	(1878 - 1941)	Underground railway pioneer	127
PITMAN, Isaac	(1813 - 1897)	Inventor of shorthand system	128
POUCHER, William A.	(1891 - 1988)	Chemist, walker and photographer	129
PRYME, Abraham de la	(1672 - 1704)	Clergyman and antiquarian	131
ROBERTS, Nesta	(1913 -)	Journalist and travel writer	131
SHEPPEY, John	(died 1411)	Dean of Lincoln	133
SMART, Hawley	(1833 - 1893)	Author	134
SMITH, A. E. (Ted)	(1920 -)	Naturalist	137
SMITH, Edith	(Died c.1920)	Pioneer Policewoman	135
STOCKDALE, Freddie	(1947 -)	Opera company manager	139
SULLY, Thomas	(1783 - 1872)	Portrait painter	140
SUTTON, John D.	(1932 -)	Airman and Governor of Jersey	141
SUTTON, Thomas	(1532 - 1611)	Founder of Charterhouse School	143
TAUPIN, Bernie	(1950 -)	Song writer	144
THISTLEWOOD, Arthur	(1770 - 1820)	Anarchist	148
THOMPSON, Pishey	(1785 - 1862)	Historian	149
THOROLD, Henry	(1921 - 2000)	Schoolmaster, clergyman and antiquary	150
TIPPETT, Michael	(1905 - 1998)	Composer	152

TODD, Richard	(1919 -)	Actor	153
VERMUYDEN, Cornelius	(1595 - 1683)	Drainage engineer	156
WAKEFORD, John	(1859 - 1930)	Archdeacon of Stow	157
WAND, John W. C.	(1885 - 1977)	Bishop	158
WARRENER, William	(1861 - 1934)	Artist	159
WHITTLE, Frank	(1907 - 1996)	Inventor of jet engine	160
WORTH, Charles F.	(1825 - 1996)	Fashion designer	161
WYMARK, Patrick	(1926 - 1970)	Actor	162
YORKE, James	(17th cent.)	Blacksmith and author	163

ILLUSTRATIONS

PHOTOGRAPHS and ENGRAVINGS

Where the subject of the photograph is not the copyright holder I have recorded the name of the person or organisation who gave permission for the illustration to be used in the second column in the list below.

Allwood, Montague, Edward and George	Allwood Bros	2
Allwoodii Pinks	Allwood Bros Front Cover	
Arundel, James	Maple Bedford	5
Baker, Tom	*Hull Daily Mail*	9
Brandon, Charles Duke of Suffolk	*	16
Broadbent, Jim	Patrick Markham	Front Cover
Broadbent, Jim	-	18
Brown, Joe	John Middleton	20
Brown, Peter	-	21
Caleb Revd and Family	Revd Canon M. Wright	23
Coleman, Ernest	*Lincolnshire Life*	26
Collier, Brett	-	Back Cover; 29
Dadley, William	Geoffrey Hadfield	34
Dexter, Colin	-	Back Cover
Dickinson, Margaret	-	Front Cover
Dobson, Fred	*Lincolnshire Life*	39
Dyer, H. J. H.	Queen Elizabeth's Grammar School, Alford	41, 42
Dymoke, Lt Col John	-	ix

Faiers, Dorothy and Roy	-	47
Flowers, Field (Headstone)	Jennifer Ward	49
Foale, Michael	-	Back Cover
Fordyce, Keith	-	52
Frinton, Freddie	Roy Faeirs	54
Galitzine, Prince Yuri	-	Back Cover
Geranium 'Anne Folkard'	John R. Ketteringham	Back Cover
Godfrey, Robert	*Lincolnshire Echo*	59
Goodrich, Bishop Philip	David Bagley	63
Hadfield, Geoffrey	-	65
Hawke, Lord	*Vanity Fair*	68
Heath, Nurse W.	Lincolnshire Naturalists Trust	69
Henshaw, Alex	-	71
Hooley, Ernest Terah	*Hooley's Confessions*	73
Hudson, Revd Charles	*Lincolnshire Life*	76
Hurt, John	John Hurt, John Middleton	79
Hurt, John	University of Derby	Front Cover
James, Revd Henry Law	Author's Collection	83
Jolly Fisherman [John Hassall]	Skegness Town Council	Front Cover
Kerrigan, Jonathan	BBC	Front Cover
Kerrigan, Jonathan	BBC, Ralph Hodgson, Jonathan Kerrigan	91, 92
Ketteringham, John R.	*Lincolnshire Echo*	x
Knollys, Hansard	Muriel James	93
Leach, Terence	*Lincolnshire Echo*	96
Lucan and McShane	Steve King	99
Magee, John Gillespie	*This England*	107
Maloney, Mike	-	109
Marshall, Dr Philip	-	110
Mays, Raymond	Bourne Civic Society	112, 113
Mitchell, Austin	-	115
Monolulu, Prince Ras	W. H. Fry	117
Nottingham, Max	-	Back Cover
Parsons, Nicholas	-	126
Parsons, Nicholas	-	Front Cover
Poucher, W. A.	Roy Faiers	130

Smith, Edith	-	135
Smith, A. E. (Ted)	-	137
Stockdale, Freddie	-	139
Sutton, Sir John	-	142, 143
Taupin, Bernie	*Boston Standard,* Tony Taupin	146
Todd, Richard	Richard Todd	155
Wymark, Patrick	Roy Faiers	162
Yorke, James	Lincoln Cathedral Library	164

* Trustees of the Grimsthorpe and Drummond Castle Trust Ltd. Photograph:Photographic Survey, Coutauld Institute of Art

Copyright Lincolnshire County Council Heritage Services, Grantham Museum.

DRAWINGS
by David Freeman, FRSA

Carnley, Sidney Bazelgette	24
Holles, Gervase	72
Johnson, Maurice	88
Lawrence, T. E.	95
Lee, Revd Austin	98
Lunn, Sir Henry	102
Padley, James S.	122
Thorold, Revd Henry	150
Wakeford, Archdeacon John	157
Whittle, Sir Frank	160
Worth, Charles	161

The drawing of 'Cuthbert Bede' which appears on page 13 has been taken from *The Adventures of Mr Verdant Green* which was first published in 1853 – 1857.

FOREWORD
by Lt Col John Dymoke
The Honourable the Queen's Champion and former Vice Lord Lieutenant of Lincolnshire

I first met Dr John Ketteringham some years ago when he appeared with two stalwarts to look at various bells at Scrivelsby. He then produced a learned account of Lincolnshire Bells, most of which are in churches.

You may say that church bells and people go well together. For now it is my pleasure to write the Foreword to the third volume of Lincolnshire People. The number connected with Lincolnshire recorded in the three volumes totals about 270. That's some number for a county so sparsely populated! They come as Saints and Sinners, Women and Men, and even a few walking the Earth today. Several of the latter I have met, and as to the former? Well, I may meet some of them in the life hereafter, if I behave myself. And from what I have read in these excellent mini biographies I would be delighted to do so.

John Ketteringham's compilation, besides being a ready reference, so easily readable and enticing, is worthy of sincere congratulations. And there is no better introduction than Jill Rundle's poem. I hope that you, like me, will enjoy the third volume.

John Dymoke

PREFACE and ACKNOWLEDGEMENTS

This is the third and final book in the *Lincolnshire People* series. As with the other two books, *Lincolnshire People* and *Lincolnshire Women*, this book contains short biographies of people who have made their mark on the history of the county. Some were born here, others have made their home here and others have unexpected connections with Lincolnshire. The book records the story of the famous and not so famous of England's second largest county. There are actors, authors, clergymen, missionaries, saints and sinners. There are artists, gardeners, politicians and even a Russian Prince and a Governor of Jersey. Indeed just about every occupation and profession has been represented in this series.

A total of around 270 people have been profiled in the three books and in the index to this book I have cross-referenced those who were included in the first two books.

A greater proportion of those featured in this book are living people and I am grateful to them for sparing time to assist me in preparing their biographies.

I acknowledge with gratitude the assistance of David Freeman who made drawings of several of those featured herein and also to those who provided photographs.

Dr Dennis Mills, Peter Sharp, Richard Thornton and Chris Medley together with my wife, Joan, read the whole of the manuscript at various stages and Neville Birch also assisted with specific subjects. I am grateful to Dr Simon Pawley for contributing the article on Lord Hussey and to Professor John Beckett for the article on Professor Maurice Barley.

Finally, I thank most sincerely Lt Col John Dymoke for his foreword and Jill Rundle for contributing the marvellous and most original poetic introduction.

May, 2002

John ALDERTON

John Alderton will always be remembered for his rôle as teacher Bernard Hedges in the 1968 television series *Please Sir* and for the same rôle in the 1971 film with the same title.

Although John's parents lived in Hull he was actually born on 27 November 1940 in Lincolnshire. During the Second World War part of Gate Burton Hall near Gainsborough was used as a Maternity Hospital. Expectant mothers were evacuated from Hull, to escape the heavy bombing which that city had to endure, and they were billeted in St John's Church Vicarage in Ashcroft Road, Gainsborough before the birth and then moved to the Hall.

John is the youngest of three children and his parents owned a fish and chip shop in Essex Street, Hull, but later moved to an off licence and general store in Hessle Road. The shop was the centre of the local community and John to a great extent owes his self-confidence to the time he spent serving customers in the family shop. He attended Kingston Grammar School which had a very strong drama department and had already produced the actor Tom Courtney and playwright Alan Plater. John had decided on a career as an architect but when he was 'persuaded' to appear in a school production of *Viceroy Sarah* he found he enjoyed being in front of an audience and he has never suffered from nerves. With a school friend he applied for an audition with the Royal Academy of Dramatic Art and as they say 'the rest is history'.

Since John's first appearance in the television series *Emergency Ward 10* in 1957 he has appeared in around twenty television series and plays and has starred in thirteen films. He has made guest appearances in the television series *Tales of the Unexpected* (1980 and 1988), *Heartbeat* (1998) and *Peak Practice* (1999). I recently visited Woodhall Spa with the Betjeman Society and, at the Kinema in the Wood, we were shown the film *Late Flowering Love* which is a compilation of four of Sir John's poems with Betjeman himself as narrator. John Alderton took the part of Miss J. Hunter Dunne's admirer in *A Subaltern's Love Song* and he was the paratrooper in *Invasion Exercise on the Poultry Farm*. An interesting experience.

In 1969 John married the actress Pauline Collins and they have two sons and a daughter. Daughter Kate is an actress with appearances in several television series. John and Pauline have played husband and wife in several television series including *Upstairs, Downstairs* (1971), *Wodehouse Playhouse* (1975), *No Honestly* (1975), *Thomas and Sarah* (1979) and *Forever Green* (1989). They have also made several films together including *Unpleasantness at Bludleigh Court* (1976), *Rodney Fails to Qualify* (1976) and *The Rise of Minna Bordstrom* (1976).

For a number of years Pauline and John have supported the work of Oxfam and they were recently invited to tour Cambodia to see at first hand the impact which landmines have had on a nation struggling to rebuild itself. John commented that it is the women and children who are the victims because they have to gather firewood or tend the cattle. They visited the Cambodian Trust Hospital and saw at first hand the terrible injuries that these people suffer.

Montagu ALLWOOD

Montague, Edward and George Allwood at Chelsea Flower Show

Montagu William Charles Allwood was the sixth child of Robert and Emily Allwood and was born in 1879 at Grange Farm, Ludford Magna. His father was a farmer and Montagu developed an interest in gardening from an early age. The youngster was introduced to the carnation by a cousin who lived at Croxby and her enthusiasm for the plant was passed on to Montagu. The dianthus family became his obsession in later life. After his early education in the village he went as a boarder to Lincoln School (now Lincoln Christ's Hospital School) and came under the influence of the headmaster at that time, Canon Fowler. The headmaster, who was something of a horticulturist himself, told young Montagu that gardening would be a pleasant, though not a highly remunerative, occupation. In a book of reminiscences Allwood records that his interest in gardening was encouraged by the school gardener, a man called Vickers. Vickers was a kindly, old, jobbing gardener, 'wide in that lore which close contact with Nature so often brings'. He appreciated the full dignity of his calling, and sparked the boy's ambition to 'make a go' of commercial gardening.

Allwood left school in 1896 and went to work on the nursery of Messrs. Illman at Lincoln where he received a good grounding in all aspects of the nurseryman's craft. After two years he left to work at Myatt's Horticultural Company at Swanley, Kent and other nurseries before taking the post of carnation grower and breeder with the firm of Hugh Low and Co., (later Stuart Low and Co.) in Kent. His brother Edward was working with a seed merchant in London and the two were able to meet regularly and discussed the possibility of founding their own nursery.

In 1910 with his two brothers, Edward and George, it was decided to found the firm of Allwood Bros. at Wivelsfield Green, Sussex. Edward brought to the firm his experience with the seed trade and George was a skilled grower who had worked in America and brought with him a large collection of carnation plants from that country.

The firm's first success was with the Carnation 'Mary Allwood' which received an 'Award of Merit' in 1912. Soon after the Allwoodii strain of dianthus was introduced and this laid the foundation for the great success of Allwood Bros. Montagu modestly described Dianthus Allwoodii as 'the world's most glorious flower'. Some of these varieties of Dianthus are illustrated on the front cover of this book.

Montagu was elected a Fellow of the Linnæan Society in 1922 and in 1949 the Royal Horticultural Society conferred on him its highest honour, the Victorian Medal of Honour. He was a member of the Society's Joint Border Carnation and Picotee Committee, Joint Perpetual-flowering Carnation Committee and Joint Dianthus Committee and vice-president of the British National Carnation Society. Montagu published *The Perpetual Flowering Carnation* in 1907, *Carnations, Pinks and Dianthus* in 1926, *Carnations for every Garden and Greenhouse* also in 1926, *Carnations for Everyone* in 1931, as well as numerous articles in the gardening Magazines and Journals. In 1940 he published his two-volume autobiography *The Third and Fourth Generations*.

Edward Allwood was not involved in the day-today running of the firm and when he died in 1956 he was actually farming in Lincolnshire. He did, however, take an active part in the staging of the firm's exhibits at Chelsea Flower show. Montagu died on 28 July 1958 and the firm continued for a time under the chairmanship of George with his son Robert. The firm remained under the control of the Allwood family until the late 1960s and, when George and Robert retired, members of the staff ran the firm. Eventually the Selsby brothers who had joined the firm in 1946 took over. Although now retired, they still take an active interest in the firm which continues to grow a wide range of the varieties developed by Montagu. The well-known signature 'Allwood Bros' which guaranteed every packet of seeds is now the logo of the firm and the name is a registered trademark.

Edmund ANDERSON

Edmund Anderson was descended from a Scottish family which had settled in Northumberland but migrated to Flixborough, Lincolnshire where he was born in 1530.

After graduating from Lincoln College, Oxford, Anderson entered the Inner Temple in June 1550. In 1567 he was appointed reader at his Inn of Court and in the Michaelmas Term of 1577 he became a Sergeant-at-Law. By 1581 he had become a judge conducting cases of importance and, in a case brought before him whilst on circuit in Norfolk, he expressed his intention of upholding the established church against Puritanism. His prosecution of Roman Catholics earned him a knighthood in 1582 and he was appointed Lord Chief Justice of the Common Pleas in the same year.

Lord Chief Justice Anderson was noted for his harshness and impatience. He sat as presiding or assisting judge in a number of important trials including that of Mary Queen of Scots, and of Secretary Davison, for alleged rashness in proceeding with her execution. He also took part in the trials of the Earl of Arundel in 1589, the Earl of Essex in 1600 and in that of Sir Walter Raleigh in 1603.

Though usually firm in his support of regal authority, there were instances in which Lord Chief Justice Anderson opposed, with equal firmness. When Queen Elizabeth granted letters patent to Mr Cavendish, an agent of the Earl of Leicester, for making out writs in the Court of Common Pleas, the Lord Chief Justice and his colleagues refused to admit Cavendish to the office, on the grounds that the Queen had no right to grant such letters, and that compliance with them would be contrary to their oaths. The Queen found herself obliged to yield.

Sir Edmund was also one of the Judges who signed a remonstrance 'against the arbitrary proceedings of the court, by which, at the command of a counsellor or nobleman subjects were frequently committed to prison and detained without good cause, and contrary to the laws of the realm'. He remained in office under James I and until he died on 1 August 1605.

Although Sir Edmund was inclined to be harsh and impatient he was an able jurist and conscientious in his decisions. He married Magdalen, daughter of Christopher Smyth of Annables, Herts. and they had nine children. From him are descended the Earls of Yarborough.

His reports of cases judged in the Courts of Westminster in the latter end of the reign of Queen Elizabeth were published in 1644.

Norman ANGELL

Ralph Norman Angell-Lane was born on 26 December 1872. He was the son of Thomas Angell-Lane of the Mansion House, Holbeach. He later changed his name to Norman Angell by Deed Poll. After preparatory schooling he went on to the lycée in St Omer, France. At the age of fifteen, while attending classes at the University of Geneva, he edited a bi-weekly English paper. At the age of seventeen he went to America where he lived for seven years working as a cowboy and prospector. He also wrote for the *San Francisco Chronicle*, the *St. Louis Globe-Democrat* and other papers.

Angell returned to Europe in 1898 as correspondent for various American newspapers. He edited *Galignani's Messenger* from 1899-1903 and, in 1904, he was appointed editor of the *Continental Daily Mail* by the future Lord Northcliffe.

Norman Angell was elected Labour MP for North Bradford in 1928 and was a member of the Council of the Royal Institute of International Affairs from 1928 until 1942. In 1933 he was awarded the Nobel Peace Prize.

Angell was the inventor of the *Money Game*, which is a series of card games using paper money designed to teach the principles of elementary economics and in particular banking and currency. He published over forty books, mainly on politics. The best known, which has been translated into over 20 languages, being *The Great Illusion* which was published in 1910. A second edition, *The Great Illusion 1933*, explored the economic developments and ideas since the publication of the first edition. Angell particularly emphasised the economic futility of war even for the victors.

Norman Angel was knighted in 1931 and he died at Croydon on 7 October 1967.

James ARUNDEL

James Arundel was born in Bradford in 1875 and after leaving school joined the family firm which undertook contract work for the Service Departments and Trinity House. The firm also maintained lighthouses throughout the country and in 1908 built the remotely controlled lighthouse at Platte Forgete, Guernsey.

From an early age Arundel had artistic leanings and would often go up onto the Yorkshire Moors with his painting materials. Although Arundel had no artistic training, his work became highly regarded and in 1905 he was elected to the Bradford Arts Club. As well as exhibiting in his home town of Bradford, he exhibited in Batley, Hull, Leeds, Liverpool, London, Newcastle-on-Tyne, the Paris Salon, Rotherham, Salford and Wakefield.

In 1921 Arundel painted the *Stations of the Cross* for his friend, the Roman Catholic priest, Father O'Connor. O'Connor was the model for G. K. Chesterton's clerical detective 'Father Brown'. Other Bradford friends included a number of well-known artists and Bernard Fleetwood-Walker, who was a member of the selection committee of the Royal Academy, painted portraits of Arundel's family.

Arundel's painting *Canna* was hung by the Royal Academy at its summer exhibition in 1938. The catalogue of an exhibition of James Arundel's paintings mounted at the Cartwright Memorial Hall, Bradford in 1958 included a number of paintings with a Lincolnshire theme including *Torksey Lock, Grimsby Docks, Welton-le-Wold* and *Locksley Hall*. This exhibition was in connection with the conferring on him of the Freedom of Bradford.

James Arundel travelled widely and in 1912 he, together with his four oldest children, went to Canada. His wife, Violet, and the youngest three children followed in 1913. Maple was born in Canada and the family returned to England in 1916. Arundel's son, Joseph, remained in Canada as a Naval Cadet. The remainder of the family lived for a time in Bradford and Morecambe before moving to Saltfleet in 1918. In 1921 Arundel purchased the Old Hall in North Somercotes. He also had a house in Bradford where he and his wife lived from Monday to Friday. After Arundel purchased the Old Hall he reverted to the earlier name 'Locksley Hall'. From at least 1865 the house had been known as 'Locksley Hall Farm' and it seems possible that the farm had been renamed after Tennyson's poem of that name. Arundel built new rooms and passageways on to the original Georgian building. His use of genuine Tudor material has caused confusion in dating the building. Bricks and timber were purchased when the Old Mill House at North Somercotes was demolished and, when the bell frame from the parish church of Theddlethorpe St. Helen was replaced in 1925, Arundel purchased the timber which was used to make the doors in the small sitting room. Jacobean panelling was purchased from Penwortham Priory, near Preston, Lancashire. Furniture, paintings and ornaments were purchased from a wide area. However, the many panels of stained and painted glass which Arundel brought to the house are by far the most important of all his purchases.

After his retirement at the age of fifty, James Arundel spent much of his time travelling and painting. He would spend all day in his studio at Bradford or North Somercotes with a bottle of claret putting on canvas a wide variety of subjects including exotic fruits sent to him by Fortnum and Mason!

Each January he left with a party of friends to stay for several months in the south of France, Tuscany, the Dordogne, Jamaica and the Canary Islands. In 1938 he sailed from Swanage to the South Sea Islands accompanied by his great friend Marcus MacCausland who was a sculptor, doctor and retired naval captain. The crew of the twenty-five foot motor yacht *Satanella* was completed by two Cambridge graduates. Engine failure caused a delay whilst new parts were obtained and Arundel decided to join a Russian, Akim Kouprianoff, who was on a peace mission sailing round the world. The two sailed to Panama where Arundel decided to return home as war was imminent. The Russian sailed on but died of starvation off the Australian coast.

During the Second World War, Locksley Hall was used by the Coldstream Guards as an Officers' Mess and Mr and Mrs Arundel lived at their house in Bradford. When Locksley Hall was released by the Army the Arundels decided to remain in Bradford and sell their Lincolnshire home.

FURTHER READING : Ketteringham, J. R. *James Arundel and Locksley Hall, North Somercotes* (1995)

Thomas de ASTON

Thomas Coterel was born in Staffordshire *circa* 1325. He appears to have used the surname de Aston from *circa* 1354. The reason for this change is unclear, but it may have been because the Coterells were notorious outlaws throughout Staffordshire. Thomas's relative, William Wilde who was a prosperous yeoman, lived at Wheaton Aston and Thomas probably thought that this would help to achieve respectability, especially as he was following a career in the church. Of course, it could well be that Wheaton Aston was his place of birth.

Thomas de Aston is known to have studied at Oxford University. He was still at Oxford in 1363 and he may well have been a fellow. By 1370 de Aston was at Cambridge and was a Bachelor of Common Law.

From his will it can be deduced that de Aston had an extensive library and this suggests that he was of a scholarly disposition. He devoted his early life to the study of medicine and, amongst other things, became physician to Edward III's wife, Queen Philippa. He was ordained in the 1340s and had been presented to the Vicarage of Lapley, Staffordshire, the Rectory of St James, Garlickhythe, London and then the Rectory of Warboys, Huntingdonshire. About 1366 he had been installed to the prebend of Norton in the Diocese of Durham and in 1367 to a prebend in the Diocese of Wells. In 1374 he was installed to a prebend in the Diocese of St Paul's, London and finally in 1382 to a prebend in Lincoln Cathedral.

De Aston's elevation to the Archdeaconry of Stow in 1386 meant that he had a permanent base in Lincoln. He most likely witnessed the installation of Henry Bolingbroke (Henry IV) to the confraternity of Lincoln Cathedral in 1386 and Richard II in 1387. He may have also witnessed the marriage of John of Gaunt to Katherine Swynford in 1396.

Thomas de Aston is particularly remembered in Lincolnshire for his refoundation of the Hospital of Spital-in-the-Street, which is twelve miles north of Lincoln. This provided a chantry and almshouses for seven needy people. Richard II made this possible by the grant in 1395 of the land at Spital. The foundation charter was dated 26 June 1397 and the chantry was dedicated 'in honour of the holy and undivided Trinity, of the blessed Mary the Glorious Virgin and of Saint Edmund King and Martyr'. When the De Aston School at Market Rasen was built in 1858 some of the endowments of Spital Chantry were used to help defray the cost.

Thomas de Aston died on 7 June 1401 and was buried in the nave of Lincoln Cathedral. His monument was destroyed at the Reformation

The chantry chapel at Spital in the Street is now maintained by the Spital Chantry Trust of St Edmund and can be visited by arrangement.

FURTHER READING : Bennett, N. and Marcombe, D. *Thomas de Aston and the Diocese of Lincoln* (1998)

Tom BAKER

Frederick Thomas Baker was born at Elm House, Upper Long Leys Road, Lincoln in 1911 and was the son of an architect. It is to this early background that he attributed his life-long interest in architecture and historic buildings. It is perhaps appropriate that his birthplace is now part of the Museum of Lincolnshire Life. Tom was educated at St John's Preparatory School, Newport and at the City School. It was his intention to become a teacher of natural sciences but instead he was successful in obtaining the first junior museum appointment to be made in Lincoln. He soon became interested in every aspect of this work and he continued his studies at Nottingham University by extra-mural visits under the supervision of Professor H. H. Swinnerton which led to an MA in archaeology. Tom also took the Museums Diploma and qualified for Fellowship of the Museums Association. In 1946 he was elected to a Fellowship of the Society of Antiquaries of London and for a time served on its Council.

During the war, Tom was seconded to the staff of the Midland Agricultural College under the Ministry of Agriculture and among other jobs his specialist knowledge led him to do research on the wood mouse that was ruining wheat crops in the East Midlands. Other research in which Tom was involved at this time was into the control of pests which included wireworm, mangold fly, leather jacket, carrot fly and aphid.

After the war and while he was Deputy Director of the City Libraries, Museum and Art Gallery, Tom Baker read for a further Master of Arts degree at Nottingham University. His thesis, which was submitted in 1954, was on 'The pre-historic settlement of Lincolnshire'.

In 1945 Tom helped to found the Lincoln Archaeological Research Committee and he was its first secretary. Amongst the highlights of the excavations which took place under Tom's supervision were the military defences of the City, the Roman aqueduct, the East Gate of the *colonia* and the first Christian church on the site of St Paul in the Bail. The enamelled ceremonial bowl which was discovered on this site is now in Lincoln Cathedral Treasury. Tom was also a founder member and chairman of the Lincolnshire Local History Society and of the Lincolnshire Historic Buildings Joint Committee. Tom represented Lincolnshire on the Council for British Archaeology and in 1961 he was appointed Director of the City Libraries, Museum and Art Gallery, a post which he held until his retirement in 1974.

When the Lincolnshire Trust for Nature Conservation was founded in 1948, Tom became its first Hon. Treasurer and continued in that office until 1959. He remained a member of the Council of that body until 1989. He was Hon. Assistant Secretary of the Lincolnshire Naturalists' Union from 1930 until 1932 becoming Secretary in 1933 and remained in that office until 1960. He also edited the *Transactions* for that organisation from 1934 until 1966 and was President for the year 1961-62. Tom was Patron during the Union's centenary year 1993-94.

During this period his responsibility for the Usher Gallery gave rise to many notable exhibitions. These attracted to the Gallery a considerable number of distinguished artists who thus made their first acquaintance with the historic city. Tom was later appointed a member of the Heslam Trust that awarded grants for the purchase of pictures for the Gallery.

In 1972 his work for history and archaeology in Lincolnshire was recognised by the award of an OBE. Although Tom always said that he had been an administrator for most of his career this is not entirely true. In 1937 he published the first book on *Roman Lincoln* and later, along with Sir Ian Richmond, he assisted Ben Whitwell in the preparation of *Roman Lincolnshire* which was the first volume in a series published by the History of Lincolnshire Committee of the Society for Lincolnshire History and Archaeology. In 1970, Tom was responsible for the revision of Arthur Mee's *Lincolnshire* in the King's England series.

After retirement Tom was elected Vice-Chairman of the Lincoln Archaeological Trust and Chairman and later President of the Lincoln Civic Trust. He was chairman of the Lincolnshire and South Humberside Historic Buildings Joint Committee which is responsible for monitoring any plans which involve alterations to historic buildings throughout the historic county of Lincolnshire. Tom also served as chairman of the Tennyson Society in succession to Lord Ancaster and was deeply involved in the Queen's Jubilee Project 1977-80. He supervised the establishment of the Tennyson Research Centre which is now known world-wide by Tennyson scholars.

Amongst projects of the Lincoln Civic Trust in which he was actively involved was the restoration of Dernstall House, Ellis' Mill and St Mary's Guildhall which is now the Trust's headquarters. In 1995 it was a great joy to him to see Ellis' Mill transferred to the Lincolnshire County Council and attached permanently to the Museum of Lincolnshire Life. The Mill is one of Lincolnshire's most exciting working restorations and a City landmark, which is floodlit at night.

Natural history, archaeology and local history have always been Tom's hobbies as well as his work and everyone with an interest in the heritage of the City owes much to Tom. His work led to the preservation of many buildings which could well have disappeared.

Tom Baker died on 24 January 1998.

Maurice BARLEY

Maurice Willmore Barley, archaeologist and historian, was born in Lincoln in August 1909. His parents, Levi Barley and Alice Willmore, met at the Wesleyan Chapel in Bailgate, and they spent the whole of their married life at the family home, 52 Lindum Avenue, Lincoln. Maurice's father worked at Ruston's Engineering Works in Lincoln

In 1921 Maurice won a scholarship to Lincoln School and in 1928 he went up to Reading University. During vacations in Lincoln he struck up a lifelong friendship with Frank (Sir Francis) Hill from whom he imbibed his fascination with local history. After graduating,

Maurice was appointed Assistant Master at the Corporation Grammar School in Grimsby, a post he held until, in 1935, he was appointed extra-mural tutor in local history at the University of Hull.

Maurice never returned to Lincolnshire in a formal capacity. From 1935 until the Second World War he lived and worked in Hull. After war service in the Ministry of Information he was appointed organising tutor in Adult Education at Nottingham University. He held appointments at Nottingham in Adult Education (1946-62) and subsequently in the newly formed Archaeology Department (1962-74). He was appointed Professor of Archaeology in 1971.

During those years he was associated with a wide range of national institutions including the Royal Commission on Historical Monuments, the Council for British Archaeology (of which he was a founder member and subsequently Secretary and finally President), the Vernacular Architecture Group, and the York Archaeological Trust, of which he was chairman 1972-90. He was also a vice-president of the Society of Antiquaries (1966-70), having been elected to a fellowship in 1941. His training was in history; indeed, he was a self-taught archaeologist in an age when the amateur was a vital player in excavation and recording and there was no first degree course in the subject.

Despite living a busy and varied life, Barley never lost his love of Lincolnshire. When in 1946 he moved to North Muskham he thought of it as 'no more than twenty miles from my birthplace', and he was a frequent visitor to the county for professional, academic, and personal reasons for the rest of his life. In 1949 Barley teamed up with Philip Corder to begin a series of archaeological excavations of Roman Lincoln. The following year, he and F. T. (Tom) Baker brought together Lincolnshire and Nottinghamshire to form regional Group 14 of the Council for British Archaeology. In 1952 Barley completed a Nottingham MA dissertation on farmhouses and cottages in Lincolnshire and Nottinghamshire and published his first book, *Lincolnshire and the Fens*, an account of the county in a new series of landscape studies launched by Batsford. In subsequent years he took adult education classes in Sleaford, and promoted and led summer schools in Lincoln designed to study historic houses using probate inventories.

In the 1960s Maurice persuaded Nottingham University (largely through the good offices of Sir Francis Hill, by now President of the University Council) to purchase the site of the Roman town of Ancaster, where he led annual training schools until 1971. He also excavated at Great Casterton and Torksey (where he worked, among others, with Hilary Healey). During the 1970s Barley found time to mount a vigorous campaign against planning proposals which he feared would do irreparable damage to the historic heart of Lincoln.

In the later years of his retirement (1978-91) he was General Editor of the *History of Lincolnshire* series, and brought his critical faculties to bear on ensuring the production of high quality studies of the history of the county.

Maurice Barley was a kindly man with a deep love of his native county. From his teenage cycling years, through family holidays on the Lincolnshire coastline, to his later excavations, he retained an active interest in the county throughout his life. He maintained an array of friendships, many of them dating back to his childhood days, and Lincolnshire examples featured prominently in his published work on vernacular buildings.

Professor Maurice Barley died at his Chilwell home on 23 June 1991, leaving a widow, Diana (nee Morgan) and three children.

SOURCE : I am grateful to Professor John Beckett of Nottingham University for assistance with this article.

George BOHEME

George Boheme was born in 1628 in Colberg, Pomerania (now Kolbrzeg on the Polish Baltic coast). His uncle, Dr Johannes Bergius, who was born in Stettin on 24 February 1587 and died in Berlin on 27 December 1658, was chaplain to the Calvinist Elector of Brandenburg, Georg Wilhelm, who had succeeded his Calvinist father, Johann Sigismund, December 1619.

George's brother, Maurice, also born in Colberg, was rector of Hallaton, Leicestershire which is seven miles north-east of Market Harborough, and was ejected in 1662, after which he returned to Germany.

When George was born, central Europe was already in the throes of the Thirty Years War, and, in the summer of 1630, it is recorded that, in Colberg, the soldiers

> 'burnt five churches with all the barns and storehouses...and this as often for the fun of the bonfire as for any other purpose; they would let off their pistols for sport into the haystacks, and once they deliberately set fire to a quarter of the town...and came back...to plunder the people who were camping in the church'.

It is not known why or when George and Maurice Boheme came to England, but it must have been before 1647, when George was admitted sizar at Queen's College, Cambridge. On 14 March 1651 he was installed as vicar of Foxton, Leicestershire (three miles north-west of Market Harborough), and he was admitted to the living of Sleaford on 22 August 1655. He was ejected at the Restoration and succeeded by Henry Allen who was vicar from 1660 until 1682.

During his time at Sleaford, he signed the registers for the five years from 1656 to 1660 and three children were born to him and his wife, Ann. John was born on 16 January 1658 and buried on 8 November in the same year; Mary was baptised on 21 August 1659 and Samuel was baptised on 9 September 1660.

After his ejection in 1660 George Boheme lived at Walcot, which is seven miles south of Sleaford, where he taught and for some time preached in the village church. Even though Walcot was said 'not to have had a settled minister in it for sixty years' he was eventually forbidden by Bishop Gardiner of Lincoln to take part in services because he was not episcopally ordained. Among his pupils from 1674 to 1678 was Thomas Emlyn the first Unitarian minister in England.

Boheme's wife Ann was buried at Walcot on 20 December 1695 and George moved to live with his daughter at Folkingham in about 1704. He died there on 9 September 1711 at the age of 83 and was buried in the church near the west door.

SOURCE : Hoare, Douglas, 'George Boheme : A Commonwealth Vicar of Sleaford' in *SLHA Newsletter* No 60 April 1989 pp 28-29

Webster BOOTH

Leslie Webster Booth was born in Birmingham on 21 January 1902 and was a choirboy in Birmingham before entering Lincoln Cathedral Choir School in 1911. The organist at the Cathedral at that time was Dr George J. Bennett and one of Booth's fellow choristers was Reginald Goodall who was to become a great Wagnerian conductor (see *Lincolnshire People* page 43). It was this basic training at Lincoln which helped to make Webster Booth into such a wonderful singer and in later years he often expressed his appreciation of his time at Lincoln Cathedral as a chorister. At the age of fourteen he returned to Birmingham to work as an articled accountancy clerk, in his spare-time having his voice trained by Dr Richard Wassell.

Booth joined the D'Oyly Carte Company and, in 1924, made his debut with *The Yeoman of the Guard*. Because there was a number of established tenors in the company he had to be content with understudying the main tenor rôles. However, Booth's *Wand'ring Minstrel* and *Take a pair of sparkling eyes* with the Hallé Orchestra conducted by Leslie Howard, is arguably the finest Gilbert and Sullivan recording ever made. He left the company in 1928 and became a freelance singer. He took engagements with concert parties, often with Arthur Askey as a colleague.

In 1929 Webster Booth's first recordings appeared and he sang in *The Three Musketeers* at Drury Lane in 1930. After Malcolm Sargent heard him sing, Booth was engaged for a Royal Choral Society production of the *Messiah* and he was a soloist in Beethoven's *Ninth Symphony* at a Royal Philharmonic Society concert. A particularly memorable occasion was Booth's appearance in *Der Rosenkavalier* during the Covent Garden International Season of 1938. Booth's skill as a Strauss interpreter was also evident in his recordings of *Morgen* and *Allerseelen* both sung in English.

The deciding factor in his career was his second marriage to Anne Ziegler whom he met while they were filming *Faust* in 1938. They were ideally matched and they embarked on a career as duettists mainly in the field of light operetta and ballads. Their frequent broadcasts and recordings earned them great popularity throughout the war years and after. Alongside this, Booth's solos in Bach's *Mass in B Minor* and the first televised *Messiah* produced much favourable comment. A work which Booth made especially his own was Elgar's *Dream of Gerontius*, which he sang with the Royal Choral Society conducted by Malcolm Sargent at the last concert at Queen's Hall, London before it was destroyed by enemy action. It is unfortunate that Booth was never invited to record this work. Webster Booth did, however, record an extremely wide variety of music which was unmatched by any other British singer of his time.

By the mid-1950s there was less demand for their kind of music and in 1956 they emigrated to South Africa where they lived and worked for 22 years. They returned to Britain in 1978 and settled in North Wales, teaching and occasionally singing. Webster Booth died at Llandudno on 22 June 1984.

Peter Rushton of the Lincoln Old Choristers' Association says that 'Webster Booth was a fairly regular attender at the annual Reunions. He had great personal presence and charm, and always delighted us with his singing following the dinner held after evensong.'

Webster Booth and Anne Ziegler wrote a joint autobiography, *Duet*, which was published in 1951.

BOTOLPH

Saint Botolph was born in England *circa* 610. In his youth he became a monk in Gaul. By 654 he had returned to England and founded the monastery of Ikanhoe in East Anglia. This place became known as 'Botolphston' from either 'Botolph's stone' or Botolph's town' which was later contracted to 'Boston'. Having led many in the way of salvation and renowned for his sanctity and miracles, Saint Botolph died in *circa* 680. He was greatly revered by his Christian countrymen in antiquity and is commemorated by the name of two towns - the original Boston in Lincolnshire and its namesake in Massachusetts. The feast of St Botolph is celebrated on 17 June.

Edward BRADLEY

Edward Bradley was a hard-working and popular clergyman. He was vicar of Lenton-with-Hanby, Lincolnshire but he originated in Worcestershire and he was born on 25 March 1827 at Kidderminster. He was the second son of Thomas Bradley who was a surgeon. After education at Kidderminster Grammar School he went up to University College, Durham, in 1845. Bradley graduated BA in 1848 and was awarded a further degree in Theology in the following year. He was still too young to be ordained and appears to have studied at Oxford and worked in the clergy schools at Kidderminster before ordination by the Bishop of Ely in 1850 to the curacy of Glatton with Holme, Huntingdonshire.

In 1857 Bradley was appointed to his first parish as vicar of Bobbington in Staffordshire. In 1859 he became rector of Denton with Caldecote in Huntingdonshire where he stayed until 1871 when he moved to Stretton, Rutland. His final move came in 1883 when he was appointed vicar of Lenton where he remained until his death in 1889.

His claim to fame is as a writer of novels, verse and articles for a great many periodicals including *Punch*, *All the Year Round*, *Illustrated London News*, *The Field* and the *Boys Own Paper* amongst many others. He also appears to have earned a quite substantial income by lecturing on 'Modern Humorists' and 'Wit and Humour'. Bradley wrote under the name Cuthbert Bede which comes from the two ecclesiastics associated with Durham, St Cuthbert and the Venerable Bede. Bradley was clearly much influenced by his Durham experiences and named his eldest son Cuthbert.

Bradley's best-known book is *The Adventures of Verdant Green : An Oxford Undergraduate* which was first published in three instalments : *Adventures* (1853), *Further Adventures* (1854) and *Married and Done For* (1857). By 1870 the complete volume had sold 100,000 copies, but Bradley only received £350. In 1878 a sequel entitled *Mr Bouncer and His Friend Verdant Green* was published, but this was not so successful. Bradley illustrated his own novels.

He was friendly with John Moyer Heathcote who stood as a Liberal candidate for the Huntingdonshire constituency at the Parliamentary elections in 1857 and 1859. The successful candidate was Conservative James Rust and a letter which Bradley wrote to Heathcote on 30 August 1855 serves to illustrate his sense of humour :

'I was told last night that you were coming forward to contest the county against Mr Rust, whose name is suggestive of many epigrams, and I could not go to bed last night without stringing together one or two epigrammatic lines, which Rusty poetry is at your service but, if you should make it public, conceal the author's name.

His glittering arms he will commend to Rust (Richard II act iii, 3)

Like as Macbeth cut short Duncan's life,
So Mr Heathcote can cut short the strife;
For he's the sharp blade that in victory must
Cleave down the glade that is nothing but Rust.

A Word to the Wise.
If you're wise, your opinions to Heathcote you'll trust;
If you lack keenness, you'll then go to Rust

An Echo of Truth.

Whom, in this iron age should men distrust?
And Echo, loving sharpness, answers 'Rust'.

> Adieu, valour! Rust! (Love's Labour Lost, ii, 2)
>
> Brother Electors, to yourselves be just,
> And in this polish'd age, vote not for Rust.
>
> For he's the sharp blade that in victory must
> Cleave down the glade that is nothing but Rust'.

In 1858 Bradley married Harriet Amelia Hancocks and they had two sons Cuthbert and the Revd Henry Waldron Bradley. The Revd Edward Bradley died on 12 December 1889 and was buried at Stretton beside his wife.

Charles BRANDON

Charles Brandon was the son and heir of William Brandon, Henry VII's standard-bearer at the battle of Bosworth in 1485, who was killed by Richard III himself. It is uncertain when Charles Brandon was born but it was probably not many years before the battle of Bosworth. No mention of him has been found before the accession of Henry VIII with whom he appears to have been a favourite from the first. In many ways he resembled the king, being tall and sturdy, with rather a tendency to corpulence. In 1509, the first year of Henry VIII's reign, Brandon was appointed a squire of the royal body, and many other honours followed in quick succession culminating in his creation as Duke of Suffolk in 1514.

As a young man, during the reign of Henry VII, he made a contract of marriage with a certain Ann Brown; but before marrying her he obtained a dispensation and married a widow named Margaret Mortymer. Some time afterwards he separated from her, and obtained from a church court a declaration that the marriage was invalid. He then appears to have married Ann Brown, and had by her a daughter. The fate of Ann is not clear but about four weeks after Louis XII of France died on 1 January 1515, Brandon married the King's widow Mary, a sister of Henry VIII.

When Lord Willoughby de Eresby died in October 1526 the wardship of his daughter Catherine was granted to the duke. It was intended that Catherine should marry Henry, Brandon's second son, who had been created earl of Lincoln in June 1525 but Suffolk's wife Mary died in 1533 and he decided to marry Catherine himself. He thus brought under his control a considerable Lincolnshire estate and when the Lincolnshire Rising erupted in 1536 Suffolk had considerable power in the county. It is not surprising that the king sent him to deal with the revolt. He obeyed the king's instructions and quickly put down the Rising with the assistance of the Earl of Shrewsbury. However, the resulting executions did not entirely put an end to disquiet in Lincolnshire and in 1537 the king ordered Suffolk to move his main residence into the county.

Suffolk preferred to reside at Tattershall Castle which was given to him by the king in April 1537 but he also had residences at Eresby and Grimsthorpe. Although he spent considerable time in the county he remained throughout his life a confidant of the king and undertook many important missions on his behalf.

Charles Brandon, Duke of Suffolk

On 24 August 1545 he died at Guildford and some measure of the regard which he had for Lincolnshire is demonstrated by the request which he made in his will to be buried at Tattershall. However, the king caused him to be buried at Windsor at his own charge.

FURTHER READING : Gunn, S. J. *Charles Brandon Duke of Suffolk 1484-1545* (1988)

Jim BROADBENT

Early in the Second World War (1939-1945) around forty pacifists who were registered as Conscientious Objectors joined the agricultural community established in Holton-cum-Beckering near Market Rasen. They came from all corners of the country and from very varied backgrounds. The Community formed a Drama Group and eventually they were joined by friends from the village and became known as the Holton Players. After the war the group continued and performances were staged in a large room at Holton Hall and later in a Nissen hut on the former RAF Station at Wickenby. When the hut was burned down in 1960 the Players returned to Holton Hall until, in 1970 the redundant chapel at Wickenby was purchased and the name was changed to the Lindsey Rural Players. Roy Broadbent and Douglas Ballard did most of the work of converting the chapel for use as a theatre. Roy died shortly before the new theatre was completed and it was decided to name it the Broadbent Theatre.

James Broadbent was born at Glebe Farm, Holton on 24 May 1949 and he is the youngest of Dee and Roy Broadbent's three children. Jim's parents were both enthusiastic actors. His mother was a sculptor and his father a self-employed furniture designer. After primary school at Legsby near Market Rasen, Jim went to the Dolphin Preparatory School, Newark, before public school at Leighton Park, Reading. He then studied at Hammersmith College of Art before being accepted by the London Academy of Music and Dramatic Arts.

Jim first appeared on the stage at the age of five in a production of *A Doll's House*. At Leighton Park he appeared in every school play. His professional career began as Acting Assistant Stage Manager at the Regent's Park Open Air Theatre and he then went on to 'rep' at various locations including York, Stoke and Ipswich. In 1976 he joined the Science Fiction Theatre of Liverpool. and appeared in Ken Campbell's *Iluminatus!* This was a twelve-hour science fiction extravaganza in which Jim played twelve characters! This was followed by the twenty-four hour play *The Warp*.

In 1983 Jim joined the National Theatre of Brent and appeared in *The Messiah*. In 1984 he appeared in, and was joint writer, of The *Complete Guide to Sex*. He was also joint writer of *The Greatest Story Ever Told,* in which he appeared in 1987. He has appeared in numerous productions with the Hampstead Theatre, National Theatre, Royal Court and the Royal Shakespeare Company.

Jim's first film was in 1981 when he appeared in the *Time Bandits* and he has to date appeared in a total of some nineteen films. At the Venice Film Festival in 1999, he received the Volpi Cup for Best Actor for his portrayal of W. S. Gilbert in *Topsy-Turvy*. This same film also

Some of Jim Broadbent's film rôles

Top left : Warner Purcell in *Bullets over Broadway* (1994)
Top right : Mr Boo with Michael Caine in *Little Venice* (1998)
Bottom left : W. S. Gilbert in *Topsy Turvy* (1999)
Bottom right : John Bayley, Iris Murdoch's husband, in *Iris* (2001)

brought him the *London Evening Standard* Award for Best Actor and the London Film Critic's Award for British Actor of the Year. He also received nominations from BAFTA, the Chicago Film Critics Association Awards and British Independent Film Awards. He was nominated by the Screen Actor's Guild Awards for an outstanding performance in *Little Voice* and, in February 2002, he received the British Academy of Film and Television award for Best Supporting Actor for his part as Harold Ziglar in *Moulin Rouge*. In Jim's latest film, *Iris*, he is cast as the novelist Iris Murdoch's 77 year-old husband a rôle for which he was awarded an Oscar on 24 March 2002 as Best Supporting Actor to add to the earlier award of a Golden Globe.

Jim has made television appearances in *Victoria Wood as Seen on TV, Blackadder, Only Fools and Horses, Gone to the Dogs, Gone to Seed* and he starred in *The Peter Principle*.

Jim is one of this countries most versatile character actors and his credits range from comedy through to serious drama. In a career spanning over thirty years he has had very little spare time, but when he does have some time for himself and family he says he enjoys walking, cooking, golf, woodcarving, cinema and reading!

Jim now lives in London but returns to his home county whenever he has the time. He married Anastasia Lewis in 1987 and they have two sons.

I am grateful to Vicki and Noel Makin, David Broughton and Patrick Markham for assistance with background material relating to the Lindsey Rural Players.

Joe BROWN

Joe Brown is usually regarded as a typical Cockney but he was in fact born on 13 May 1941 at Swarby, near Sleaford. His father, who was crippled with bronchitis for most of his life, was also born in Swarby and had met his wife on a visit to London. After they married they lived in Sleaford but later moved to Swarby. Joe's grandparents were George and Alice Brown who had moved from Grantham to live in Swarby. George was a boot repairer

Joe was very young when the family went to live in London and his early education was at the Pretoria Road School, Plaistow. He passed the eleven-plus and went to Plaistow Grammar School and at the weekends he pushed a barrow fifteen miles round the East End selling shrimps, winkles, whelks and other shellfish and followed this in the evening with a jellied eel stall. His day started on Saturday morning at five thirty and finished at two on Monday morning - not bad for a thirteen year old! Eventually, and perhaps not surprisingly, Plaistow Grammar and Joe parted company and he returned to Pretoria Road School.

After leaving school Joe became an electrician's apprentice but soon moved on to become a packer with a firm of printers in Covent Garden. Joe says that he really enjoyed his next job working on the railway starting as a cleaner and finally as a fireman - this was, of course, in the days of steam. Because this was shift work Joe was able to spend more time playing with the Spacemen Skiffle Group he had joined. He had started a skiffle group called the Ace of Clubs Rhythm Group whilst he was still at school.

Joe prefers to forget his first break into the big time.   He was asked to join a band called *Clay Nicholls and the Blue Flames* at Butlin's Holiday Camp at Filey. The band's lead guitarist had let the band down and he says 'They were the worst group I've ever played in'.

Joe's real break came when Larry Parnes spotted him in 1959 and he became a guitarist in Jack Good's Television show *Boy meets Girls.*   In 1960 he formed his own group, *Joe Brown and the Bruvvers* and had numerous top ten chart entries, the best known of which, *Picture of You,* reached number one and stayed in the charts for many months.

Joe with two fans at the Ritz in Lincoln 1962.

Joe's early musical career included playing guitar with Johnny Cash, Gene Vincent and Eddie Cochran.   He also appeared with Bill Haley, Jerry Lee Lewis, Little Richard and Chuck Berry.   In 1965 Joe starred at the Adelphi opposite Dame Anna Neagle in the musical *Charlie Girl.*   At that time it was a real achievement for a pop star to appear in a West End show and even more so to actually have a starring part.   After two and a half years Joe left *Charlie Girl.*

In the early 1970's Joe formed a band known as *Brown's Home Brew* which included his late wife Vicki and Joe Fagin.   Their music consisted of a mixture of Country, Rock and Gospel and they released two albums.   Joe's hit records include *A Picture of You, It took only a minute, That's what love will do, 'Enery the Eighth* and *All things bright and beautiful.*

Although Joe is probably best known as a stage artist he has starred in six films among which are *What a Crazy World, Three Hats for Lisa, Spike Milligan Meets Joe Brown* and *Mona Lisa.*   His television appearances include Set *'em up, Joe; Oh, Boy!* and *Square one.*

In 1986 Joe, with the assistance of Graeme Wright, wrote *Brown Sauce* which is an entertaining and irreverent look at life.   As Joe says, although the book is about him '…it's just as much about the people, the characters, I've met during my life'.   In his foreword to the book, George Harrison says that Joe is at his happiest '…as a musician, playing the guitar, mandolin, banjo, harmonica and fiddle, and composing songs.'   George added '…he is also not bad with an odd joke or two or three …'

In 1963 Joe married Vicki Haseman whom he had first met on *Boy Meets Girls* when she was singing with the *Vernon Girls.* They had a son, Peter, who is a record producer and a daughter, Sam, who is a singer with four albums to her credit, one of which, *Stop,* sold two and a half million copies. Sadly Vicki died almost ten years ago.

After almost forty years Joe is still working hard and usually returns annually to the Embassy in Skegness. In 1997 he presented a thirteen-week series *Joe Brown's Good Rocking Tonight* on BBC Radio 2 and a second thirteen-week series entitled *Joe Brown's Let it Rock* was broadcast in 1999. Joe, with Roger Cook, has written a musical play, *Skiffle,* for the West End stage which is expected to be in production in the near future.

Joe has other interests than music and is a skilled carpenter. He enjoys making wooden toys for his grandchildren and, perhaps appropriately, he has restored an old costermonger's barrow. Long may the yellow belly cockney continue to entertain.

Peter BROWN

Peter Brown in his day job and as Pedro the Clown.

Five days a week, he is the Lincolnshire Echo's longest-serving journalist, writing the daily Gossiper page, combining news, views and memories of the county.

But most weekends, you will find Peter Brown putting on an outrageous curly red wig, slipping into a striking tartan suit and covering his face with make-up, to become Pedro the Clown.

Lincoln born Peter has been a journalist in the city since the age of 17, and for most of the last 40 years he has also been a semi-professional circus and cabaret artiste as well.

And he just couldn't be happier.

"The only two things I ever wanted to do in life were to be a newspaper reporter and to work in a circus, and I have been very lucky to be able to do them both, and at the same time," says Peter.

"The two jobs seldom conflict. In my younger days, there were times when I have left the office at the end of a busy eight-hour shift, got into my car and driven 100 miles or so, done a show, driven back home again, and still been back in the office again at 8.30 the following morning. It's a great way to relax.

"Over the years, I have been lucky enough to appear in theatres with some of the biggest names in show business, like Ken Dodd, Norman Collier and Keith Harris.

"I once got through to a regional final of a national talent contest, and found myself competing against an unknown Canon and Ball and Les Dennis. And none of us won. Still, it didn't seem to do their careers any harm!"

Occasionally Peter has been able to combine both his interests into one. Like the time he wrote his Gossiper column while sitting at his desk inside a lions cage at the circus. And to this day, he is still not sure why he did it!

Although Peter reckons he must have appeared in most of the towns and cities between Lincoln and London, in the years he was regularly entertaining under the Big Top, these days he is more likely to be found appearing in galas, carnivals, charity shows and fairs with his partner Lynn, who is taking time out of her professional career to be a part-time face-painter, fire-eater and fellow clown, following the recent birth of their daughter.

Educated at Lincoln schools, Peter is a keen fairground enthusiast and was for many years on the organising committee which ran the Lincolnshire Steam Spectacular.

In his spare time, he is a regular contributor to BBC Radio Lincolnshire, an after-dinner speaker and travels extensively around the county, giving talks to organisations.

"I am very interested in local history," says Peter. "After all, I have lived through quite a large part of it!"

Very much a family man, Peter has two daughters, born almost 31 years apart, and four grandchildren.

Theophilus CALEB

Sir John Betjeman, when staying with his friend Jack Yates at Louth in the late 1940s, visited Huttoft church and, as a result, wrote the poem entitled *A Lincolnshire Church*. Unfortunately, for copyright reasons I cannot quote from this poem, but would recommend every lover of 'the forgotten county' to read it.

Sir John sent the poem along with his letter of thanks to Mrs Yates, Jack's mother, and later it appeared in *Collected Poems,* which was published in 1958. The reference in the poem to 'an Indian Christian Priest' particularly concerns us here. It seems probable that Sir John with his friend attended Evensong and were taken aback to find in deepest rural Lincolnshire an Asian priest!

Theophilus Caleb was born in North India in 1878. His father had financed the printing of the first Bible in Hindi and clearly they were a Christian family. After Theophilus graduated with a degree in Persian at the University of Allahabad he went to London and was called to the bar.

After his father died, Theophilus was able to pay for training at Chichester Theological College and it was in Chichester where he met his future wife, Annie Elizabeth. Caleb was ordained in 1907 and served curacies in the St Albans Diocese before moving to Staffordshire in 1916. He was curate of Caverswall and than moved to Meir where he remained until 1923. He was appointed vicar of No-man's Heath, Tamworth in 1923 and moved to Lumb in Rossendale in 1926 before moving to Lincolnshire to become vicar of Mareham-on-the-Hill in 1934.

Mareham is and was a small hamlet with most of the parishioners being connected with agriculture in one way or another. The word went round that the new vicar looked like Gandhi. At that time Gandhi was not receiving a good press because of his civil disobedience campaign. However, it should be realised that at that time someone from as near as ten miles away would be regarded as a 'foreigner' in rural Lincolnshire.

The Caleb family at Huttoft

Caleb did not always help himself to make friends. The organist at Mareham church sometimes assisted at the Methodist chapel. However Caleb issued a severe reprimand and told her 'she could not expect to go to heaven'. He denounced those 'pleasure seekers' who spent their Sundays at the seaside when they should have been in church. No doubt he didn't realise that many of his flock would be setting off for Mablethorpe after the service. On one occasion he visited the parents of John Timms who owned the local farriers and blacksmith's shop. He noticed a framed print of Robert Burns and was amazed that anyone in Mareham-on-the-Hill should have any knowledge of poetry!

John Timms recalls the occasion when the village school children were attending a service in the church and Caleb questioned them on their knowledge of the scriptures. He asked young John what God would want from us. The boy replied 'God would want us to be good'. This annoyed the priest and he shouted at length 'GOOD! GOOD! God wants you to do his work...'

In 1943 Caleb moved to Huttoft and he died in 1959. His first wife, to whom he was devoted, had predeceased him and he was buried with her in Huttoft churchyard.

To have an Asian vicar in this area of Lincolnshire was, to say the least, unusual at that time and there is little doubt that he had to endure considerable prejudice. However, Caleb was a well-known Anglo-Catholic priest and his devout spirituality and pastoral care were much valued and appreciated.

Sidney Bazalgette CARNLEY

Sidney Carnley was born at Ivy House, East Torrington in 1861 and was the son of William Carnley and Emma Bazalgette. Although Sidney's father was a farmer, his grandfather and great-grandfather were both solicitors practising in the building which still stands opposite the South Market Place in Alford close by the parish church. It is, therefore, not surprising that young Sidney should decide to follow that profession. In 1881 he is recorded in the census return for that year as lodging with Dr and Mrs Bosson, of Hanby Hall, Alford and he is described as a law student. It would seem that soon after his marriage on 10 December 1884 to Ellen Cartwright of Well he became a partner with Frederick Jackson Rhodes. His marriage was not to be a happy one and within a short time Ellen became an invalid.

Carnley became friendly with Miss Florence Wilson who was the daughter of the clerk to the Alford Justices and lived at Bleak House which is next door to Norbury House, the residence which Carnley had built and which is now part of Queen Elizabeth's Grammar School. By 1894 Mrs Carnley had become bedridden and Sidney's relationship with Florence had become more than just friendly and he had promised to marry her as soon as he was free of his wife.

Sidney left many passionate letters in the hedge separating the two houses but it seems that it was not until 1900 that he finally seduced her but having satisfied his carnal desires he immediately rejected her. However, Florence became pregnant and she left Alford to live in Southwell for a while and then moved on to Wimbledon where the baby was born but died within a week.

On her return to Alford, Carnley declared that he still loved her but Florence, at that time, would not renew the relationship. However, in 1902 she had become worried about her finances and tried to renew their friendship. A long campaign of poison pen letters then ensued and in January 1906 Mrs Carnley died, but Sidney was no longer interested in Florence who became the traditional 'woman scorned'. In October 1906 she wrote to Carnley demanding that he marry her 'or I shall expose you as a dishonourable man'. She took to following him around the town and arranged to have photographs taken of him with other women, which she had printed on postcards with various insulting messages attached. Obscene messages were chalked on the doors and walls of his house

Eventually Florence decided to sue for breach of promise and Carnley put forward the defence that a promise of marriage made while a man was still married was not a legal promise and he counter-sued for libel. The jury decided that both cases were true and Florence was awarded £100 damages and Carnley a farthing's damages for being libelled!

There were numerous rumours of Carnley's activities with housekeepers but he was a man who, because of his wealth, was able to achieve quickly a rôle as a leading citizen of Alford. He became well known for his stud of horses at Norbury House and he was a member of the Hackney Horse Society. In the 1890s he had a lot of success in showing a harness horse named Norbury Squire and he bought a very good stallion and two mares at the dispersal of the Earl of Londesborough's horses at Market Weighton in 1898. He continued to breed horses until about 1930.

This larger than life character died on 24 June 1947.

Nathaniel CLAYTON

Nathaniel Clayton was born in Lincoln on 25 August 1811. His father, who was also named Nathaniel, ran a packet boat service between Boston and Lincoln. When his father died in 1827 Nathaniel junior took over the management of the business for his mother and eventually became its owner. The business amalgamated with the boat yard owned by Clayton's brother-in-law, Joseph Shuttleworth, and low lying land west of the dock was reclaimed.

Nathaniel Clayton junior had commenced his working life at the Butterley iron works in Derbyshire and, in 1842, the iron works of Clayton and Shuttleworth was established on the reclaimed land at Stamp End.. The firm started with twelve men, a foundry, two forges and a lathe and their first major contract was to make iron pipes for Boston Waterworks. They also made iron girders for roofs and bridges but their reputation was established when, in 1845 they made their first portable engine. Their engines were exhibited at the Great Exhibition in 1851 and this helped to make known the products of Clayton and Shuttleworth world wide.

The firm had two wealthy sleeping partners, Keyworth and Seely, and invested heavily in the development of portable engines. The firm was now registered as Clayton, Shuttleworth & Co. Ltd. They were the first to produce a portable engine with horizontal cylinders on top of the boiler, a practice which became the general arrangement. These engines won awards at exhibitions both nationally and internationally.

This created for Lincoln an entirely new industry and the city became a major British manufacturing centre. Clayton engines were known worldwide and the firm also manufactured threshing machines which also became well known internationally. By 1870 they had manufactured 10,000 engines and were producing three a day. When Nathaniel Clayton died a millionaire on 21 December 1890 the firm had manufactured 26,000 engines and 24,000 threshing machines. The area of the foundry site had grown from $1\frac{1}{2}$ acres to 18 acres!

In 1875 Clayton purchased the Withcall estate consisting of a farm of 2,500 acres. He installed an irrigation system, new roads, built new farm buildings and cottages. Clayton even rebuilt the village church. Withcall farm was said at that time to have been the largest cultivated farm in the country.

Nathaniel Clayton was a very well respected citizen of Lincoln and generous benefactor. He contributed to the building of St Swithin's and All Saints' churches and to the building of the new county hospital in Lincoln. He held many offices and was a magistrate for a number of years. He was also a member of the City Council and Mayor in 1857. He was the first President of the Lincoln Liberal Association, Deputy Lieutenant of the county and High Sheriff of Lincolnshire in 1881.

Ernest COLEMAN

Although born in Lincoln in 1943 Ernest Coleman's family moved to Grantham three years later and it was here that he received his education. He attended Huntingtower Primary School and then went on to the Boys' Central School. From an early age he had yearned for a life at sea, which he attributes to the fact that his father was a trawlerman.

Unfortunately, for Ernest, he was too young to enter the Navy when he left school at the age of fifteen and he had to be content to work in the drapery department of the Co-op in Grantham. At the age of seventeen he became Junior Electrical Mechanic, Second Class Coleman – he describes this rating as 'so low down on the social scale that I looked up to pond life.'

His first draft was to the shore training establishment H.M.S *Collingwood* in Fareham, but his first sea-going ship was no less than H.M.S *Ark Royal*. For a seventeen-year-old raw recruit joining a ship with 2,000 men was certainly being 'thrown in at the deep end' and on this first voyage he sailed round the world and crossed both the Equator and Arctic Circle. Ernest Coleman has served on every type of ship from aircraft carrier to submarine and he has led a life full of interest. He served aboard seven sea-going ships and also in Nelson's flagship, H.M.S *Victory*. Ernest reached the rating of Chief Petty Officer and was awarded a commission as a lieutenant. In 1980 he was responsible for mounting the central display at the Centenary Royal Tournament commemorating 250 years of naval gunnery. This event provided him with one of the most embarrassing moments of his Naval career. 'When I gave the order to 'Quick March' out of the arena the band drowned my orders and I marched off alone in the belief that the Guard of Honour was behind me - all in front of the Queen'.

When he was Officer of the Day in H.M.S. *Victory,* Chief Petty Officer Coleman met Lord Mountbatten twice and had the same conversation with him on both occasions - Lord M : 'Good Evening, Chief'. Ernest : 'Good evening, Sir', end of conversation. It was at this time whilst Officer of the Day on H.M.S. *Victory* that Ernest was able to achieve a small ambition – 'I was taking the salute on behalf of the Commander-in-Chief from the poop deck as my old ship, the *Ark Royal*, entered Portsmouth harbour. I delayed giving the order 'Carry on' to the Bugler for a fraction of a second in memory of all the times I had stood to attention in exactly the same manner on her flight deck'.

After 22 years of sea-going service Ernest joined the Royal Navy Career Service and was appointed first to Sheffield and then Watford before applying for an appointment in Lincoln. In 1988 he was pleased to return to his birthplace as the county's Naval recruiting officer.

Lincolnshire is often regarded as the stronghold of the Royal Air Force but long before the R.A.F was created the Navy was here. Lincolnshire's Naval traditions have been recorded by Ernest in his book *The Royal Navy in Lincolnshire* which was published in 1992.

Although Ernest Coleman is an author, naval historian, lecturer and a popular after-dinner speaker, it is as an Arctic explorer that he is known world wide. Spilsby-born Sir John Franklin's search for the North West Passage and his subsequent disappearance with 128 men at some time between 1845 and 1848 has had considerable influence on Ernest. He has led several expeditions into the Arctic in search of Franklin's grave. The first attempt was in 1990 when he led a two-man expedition to King William Island in the Arctic and found a human skull on Todd Island and a Caribou carving that appeared to be an attempt to repair a musket. Both of these artefacts were on the expedition retreat route.

Two years later Ernest returned alone to the north-west corner of King William Island and found two large man-made mounds, which he is convinced contain the graves of Franklin and others who died with him.   It was during this solo expedition that Ernest became disorienated and spent over thirty hours searching non-stop for his tent and he went without food for six days. He says 'Pathetically, I got to the point where I thought I wasn't going to survive and pulled out a sheet of paper and a pencil from my top pocket.   I managed to write in wavering script 'Franklin might be in mounds one mile north of summer camp' and tucked it back into my jacket.'

However, through sheer determination he survived and in 1993 Ernest joined an international team mounted to look at the discoveries of the previous year.   Eskimos showed him the remains of a ship's whaler which is almost certainly a relic of the Franklin expedition. This site was last visited by Lieutenant William Browne R.N. during his search for Franklin in 1851 and the site remains exactly as he left it almost 150 years ago.   In 1995 Ernest returned for a fourth time to the Arctic in an attempt to prove his personal theory that Franklin's men went overland down the Island rather than over the ice of Victoria Strait. On the route he found a wooden toggle that could well have been used on a flag or more likely as part of sledge-hauling harness. It was during this expedition that a hitherto unknown Franklin camp-site with remains of a tent 'ring', stone cairn and outline of a whaler made out in rocks was found. His theory having been justified, he named the site of the camp 'Fort Crozier' in memory of Franklin's second in command.

Ernest has been to visit the grave of another of his interests - Sir Ernest Shackleton, who died on board the Quest in 1922.   Shackleton died at the now abandoned whaling station of Grytviken in South Georgia, Antarctica. It was during this expedition that Ernest had to fend off ferocious fur seals. He said 'Although it sounds cruel you have to kick sand in their eyes - they soon get the message.'

Ernest's passion for practical research into naval history has led him into some very difficult and uncomfortable situations.   'Probably the greatest surprise in the Arctic', he says, 'was the mosquitoes. I could use modern repellents to keep them at bay, but Franklin's men must have suffered grievously'.   In 1999 in a remote part of South Georgia he became stuck 80 feet up the side of a cliff and it seemed that inevitably he would fall to his death.   After over an hour when all hope was gone he saw a lone figure walking about a hundred yards away. He managed to blow 'SOS' on his whistle and the man, who turned out to be a Chilean mountain climber, rescued him.

After 36 years service Lieutenant Ernest Coleman, R.N. is now on the Navy's Retired List.   In 1991 Ernest was elected a Fellow of the Royal Geographical Society and delivered the prestigious Nelson Birthday Lecture using the title 'Manning the Fleet'.   In 1994 he was elected a member of the Arctic Club and lectured at the Scott Polar Research Institute, Cambridge and in the same year delivered a second Nelson Birthday Lecture.   This time the subject was dear to his heart : 'Franklin and his searchers'.   In 1997 Ernest lectured at the National Maritime Museum using as his subject 'The Franklin Expedition'. He read the prayers at the 150th

Anniversary Commemoration of the death of Sir John Franklin in Westminster Abbey and on the same day he broadcast live to Australia and Canada, and appeared on B.B.C's 'Today' programme - such is the appeal of the Franklin mystery.

Ernest's biography, *Captain George Vancouver* was published in 2000 and his transcript of *The 1766 Navy List* in 2002.

Ernest now lives with his wife in the quiet village of Bishop Norton in a cottage packed with memorabilia which cannot help but remind him and his visitors of those heroes of England's naval history. He is immensely proud and delighted that both his sons decided to follow in his footsteps. One of the Coleman offspring has served on board the Royal Yacht and the other is a Chief Petty Officer in the Naval Air Service.

Brett COLLIER

Above : Brett Collier in 1951
Back cover : Brett with the Ramblers' Church at Walesby in the background

All of us who enjoy the Lincolnshire countryside, but especially walkers and ramblers, owe a great deal to Brett Collier. He has been an indefatigable campaigner for the rights of walkers for many years and has written nine very popular books on walking in the county. His voluntary work in respect of public access has recently been recognised by Lincoln City Council by the award of the Mayoral Medal.

Brett's activities have not however found favour with everyone and he tells, with some amusement, of the occasion when the squire of the Lincolnshire village in which he and his wife were then living told him that, as a retired regular army officer, he was a traitor to his class! This comment was ludicrous as Brett's father, Henry Collier, over a hundred years ago at the age of twelve, went to school in the morning and then worked an afternoon shift in a Lancashire coal mine pushing loaded bogeys underground. He eventually became a main-line engine driver on the old London, Scottish and Midland Railway and always prided himself as being the cream of the working class.

Henry Brett Collier was born on Merseyside in November 1920 and educated at the Wade Deacon Grammar School. He entered teacher training college but on the outbreak of World War Two in 1939 he volunteered for the Army. On commissioning he was posted to a Lancashire regular infantry battalion serving in the Far East which was still at peace. The British Army was completely unprepared for tropical warfare even after many years service in the Far East. The men should have become acclimatised but they were ordered to be in bed between two and four in the afternoon and it was also a chargeable offence to remove one's shirt and thereby risk sunburn! These precautions were clearly unnecessary, as it quickly became apparent after the Japanese came.

Singapore was subjected to an undeclared air attack by the Japanese in December 1941 some hours before Pearl Harbour was bombed. Brett's battalion moved up-country into the Malay Peninsular and fought at Yong Peng and Batu Pahat in a desperate attempt to break through to Australian troops who were surrounded at Parit Sulong Causeway. Unfortunately they did not succeed and all the wounded Australians and the padre who had volunteered to stay with them were massacred by the Japanese Imperial Guard.

After withdrawal to Singapore Island, capitulation came in February, 1942 and at that time there were only 129 men left in Brett's battalion. At Easter 1942 Brett sailed with the first draft of 1,000 Far East prisoners of war to leave Changi in an old Clyde-built tramp steamer. Initially there were 250 men in each of the four holds, including the Governor and senior officers of all three services. Conditions aboard were appalling and many prisoners died. They lived in semi-darkness with two toilet buckets for each hold and very little drinking water. The voyage took forty days and, after landing in Korea, Brett's group were taken to work in quarries and a goods yard in the capital, Keijo. After one dreadfully cold winter batches of 100 men were literally sold to various firms in Manchukuo and Japan. Brett went with his group to Kobe, Japan and he became a riveter in the Kawasaki Shipbuilding Yard working on small escort carriers. Every gang of prisoners of war was forced to complete a strict daily quota. Early in 1945 Kobe was completely destroyed in a napalm fire raid by American B29 bombers.

Brett's group of prisoners were then sold to a mining company in Nagasaki. They worked from 5 a.m. to 7 p.m. in a very wet drift coal mine under the sea. Roof falls were common and as men died the length of the daily stint increased.

As the war situation worsened for the Japanese, orders were given to all prison camp commanders throughout the whole of South East Asia that, if the Allies landed on the Home Islands of Japan, all prisoners of war were to be killed. In Brett's camp, and in many others, a large pit had been dug at the end of the parade ground as a communal grave. Each day as prisoners stumbled bare-foot to and from the mine they passed the pit knowing only too well its eventual purpose.

One day, half way through their shift in the mine, all power stopped, lights went out, the pumps no longer worked and there was no fresh air. The mine exit had been blocked by many tons of earth and there appeared to have been a major earth tremor. When help did not arrive, six men using their picks and shovels started digging at the top of the blocked shaft. For many hours the spoil had to be moved back down the shaft in pitch darkness with the water rising, the air becoming foul and rats scurrying up the tunnel. Just before dawn the prisoners broke out and only then was it realized that the destruction had been caused by some kind of bomb. Later it was learned that the second atomic bomb had been dropped at one minute after twelve on the afternoon of the previous day, so the prisoners must have been digging their way out for 15 or 16 hours.

Brett sincerely believes that the two atom bombs dropped on Japan saved at least a million lives. They certainly saved his life and many thousands of Far Eastern prisoners of war. This precious gift of life and freedom has coloured his whole outlook on living for the remainder of his days. He feels that, providing one was not embittered, life had been enhanced by the experience of hardship together with the depth of comradeship experienced in such dire circumstances.

In 1946 Brett was placed on reserve with the rank of Lieutenant and he completed his teacher training. He taught in two Lancashire schools until, in September 1950 on the outbreak of war in Korea, he was recalled and seconded to the Royal Malay Regiment during the Communist Emergency. After discharge with the rank of Major, he went to the Cambridge Institute of Education and then returned again to Malaya as headmaster of a school in Ipoh, Perak. This was followed by a tour in Kenya training future teachers. In 1969 he took up a similar appointment at Bishop Grosseteste College, Lincoln.

Many people throughout Lincolnshire have been moved by Brett's talk *Far East Odyssey*. The Liverpool School of Tropical Medicine, which researches the diseases contracted by prisoners of war in the Far East, has benefited financially as a result of collections taken at these talks. In 1998 Brett accompanied a small group of former prisoners of war who returned to Japan as Pilgrims of Reconciliation, and he carried a message of peace from Lincoln Cathedral to the people of Japan. This visit led to another talk entitled *The value of reconciliation* which Brett has delivered to a number of groups and organisations.

Brett's love of the countryside and wide knowledge of public rights of way in the county has enabled him to write a series of books on walking in Lincolnshire which have proved very popular and sales have reached several thousand. He helped to establish the route of the Viking Way, the first long distance recreational path in this country, and later he wrote *Lindsey Loop* which describes a 95-mile walk in the Wolds linking six market towns in East and West Lindsey. This was followed by *Plogsland Round Lincoln* which describes a 47-mile circular walk around Lincoln with the cathedral in view for much of the way. The title of this book is taken from the Norse word for 'ploughed land'. Brett contributed a chapter for John Hillaby's book *Walking in Britain* which was very critical of the state of footpaths in Lincolnshire and the attitude of farmers. This brought a response from a councillor who, as Vice-chairman of the County Council committee responsible for the countryside made the comment that 'It is the policy of this council not to interfere with the farming community'.

As Area President of the Lincolnshire Branch of the Ramblers' Association he formed a number of local walking groups. The Lincoln Group has a membership of well over five hundred and one of Brett's minor worries is that one day all the members will turn up together for a ramble!

Brett celebrated his eightieth birthday by swimming eighty 25-metre lengths and the sponsorship from this enabled a substantial donation to be made to the Star and Garter Home. With the help of some fellow ramblers he also marked the occasion by planting 80 oak trees in a new wood for the Woodland Trust at Aubourn, with a proviso that if the cathedral needed some oak timber 200 years hence they could have Brett's oaks!

He has served as President of Jubilee Probus and he is Vice-Chairman of the Friends of Walesby Old Church (The Ramblers' Church). He is a member of the executive committee of the Lincolnshire Branch of the Council for the Protection of Rural England and he has served as a judge for the Best Kept Village in Lincolnshire for fifteen years. Brett is also a member of the Nature and Countryside Group of the Lincolnshire Environmental Forum.

Brett has two daughters, Elaine and Julia. Both read History at Oxford University and Elaine was awarded a D.Phil. Brett met his second wife Janet on a mountain in Kenya where she was training for an eventually successful climb of Kilimanjaro. They had met briefly before at an Overseas Orientation Course at Farnham Castle in Surrey. Janet was Head of Geography at the Aga Khan High School in Nairobi and later at Branston Community College.

It has been as long journey for Brett from his native Merseyside which has brought him to his home in Lincoln where he and Janet have lived since 1970. The county has many reasons to be grateful that they settled here. Long may he continue his work for walking and the environment in the County.

John COTTON

In 1612 the vicar of Boston, Thomas Wooll, was appointed to the rectorial living of the neighbouring parish of Skirbeck. His opinions, like those of many others in the area, were decidedly Puritan and a careful search was made for a successor of similar opinions. The choice was John Cotton, who accepted the post.

John Cotton was born in 1584 at Derby and went up to Cambridge University. In 1610 he was ordained a priest in the Church of England and was appointed lecturer at Emmanuel College, Cambridge, which was a strong centre of Puritan teaching. His sermons at the University attracted large congregations and he soon made a deep impression in Boston, where he remained for eleven years.

Cotton erected a pulpit in St Botolph's church, which still remains. It bears on each of its panels a bunch of ostrich feathers in tribute to the memory of Henry, Prince of Wales, who died in the same year in which Cotton took up his appointment in Boston. Prince Henry had refused to marry a Roman Catholic and the Puritan party had set high hopes on his leadership. Although the policy of most Protestants was to destroy churches and monuments, Cotton did much to repair and maintain the fabric of St Botolph's.

In 1633, because of his Puritan leanings, Cotton was summoned to appear before the archbishop of Canterbury, William Laud, at the Court of High Commission. However, he decided to leave the country, and in September 1633 he arrived at the town of Boston, in the Massachusetts Bay Colony. There he was ordained teacher of the First Church, a post he held until his death.

Because of his learning and piety Cotton had a powerful influence in New England. He approved the exile from Massachusetts of the Puritan clergyman Roger Williams and the religious reformer Anne Hutchinson, whom he had first supported in her controversy with church authorities. Cotton became one of the heads of the Congregational church in Massachusetts, promulgating his teachings in more than 50 volumes, including *The Keys of the Kingdom of Heaven* (1644), *The Way of the Churches of Christ in New England* (1645), and *The Way of the Congregational Churches Cleared* (1648). He staunchly upheld the right of Puritan magistrates to enforce uniformity of religious beliefs.

John Cotton died in 1652.

William DADLEY

Poaching was almost a necessary means of survival for country people until quite recent times. Small birds as well as rabbits were caught and eaten and most farmers would allow their workers to 'poach' a couple of rabbits on a Saturday afternoon to feed their family.

In the eighteenth century a law was made which forbade anyone who was not a squire or a squire's eldest son to kill game. Fines were severe and the Justices of the Peace, who were mostly from the gentry class, showed no mercy. A poacher could be deported for seven years for being in possession of nets at night. Unfortunately poaching attracted hooligans who would come out from the towns in armed gangs and pitched battles often took place between poachers and the gamekeepers.

By the second quarter of the nineteenth century the large poaching gangs had disappeared but, despite the penalties, the tradition was still carried on by one or two men, usually out of necessity to feed their own family or supply the village shop. Some poachers were vicious and several murders of gamekeepers took place.

William Dadley came to Well near Alford in April 1838 from Aylsham in Norfolk to work as head gamekeeper for Robert Christopher, a Member of Parliament who owned Well Hall but lived at Bloxham Hall. On April 28 he wrote home to his parents describing his two-day journey from Aylsham with an overnight stay in Boston. He mentioned the extremely cordial welcome he received from Captain Mansell, who lived at Well Hall and from Mr Higgins, the agent for the Well Vale estate. There seemed to be a real bond between master and servant and William worked well. He quickly became respected for his responsible attitude to his duties.

Left to right : William and Mary Dadley's cottage; Stone marking the spot where William Dadley was killed; William Dadley's headstone in Well churchyard.

On 5 January 1839 at St. Botolph's Church, Boston, he married Margaret Brown and they set up their home in the gamekeeper's house not far from Ulceby Cross near Miles Cross Hill, Alford. Five nights after the marriage on 10 January 1839 the Dadley's held their wedding party. During the celebrations, the noise of disturbed game was heard and William got up and said he would have to investigate. Members of the party tried to persuade him not to go, but he went unarmed with Charles Harrison of Sloothby. Together they went in pursuit of the poachers and they caught up with them. There was a shot and William was killed.

Poaching in the area had become a real problem and the local newspapers record that three poachers had been sent to the house of correction in February 1839 for snaring hares at Well. Later the same month four men were sentenced to three months imprisonment for poaching with arms also at Well.

The local farmers and landowners were so concerned that they were prepared to pay for information leading to the arrest of Dadley's murderers and also promised a Queen's pardon to the other poacher in return for information.

One John Baker of Partney who was aged about 25 was well known as a thief and poacher. He was the terror of the Spilsby area and he was strongly suspected of the murder of a gamekeeper at Normanby, shortly after the murder of Dadley. The authorities were convinced that Baker was also guilty of the murder of Dadley and he was arrested in Candlesby after having been found heavily armed in a loft. Apparently the house where he was found was occupied by a notorious family. Baker was taken to Spilsby prison and committed for trial at Lincoln prison. He was acquitted on a charge of burglary and theft from Mrs Ingall's house at Burgh, but on a charge of burglary at the house of Mr Thomas Stainton of Spilsby he was found guilty and sentenced to death, but he was actually transported for life. It seems clear that although the authorities believed that Baker was guilty of Dadley's murder, there was insufficient evidence to try him for that crime. Baker was deported to Van Diemen's Land (now Tasmania) and sailed on the *Layton* from Portsmouth on 13 July 1839 arriving on 7 December 1839.

There is an interesting twist to this sad tale. Apparently on his deathbed one Stephen Cowley confessed that it was actually he who fired the shot which killed William Dadley. After over 150 years it is impossible to be certain of the facts, but the most likely conclusion seems that both Baker and Cowley were capable of murder and in this case no doubt it was Cowley who was guilty, but there is also the murder at Normanby to consider and Baker is the most likely suspect of that crime.

Whatever the truth of the matter, a man of 31 years of age of irreproachable character who had married only five days previously had lost his life. There is a headstone in the churchyard at Well inscribed as follows :

'Sacred to the Memory of William Dadley, late Gamekeeper at Well. The faithful and devoted servant of Robert Adam Christopher, Esq. Who was hurried into his Redeemer's presence by the hand of a murderer. In the 32nd year of his age, on the 10th day of January. In the year of our Lord 1839'.

A stone marks the place of the murder and this is inscribed 'W. Dadley murdered by poachers on this spot 10th Jan. 1839.' Maps of the locality record the place as 'Dadley Stone Wood'.

SOURCES : Information communicated by Geoffrey Hadfield and Peter Taylor.

Harold Francis DAVIDSON

The Revd Harold Davidson was appointed rector of the parish of Stiffkey, Norfolk in 1906 and he was, apparently, a popular parson. Soon after the end of the First World War his character seemed to change and he was rarely seen in the parish except on Sundays. For the remainder of the week he was in London where he was to be found in restaurants talking to the waitresses during the day and at night he wandered the streets of the West End supposedly rescuing the ladies of the night.

Davidson was obsessed with this work and he would reward his favourites by taking them to Paris. He had a wife and five children and the expense of his welfare work led him to the verge of bankruptcy. In 1931 one of the ladies he had been 'reforming' for about ten years sold her story to a Sunday newspaper and in March 1932 he appeared before a Consistory Court held in Church House, Westminster, to answer five charges of immoral conduct. As the trial proceeded the newspapers regaled their readers with startling revelations of the activities of the self-styled Prostitutes' Padre.

During the trial Davidson returned to Stiffkey to conduct the Sunday services and not surprisingly the congregation became very large and coach trips took place so that the curious could see and hear him preach! The trial lasted for more than three months but he was eventually found guilty on each charge and Davidson was stripped of all his clerical offices. He appealed to the Privy Council without success and he then embarked on a long crusade to establish his innocence. During the summer season of 1936 he exhibited himself on Blackpool's

Golden Mile, fasting in a barrel, and during the following season he came to Skegness to publicise himself on a fairground where 'Captain' Freddy Rye displayed his lions. The 'captain' was a local farmer and fellmonger who had taken to breeding lions on his farm near Burgh le Marsh. Two of his lions were exhibited in the amusement park and he allowed the former rector of Stiffkey to conduct his campaign in the lion pavilion.

Davidson gave a set speech describing his work of rescuing the fallen women of Soho by offering them friendship. The door of the cage was then opened and he entered the lions' den with the young lady lion trainer shepherding the lions away from him. Towards the end of July the Skegness Police attempted to serve a warrant on Davidson for the non-payment of a fine, but he would not leave the cage saying, 'You will have to come in and get me!' Not surprisingly, the police refused the invitation and remained outside. Sometime later, Davidson gave up and was taken to the police station where he paid the fine. A week or so later on 28 July 1937 one of the lions attacked him and he died in Skegness Hospital a few days later at the age of 62, but not before he is alleged to have given an instruction that the London newspapers were to be informed of the incident!

Colin DEXTER
(See photograph on back cover)

Colin Dexter began writing detective fiction comparatively late in life and his first Inspector Morse novel appeared in 1975 when he was aged 45. This book was written during a depressing rain- soaked holiday in North Wales. Colin submitted the manuscript to the crime publisher Collins, which resulted in his one and only rejection letter!

Nothing daunted, he sent the manuscript to Macmillan and it was snapped up by Lord Hardinge, who ran the crime list. Colin has remained with Macmillan ever since.

Norman Colin Dexter was born in Stamford in 1930 and is the son of Alfred and Dorothy Dexter. He has an older brother, John, and a younger sister, Avril. He was educated at St John's Infants' School, the Bluecoat Junior School and Stamford School. After completing his national service, he went up to Cambridge, graduating in 1954 with a classics degree. Colin then became Classics Master at Leicester, Loughborough and Corby Grammar Schools before moving to Oxford in 1966 to work for the Oxford Examinations Board. He took early retirement in 1988.

Since the first Inspector Morse novel *Last Bus to Woodstock* was published in 1975 there have been 13 books and Colin Dexter has been responsible for 81 body bags! All the books have been adapted for television with huge success and John Thaw has played the inimitable Chief Inspector, with Kevin Whately as his long-suffering Sergeant. Colin wisely decided to 'kill off' Morse whilst the series was still popular and before he ran out of ideas. He has followed in the Hitchcock tradition and has appeared in cameo rôles in each of the 33 episodes. The last Inspector Morse novel was screened on 15 November 2000 with Colin appearing as a wheelchair bound tourist. Sadly, John Thaw died in February 2002.

Colin has received many awards for his novels, including the Crime Writers' Association Silver Dagger twice, and the Gold Dagger for *The Wench is Dead* and The *Way Through the Woods*. In 1997 he was presented with the Diamond Dagger for outstanding services to crime literature. He was awarded an OBE in the year 2000 Queen's Birthday Honours List and he has recently been made a Freeman of the City of Oxford for 'helping enhance the profile of the city around the world'.

Colin is a crossword setter and several times has been national champion in the Ximenes and Azed crossword competitions. He plays bridge and is an avid *Archers* fan. Among his unfulfilled ambitions are opening the batting for England and crossing swords with fellow Lincolnshire 'Yellow Belly', Baroness Thatcher, in a parliamentary debate!

There are no plans for any more books and Colin's time is spent on work for various charities and answering mountains of correspondence. Colin Dexter still visits Lincolnshire and has an affection for his 'home town', Stamford. It gave him great pleasure to be asked to present the prizes on Speech Days at both the Boys' and Girls' schools in Stamford.

Colin and his wife, Dorothy, live in Oxford. They have two children and two grandchildren.

Margaret DICKINSON
(See photograph on front cover)

Margaret Dickinson has seventeen books to her credit, with another due for publication in May 2002 and a sequel planned for 2003. For as long as she can remember she has had stories, plots and characters coming into her head and she says she has no real idea what triggers them off. Her first story was written when she was fourteen years old and, in 1964, she had her one and only short story published in a magazine. Her first novel was published in 1968 and eight others followed between 1969 and 1984 but then, because of family commitments, Margaret did not write for seven years.

Margaret was born in Gainsborough in 1942, but her family moved to the Skegness area when she was seven years old and she has lived there ever since. She has a creative background going back at least three generations. Her mother taught embroidery and other members of her family were artists. Her sister embroiders and her brother is a wood carver and water colour artist, but Margaret creates her pictures in words.

As with most authors, she has had her fair share of rejection letters and the breakthrough came when her historical romance *Pride of the Courtneys* was accepted for publication. She returned to writing when her family became more independent and decided to follow up one of her ambitions - to reach a wider readership by having her books published in paperback. In 1991 Margaret approached the agent Darley Anderson who specialises in twentieth century regional romantic sagas. He advised her to write about the place she knows best - Lincolnshire - and was instantly impressed with the manuscript she sent him. Pan Books published *Plough the Furrow* in 1994 and they have now published eight of Margaret's books. *Plough the Furrow* was the first in the *Fleethaven Trilogy* with its sequel, *Sow the Seed*, appearing a year later. Margaret had clearly found her niche as an author of romantic fiction, inspired by her love of the sea, the Lincolnshire landscape and its people. *Reap the Harvest*, published in 1996, completed the trilogy. These stories revolve around Brumby's Farm which is modelled on the 'living museum' at Church Farm, Skegness with the setting at Gibraltar Point.

In 1997 *The Miller's Daughter*, which was inspired by the windmill at Burgh-le-Marsh, near Skegness, was published and in the following year *Chaff Upon the Wind* took the Manor House at Alford as the setting for the characters. In 1999 *The Fisher Lass*, which tells the story of those who are born to the fishing way of life, was based on Grimsby. Much of the research for this book was carried out with the assistance of the staff of the National Fishing Heritage Centre. As with all of her books, once the central character had been decided, the others followed along with the beginning and the end. Having worked out the skeleton of the plot the book begins to take shape and the hard graft of actually putting pen to paper begins. Margaret tries to produce 1,000 words a day with an eventual total of about 120,000. Of course, as with most authors, a time comes usually around the middle of the book when a difficult point is reached and it seems as if the work is just not going to be good enough. This passes and through sheer hard graft the book is completed. *The Fisher Lass* was described by the publishers as '...a love story as powerful and restless as the mighty North Sea'.

Spalding and district was the setting for *The Tulip Girl* published in August 2000 and *The River Folk*, which was published in June 2001 was inspired by Margaret's birthplace, Gainsborough. For *Tangled Threads*, which is due for publication in May 2002, Margaret has moved over the border to tell a story with the Nottingham hosiery and lace industries as the setting. There is a sequel to this book planned for the following year.

To celebrate the Millennium, Margaret was invited by the Skegness Playgoers to write a community play. Having worked on this for over a year *Embracing Tides* was staged at the Embassy Theatre, Skegness in late 2000 and also on 1st December as the Playgoers' entry for that year's Play Festival.

Margaret has known her husband, Dennis, since she was 16 and they have two grown-up daughters, Mandi and Zoë. Although Mandi worked for a time in the publishing industry and all of Margaret's family are very supportive, none of them have, as yet, written anything for publication themselves. Dennis says he is amazed at Margaret's resolve to keep going no matter what disappointments come her way. He usually accompanies her on her numerous book signings.

Margaret firmly believes that a writer must have a day job. She worked in Lincoln as a secretary and later returned to Skegness to work in the County Council District Education Office there until 1970. For the last seventeen years she has worked for her husband doing the administrative work for his furniture store. However, Dennis has recently retired and in future Margaret will be concentrating on her writing career.

One ambition remains. She would like one of her books dramatized for television. Margaret believes that this would really put Lincolnshire on the map. She is full of ideas and no doubt there are many more Lincolnshire sagas in the pipeline!

Fred DOBSON

Fred Dobson was born in 1913 of Lincolnshire parents at Netherfield, Nottingham. His ancestors for many generations had been true Yellowbellies and it was an 'unfortunate' quirk of fate that Fred should have been born on the wrong side of the border.

His family returned to Lincolnshire almost immediately after his birth and his home remained in the county for the remainder of his life. He always emphatically denied that he was a native of anywhere else and he only visited Nottingham twice during his life!

Fred's early education, both formal and informal, was in and around Minting, Wragby and Saxilby. It was here his mid-Lincolnshire dialect was developed and used every day. Fred eventually left school at Christmas, 1927. Although he had been head of his class for the last five years and passed the Scholarship Examination, he was not successful at the interview and he didn't go on to higher education. However, he was able to find a job as a full-time newspaper/errand/garden lad for Mr F. Pentney, the Saxilby Chemist. Later Fred moved on to the well-known nurserymen, Lawsons of Lincoln.

In early 1932 Fred joined the Coldstream Guards but to his regret was medically discharged after just a few weeks. He went on to work for several years on the farms and bulb fields of South Lincolnshire. It was here that he met Margery Bayston who became his wife on 2 September 1939 - a memorable date as many readers will remember.

Fred tried twice more to join the armed forces. When he tried to join the Lincolnshire Regiment his medical discharge was on record and when he attempted to join the Royal Marines he failed the medical examination. He did join the Home Guard though, spending the war years at Ingleby by Saxilby. He then spent some thirty years at Tanya Knitwear which is based at Fiskerton. It was towards the end of his schooldays that Fred became involved in village concerts. He was also involved with the chapel choir and blew the organ at Saxilby Wesleyan Chapel. He was unable to read music but had a passion for taking any opportunity that came his way to try his skill on the organ (or rather the blower). The writer can well understand this, having learned to play at Bilsby with his mother on the blower; but thereby hangs another tale!

Fred had another hobby as well that remained with him all his life; writing short stories, essays and verse just for the sheer pleasure of writing. He always found putting together his own stories much more interesting than merely reading other people's efforts. However, it was not until 1939 that he plucked up courage to send off his first item for publication. One can imagine his joy when this was accepted, and not only printed but broadcast 'on the wireless'! Many will envy him this achievement at the first attempt. This was due to a request by the *Radio Times* for 'Items in one or other of the Northern Dialects'. This gave Fred a lead which he followed for the remainder of his life.

After this first success Fred wrote a considerable number of items with a Lincolnshire background. He broadcast on the radio many times and also appeared on television; lectured at some 500 meetings, wrote over 400 items for a series in a local newspaper and had many items published in Lincolnshire periodicals including *Lincolnshire Life*.

His first published book *Life and Laughter in Lincolnshire* appeared in 1962. This was followed by *Lincolnshire Laughs Again*. *Fungus the Lincolnshire Cat* appeared in 1980 and this was followed by *Lincolnshire Folk*. Fred's last book was published shortly before his death and was a collection of *Lincolnshire Limericks*.

He was an enthusiastic supporter of the Museum of Lincolnshire Life and frequently entertained groups with his dialect stories and dialect quizzes both there and elsewhere.

This true Lincolnshire Yellow Belly died on 15 November 1993 at the age of 80.

Arthur DREWRY

Arthur Drewry was born on 25 March 1891 in Grimsby and educated at the Grimsby Collegiate School. In 1911 he joined the Lincolnshire Yeomanry and served in Palestine and the Western Desert in the 1914-18 War being a squadron quartermaster sergeant in the first battalion of his regiment. In the Second World War he was head warden and chief fireguard in North Lincolnshire. Arthur Drewry ran a fish merchant's business in Grimsby from 1908 until his retirement in 1953, was a member of Grimsby Borough Council and was a justice of the peace for the borough.

He had a long and distinguished record of service to football, being a director of Grimsby Town Football Club, president of the Football League from 1949 to 1955, chairman of the English selectors for some years and the first Englishman to be president of the international body, *Federation Internationale de Football Association* (FIFA).

Arthur Drewry was distinguished in appearance and gracious of manner. He was a friendly guiding light on the stormy seas of modern football with horizons broader than many of his colleagues in the higher posts of administration. He could be firm if necessary as he showed in Stockholm in 1958 when delegates from Communist China tried to address a FIFA congress after losing a motion. On being ruled out of order the Chinese said they would have to leave to which Mr. Drury replied : 'It is not a question of you wanting to withdraw; you are ordered to do so'.

Drewry saw football for what it has become - a world game. Though he stood for the ideals first set by Great Britain he could understand and move with changing times. Having given the game to the world he believed the British should be prepared to share it fairly with people of many creeds. One of his most valuable gifts was the ability to balance the needs of the moment with the requirements of tradition. He was able to achieve this so deftly that he was elected to the Presidency of FIFA, a unique distinction for an Englishman and a title he esteemed very highly.

Arthur Drewry, who was appointed CBE in 1953, married Ida May Stookes in 1919 by whom he had a son and a daughter. He died in hospital at Grimsby on 25 March 1961.

H.J.H. DYER

Henry James Herbert Dyer was born at Leamington Spa in 1902 and was the eldest son of Charles Dyer a Co-operative Society Branch Manager. H. J. H. as he was usually known received his early education at Leamington College before going up to Keble College, Oxford. After receiving his MA he studied law at Lincoln's Inn and was called to the Bar in 1931.

He taught for a short time at Huntingdon, Coventry and Bradford before he became headmaster of Queen Elizabeth's Grammar School, Alford in 1935. Dyer remained in that post for 32 years - a record for the school except possibly for a certain reverend gentleman who appears to have held the post from 1704 until 1775!

Dyer did not inherit an easy situation at Alford. It was a time of change in education and there was some unrest amongst the staff but Dyer's strength of character created a fine school which produced many who went on to achieve high office in many walks of life. He would often recall the year when the entire Sixth Form went on to read for honours degrees (three of whom were later to receive the OBE) and this was followed by a year when the school was awarded two state scholarships to Oxford.

George EDWARDES

George Edwards was born on 14 October 1855 at Old Clee near Grimsby and attended St James's Catholic College. At some time during his early life the second 'e' was added to his surname. His father, Captain James Edwards, had retired from the Army to make a new career as a customs officer. His parents decided that George should go to London to study for the Army entrance examinations. However, the attraction of the Music Hall was more important to George and he failed the examination. He was able to find employment as the manager of a theatrical company, which was about to begin a tour at Leicester.

This suited George's personality and he developed an aptitude for handling temperamental actors. He was soon launched on a promising career in the London theatre securing a post with Richard D'Oyly Carte's newly formed Opera Company. He became a good friend of Arthur Sullivan but did not get on very well with W. S. Gilbert. In 1885 he went into partnership with John Hollingshead the owner of the Gaiety Theatre and in the same year he married Julia Gwynne, a young actress.

'The Governor' as he was usually known took over the Gaiety from Hollingshead and bought Daly's Theatre in 1890 rebuilding it to his own specification. His first important venture as a theatre manager was the staging of the light opera *Dorothy* but this was not a success. However, by staging a succession of musical comedies in both theatres he made them world famous. Amongst the successes were *A Gaiety Girl* which was staged in 1893, *The Geisha* (1896), *San Toy* (1897), *A Country Girl* (1902), *The Merry Widow* (1907), *Our Miss Gibbs* (1909) and *The Quaker Girl* (1910).

By 1912 musical comedy had run its course and George Edwardes lost a considerable amount of money through unsuccessful shows, gambling and his racing stable coupled with a spendthrift wife. Following a succession of heart attacks he died on 4 October 1915. Although he died heavily in debt, the success in 1917 of *The Maid of the Mountains* which was staged at Daly's Theatre enabled all his debts to be settled and brought a considerable fortune to his heirs.

FURTHER READING : Bloom, Ursula *Curtain Call for the Governor* (1954)

William Edward ELSEY

William Edward Elsey was born on 19 May 1855 at Hemingby. His father, Edward Elsey, farmed at High House Farm in that parish. On 16 October 1879, William married Sarah Ann Scorer of Burwell and they rented a 1,200 acre farm in Baumber. This was a mixed farm but the main activity was the breeding of horses.

In 1883 Mr Elsey's young stallion, *Baumber Tom*, won the two-year old class at the Royal Show at York. Good prizes were also collected at local shows and also as far afield as Doncaster and Peterborough. At that time the Horncastle Horse Fair was in its heyday and good prices could be obtained from the buyers who came from all over Europe. However, around 1890 the bottom dropped out of the market and William decided to train his young horses for racing.

He turned a 60-acre field off the Caistor High Street into training gallops and with 40 good brood mares it was not long before his horses were in the winning enclosure. In 1891 his *Glen Helen* won the Tathwell Stakes at Lincoln.   The Carholme was then, and had been for many years, the traditional venue for the opening of the flat-racing season.   Less than twenty miles from Baumber, it was an ideal place for the new trainer to get into his stride.   In 1894 *Ella Tweed, Follyfoot* and *Plaything* all won races and in 1898 *Lord Edward II* won the National Produce Stakes at Sandown worth £5,000, a lot of money in those days. The number of winners continued to increase and in 1905 William Elsey trained no less than 124. That was the greatest number of winners in one season turned out by any trainer. It remained the record number until overtaken by Henry Cecil in 1979.

William Elsey employed 60 'lads' who lived mainly in Baumber and the surrounding villages. Their working day started by 7 a.m or earlier; any morning the long string of horses could be seen going along the Caistor High Street to the training gallops. The most successful jockey for William was Elijah Wheatley and in one year he rode 83 winners.   Wheatley married Miss Pinkett of the Fleece Public House and they lived in Queen Street, Horncastle.

William and Sarah Elsey had five children. The eldest, William Edward, was baptised on 31 July 1880 and eventually became Bishop of Kalgoorlie, Western Australia from 1919 to 1950. Charles Frederick was born on 10 December 1881. He enlisted in the Yorkshire Hussars early in the 1914-18 war and was commissioned. On demobilisation he had reached the rank of captain and assisted his father in running the stables. There were three daughters, Katherine Susan, Evelyn Mary and Marjorie.

There can be no doubt that William Elsey was a very successful trainer and for over thirty years there was a successful racehorse training establishment in the little Lincolnshire village of Baumber. It provided employment for a large number of people and trade for the village shop as well as for the shopkeepers of Horncastle.

William Edward Elsey died on 15 February 1922.

SOURCE : Adapted from Anderson, C. L.'William Edward Elsey of Baumber - Racehorse Trainer' in Society for Lincolnshire History and Archaeology *Newsletter* No 62 October 1989 pp. 22-24

Laurence EUSDEN

Laurence Eusden, who was rector of Coningsby towards the end of his life, was appointed poet laureate on 24 December 1718.   He was the son of the Revd Laurence Eusden rector of Spofforth, Yorkshire and was baptised there on 6 September 1688.   He went to St Peter's School, York and went up to Trinity College, Cambridge in 1705.   He graduated BA in 1708 and was awarded an MA in 1712.

Eusden's first printed item was a translation into Latin of a poem by Lord Halifax on the Battle of the Boyne and a poem by him drew attention to his lordship's poetic abilities. Not surprisingly this earned Eusden Lord Halifax's patronage. He gained the favour of the Duke of Newcastle who was the Lord Chamberlain by writing a flattering poem on the occasion of that nobleman's wedding. This led to Eusden being appointed poet laureate. His subsequent literary efforts provoked the following couplet from a contemporary poet, Thomas Cooke :

'Eusden, a laurel'd Bard, by fortune rais'd,
By very few was read, by fewer prais'd'

Whatever the quality of his work may have been Eusden held his position as poet laureate for twelve years. Although his work was certainly undistinguished it never aroused the venom of the great satirists of the age, as did the work of other poets of the time. A sample of his work is contained in the ode written by him in the death of George II which contains the lines :

'Thy virtues shine peculiarly nice
Ungloomed with a confinity to vice'

Pope contented himself with remarking mildly by his standards that 'Mr Eusden's writings rarely offended but by their length and multitude'. Eusden's character was attacked by Thomas Gray of *Elegy written in a country churchyard* fame who said that he 'turned out [to be] a drunken parson' but there is no evidence for this statement.

Eusden died at Coningsby in 1730 and was succeeded as poet laureate by Colley Cibber who spent part of his early life in Grantham (see *Lincolnshire People* Vol. I page 27).

Roy FAIERS

Roy Faiers was born at Cleethorpes in December 1927, the youngest of three children. His father, Phil Faiers, was a well-known local pianist and often provided the accompaniment for his great friend and eventual TV comedy star, Freddie Frinton (see page 54) when performing at clubs and pubs in Lincolnshire during the Thirties.

In 1931 the family moved to the Nunsthorpe district of Grimsby and Roy, with his sister, Betty, and brother, Philip, attended the local council school. Grimsby was subjected to heavy German air attack during the Second World War and his parents decided to send Roy to live with an aunt in Toronto, Canada. Twelve-year-old Roy was none too happy at first but was overjoyed when he and three other evacuees were offered places at De La Salle College which was a leading boarding school in North America.

He joined the school's 120-strong military style brass band and a recording of him sounding *Reveille* on his bugle was used by a local radio station for ten years to wake up its listeners every morning! Roy had inherited his father's love of music and he taught himself to play by ear popular songs on the school piano for dances and parties. He matriculated four years later and in June, 1944 he returned to Britain to join the Royal Navy.

Seventeen-year-old Boy Seaman Faiers served first in a minesweeper in the North Atlantic before being drafted to the Far East. While at shore bases in Ceylon and Malaya, he was in regular demand to play the piano for local Servicemen's clubs. Soon after the Japanese surrender he and a few other Navy pals combined their talents to get the first post-war English broadcasting service going again in Singapore. As well as presenting the daily half-hour programme of piano music called *Melody on Ivory,* Roy began writing scripts for Goon type comedy shows which he and his messmates later acted out and broadcast. This was Roy's first taste of script-writing and this set him on course for his future career.

On returning to Grimsby following demob at the end of 1946, he tried without success to find a job in broadcasting but instead found himself serving a three-month trial as a cub reporter on the *Grimsby Evening Telegraph* at 30 shillings a week. Within eighteen months, after rapidly gaining experience in news reporting and feature writing, his salary was tripled to £4.10s for a six-day, 50 hour plus week. That was just enough to enable 20-year-old Roy to marry 18-year-old Dorothy, younger daughter of local hotel manager Colin Middleton. After their simple wedding in July 1948 at St Mary's church in Heneage Road, Grimsby, they 'splashed out' and caught the bus for a two-day honeymoon at Mablethorpe.

Dorothy and Roy celebrated their Golden Wedding in 1998

In order to make ends meet, Roy followed in his father's footsteps and began playing the piano at pubs and clubs in the Grimsby area. He became the regular Saturday night entertainer at *The Ship Inn*, Barnoldby-le-Beck.

In 1950 Roy left the *Telegraph* to join the editorial team at the *Manchester Evening News* and he also began weekend freelance work for the BBC as a football reporter on the Saturday evening programme *Sports Report*. It was while at Manchester that he had hopes of going back to North America, as a radio journalist, this time assisting the *Guardian's* already well-known American correspondent Alistair Cooke. But the veteran writer and broadcaster, famous for his weekly *Letter from America*, decided he couldn't afford a second-in-command and so Roy returned to the *Grimsby Evening Telegraph* in 1952 as a sub-editor. He still worked for the BBC at weekends, and two years later gave up his staff job to become a full-time freelance journalist representing all the national daily and Sunday newspapers in the Lincolnshire area.

In 1956 Roy opened a small office near the Town Hall in Grimsby and invited journalist Charlie Ekberg to join him on an equal footing. Together they launched their first magazine, *Humber Industry and Fishing Review*, a year later and in the Spring of 1961 they brought out the first issue of the county magazine, *Lincolnshire Life*, at first published quarterly. A small printing workshop was set up in Wellowgate, Grimsby, to handle the growing output.

The new magazine eventually spawned a series of twelve similar county titles spread across the country, from Norfolk and Suffolk to the Cotswolds and Devon. Roy took over the long-established Grimsby printing company of Windles to manage the increased print demand and local artist and school friend Colin Carr joined Roy as an illustrator. This proved to be a fortuitous move as Colin's unique art-work not only graced the pages of the group's many county publications but in early 1968, with the launch of the hugely successful international quarterly *This England,* his distinctive style was seen and highly admired by the magazine's two million readers all over the world.

With editorial offices as far apart as Norwich and Salisbury, and his own printing companies in Grimsby and Exeter, Roy decided to move his headquarters to a more central site in Cheltenham. He learned to pilot his own plane in order to visit the various regional outlets and also to take a break every few weeks at the sunshine home he had built for his family, then numbering four sons, on the Mediterranean coast of Spain.

Not all his projects have been successful. In 1966 he produced a new Sunday newspaper for Lincolnshire and the north-east, entitled *The Link*. It was the first Sunday paper to be launched in Britain for several decades and the Press barons in London blocked all his attempts to distribute the paper so the title closed within six weeks.

The county magazine titles were sold in order to concentrate on the expanding success of *This England* by establishing offices in Australia, New Zealand, Canada and the USA. Then, in 1985, he launched a sister magazine entitled *Evergreen* which was also aimed at the mature majority in Britain and overseas.

In 1995 Roy was granted the Freedom of the City of London, but three years later he took the unprecedented step of revoking his position as a Freeman by returning his sealed Certificate to the Lord Mayor in protest at the Honorary Freedom being awarded to German Chancellor Helmut Kohl, a former member of the Hitler Youth and the first European politician from outside Britain to receive the honour. Herr Kohl is on record as having stated: 'The future will belong to Germany when we have built the house of Europe'. This touched a raw nerve in Roy's soul for he is a passionate opponent of a European Union super-state, as fully reflected in his editorial columns for *This England*.

At a ceremony in St James's Palace, London, in April 2000, Roy Faiers was honoured by being awarded the rare Fellowship of the Royal Society of St George in recognition of his many services to England. Now in his 75th year, he is still working every day, not only editing *This

England, but also writing articles and producing books, including a new one now in the pipeline as a tribute to the unique artistry of his great friend from schooldays, Colin Carr.

Field FLOWERS

Whilst on holiday a few years ago I visited Lindisfarne and my attention was drawn to a headstone close by the entry to the Priory. I was surprised to find that this recorded the death of a young boy from Lincolnshire. On my return to Lincoln I made some enquiries and I was eventually able to record details of a tragedy which affected several Lincolnshire families.

On the night of Wednesday, 19 July 1843, the steamship *Pegasus* set sail on its regular voyage from Leith to Hull. There were approximately 55 people on board, including a crew of 14. The steamer left at about six o'clock in the evening and six hours later it struck the Goldstone Rock and sank close by the Farne Islands. This occurred at about 12.20 in the morning and the ship had sunk by one o'clock in the morning. Only two passengers and four members of the crew were saved.

Amongst those who perished were Field Flowers aged thirteen and his sister Fanny Maria aged eleven who were the two eldest children of the Revd Field Flowers, vicar of Tealby, Lincolnshire. They were attending Miss Banks' Boarding School in Edinburgh and were coming home for the holidays in the charge of Miss Maria Barton, daughter of Zephaniah Barton, a medical practitioner living in Market Rasen, Lincolnshire. Also in her charge was a Miss Hopetoun, a pupil at the same school, who was visiting Market Rasen. They also lost their lives, as did Mr. Robinson Torry aged 27 another native of Market Rasen, who 'had been taking a trip for the benefit of his health'.

The body of Miss Barton was picked up at about six o'clock on the morning of the 20 July by the SS *Martello* which was sailing from Hull to Leith. Her body was brought back to Market Rasen and interred in the family vault on the 1st of August 1843. The Revd Field Flowers was present, as was Mr. John Torry, whose brother had perished at the same time.

The body of young Field Flowers was eventually picked up by some French fishermen who brought it to Holy Island for burial at Lindisfarne about four weeks after the tragedy. A headstone was erected to his memory together with that of his sister Fanny Maria, whose body was never recovered.

The inscription on the stone is barely legible now but from a photograph taken some twenty or more years ago most of the inscription can be deciphered and reads as follows :

IN MEMORY
OF
FIELD FLOWERS
SON OF THE REVEREND FIELD FLOWERS.
AND FRANCES HIS WIFE
OF TEALBY VICARAGE LINCOLNSHIRE
AGED 13 YEARS
WHO WAS DROWNED ON THE 19th OF JULY
1843 WHEN THE STEAMER PEGASUS
WAS WRECKED (OFF HOLY ISLAND)
Also FANNY................. SISTER
WHO…………………………..

Another who lost his life in the tragedy was the Revd. J. Morrell Mackenzie of the Theological Academy, Glasgow. By a remarkable coincidence, he had preached a funeral sermon for two of his friends who were lost when the *Forfarshire* was wrecked five years earlier near the same spot!

SOURCES : I am grateful to Jim Murray of Tealby for reading and correcting this article and to Janice Brigham a member of the staff of Lindisfarne Museum. For a detailed account of this tragedy see 'The Wreck of the Steamship Pegasus' by Jim Murray which was published in *The Northumbrian* (Vol. 27 Summer 1994) and also in the *Journal of the Open University History Society* (1994).

Michael FOALE
(See photograph on back cover)

In June 1983 Michael Foale joined the staff of NASA at the Johnson Space Centre and four years later was selected as an astronaut candidate. He completed a twelve-month training and evaluation programme and his first space mission was on board an American Shuttle flight in 1992 when he spent nine days in orbit. Two other flights followed and in February 1995 he became the first British-born man to walk in space.

In 1996 he undertook further training at the Cosmonaut Training Centre, Star City, Russia in preparation for a long duration flight on the Russian Space Station Mir. On 17 May 1997 he joined the eleven-year old Russian space station and during his time in space survived a number of potentially disastrous incidents. These included a collision with a supply ship. Michael commented that he and his two Russian companions tried not to dwell on the possible consequences of the collision but a week after the collision 'I was thinking about what really could have happened and we sort of shuddered at the thought of it and just stopped thinking about it'. Michael returned safely to Earth on 6 October 1997. In 1998 he was appointed Assistant Director (Technical) and in 1999 Chief of the Expedition Corps in the Astronaut Office of the

Johnson Space Centre of the United States National Aeronautics and Space Administration.

Michael says 'I don't intend to leave until I'm in my 50s and I hope to fly every two years or so. I want to take part in as many programmes as possible'. He went on to say 'It's the best job in the world. You couldn't find such a variety of things to challenge you physically and mentally anywhere else'.

Colin Michael Foale is the son of Air Commodore Colin Foale and his wife, Mary Katharine Foale *née* Horton, who comes from Minneapolis, USA. Michael was born at Louth on 6 January 1957 whilst his father was a pilot attack instructor at RAF Manby living at Sutton-on-Sea. When Michael was fifteen months old the family left Lincolnshire and his early schooling was at Montpelier School in Plymouth, Devon and the King's School, Canterbury. He went up to Queen's College, Cambridge graduating with a first class honours degree in Physics in 1978 and then researched, at the Cavendish Laboratory for a PhD in astrophysics which was awarded in 1982.

Whilst researching for his PhD, Michael participated in the organisation and execution of scientific scuba-diving projects and with the co-operation of the Greek Government he participated as both a member and leader of expeditions surveying underwater antiquities in Greece. In autumn 1981 as a volunteer diver he helped survey the *Mary Rose* in very low visibility conditions.

Michael was awarded the Founders' Medal of the Air League in 1993, the Barnes Wallis Award of the Guild of Air Pilots and Air Navigators in 1994 and an honorary Fellowship of the Royal Aeronautical Society in 1997. He was appointed to an honorary Fellowship of Cambridge University in 1998 and awarded an honorary doctorate by the University of Kent in 2000. In the same year he was awarded an honorary doctorate of science by the University of Lincolnshire and Humberside.

Although Michael's acquaintance with 'the forgotten county' was brief, he and his parents have a deep affection for his birthplace. Michael continues to enjoy Anglo-American dual nationality and lives in Houston with his wife and two children. Amongst his recreations he includes flying!

Oliver Goring FOLKARD

Clergymen and gardening seem inextricably entwined, and the image of a country parson gently botanising is a common one. The reality is somewhat different, as vicars are on call almost as much as busy GPs. Oliver Folkard originates from Devon where he was born in 1941. In 1963 he graduated from Nottingham University and, after training at Lichfield Theological College, he was ordained deacon in 1966 and priest in 1967. Oliver held a number of curacies in the Southwell and Lichfield Dioceses before moving to Lincolnshire as curate of the Folkingham group of parishes. He was vicar of Whaplode Drove from 1976 until 1984 when he moved to Sutton St Mary. Oliver Folkard moved to his present post at Scotter in 1994 and after some twenty-five years in Lincolnshire has come to have a high regard for the county.

From an early age Oliver Folkard had a passionate interest in gardening and is an inveterate seed sower and taker of cuttings. In the early 1970s he made a deliberate cross between *Geranium psilostemon* and *Geranium procurrens* which produced a promising seedling which he named for his wife Ann. He and his wife lived at Walcot and it was there that 'Ann Folkard' first saw the light of day although the cross and seed collection had been made in Staffordshire. After a description of the plant was published in the *Journal* of the Royal Horticultural Society Alan Bloom became interested and it was he who undertook to launch *Geranium 'Ann Folkard'* for sale to the general public. The plant produces its clear magenta flowers with a darker centre continually until late in the season. The leaves are flushed yellow and its habit of growth is also outstanding. From a small central rootstock it can make a plant four or five feet across but if hedged about by other plants it simply trails and weaves through them dying tidily back to almost nothing in autumn. It is an indispensable plant and the Lincolnshire connection makes it even more desirable. *Geranium 'Ann Folkard'* is pictured on the back cover of this book.

To date Oliver Folkard has one other geranium in general cultivation, a cross between *G. traversii* and *G. sessiliflorum*. This is a low-growing plant with pale coffee leaves and delicate pink flowers, named Kate after his daughter. His interest still continues but nothing more of the quality of 'Ann Folkard' has yet appeared.

Keith FORDYCE

Keith Fordyce became well known in the 1960s first on radio as the presenter of such popular radio programmes as *Housewive's Choice* and *World Wide Family Favourites* and then on television as the compère of the *Miss England, Miss U. K.* and *Miss World* beauty contests.

Keith Fordyce Marriott was born in Lincoln in the St Giles district to the north of the city in 1928 and he is the son of Frank and Kitty Marriott. His father was the secretary of the Tennis Club in Longdales Road and eventually became a Vice-President of the Lincolnshire Lawn Tennis Association. Tennis championships were not held during the war years and Keith, who was an enthusiastic player, was only able to compete in one Lincolnshire Junior Tennis Championship before reaching the age of eighteen and becoming ineligible. However, in 1946, he won the Championship and he was very pleased for his father's sake. Keith's father had the ability to recognise budding tennis stars and one of his discoveries was Shirley Bloomer (see *Lincolnshire Women* page 8).

After early schooling Keith continued his education at Lincoln School (now Lincoln Christ's Hospital School) from 1937 until 1947. He had joined the Air Training Corps at the age of fifteen and immediately from school he was called up to serve in the Volunteer Reserve with the Royal Air Force. He was very lucky to be posted to Germany at the time when an RAF General Administrative Order was promulgated calling for volunteers to join the recently formed British Forces Network. The headquarters of the radio station was in Hamburg and eighteen-year-old AC1 Marriott, K. F. was called for interview by two Squadron Leaders, a Wing Commander and - Raymond Baxter. They must have been impressed because Keith served for the remainder of his time with the RAF as a broadcaster! Actually, he had said at the interview that he would prefer to work as a producer in Features and Drama and he has always regarded himself as more of a producer than a performer. However, the B. F. N. needed presenters and it was more or less a case of take it or leave it. After a very gruelling test Keith asked Raymond Baxter how he had done and the reply in Baxter's rather languid manner was: 'Well, my boy, you're not exactly God's gift to radio but we'll make something of you'.

On returning to Civvy Street, having reached the rank of Sergeant, Keith went up to Emmanuel College, Cambridge and graduated with a Master's degree in law. He then worked in London as a personal assistant with Sainsbury's whilst trying to find an opening in radio. After a period of free-lance broadcasting he joined Radio Luxembourg and it was at this time that he began to use his professional name 'Keith Fordyce'. He lived in the Grand Duchy from 1955 until 1958 when he returned to England to take up free-lance broadcasting again but this time primarily in television.

At the height of his career he had two programmes each week with ITV, two with the BBC and six with Radio Luxembourg. These included hosting radio programmes which, as well as *Housewife's Choice* and *World Wide Family Favourites,* included *Twelve O'clock Spin, Roundabout, Late Night Extra* and *Open House*. On television, he co-presented *Picture Parade* with Robert Robinson and *Ready, Steady Go,* a programme which had a great influence on fellow Lincolnshire Yellowbelly, Bernie Taupin (see page 144). Keith also compèred around 100 national and international beauty contests as well as *Royal Film Performances, Come Dancing* and a programme in the *Juke Box Jury* series. Keith was commentator for the BBC at Wimbledon in 1967 and 1968. A particular landmark programme was the first day of the 1967 Wimbledon Tournament, which was the first transmission in this country to be made in colour. For ITV he presented five series from 1976 until 1979 of *Kitchen Garden* and *Star Gardens*.

In recent years Keith has presented three series of *Support Your Local* for Radio 2, eight series of *Town and Country Quiz, Sounds of the Sixties* for four years until 1987 and *Beat the Record* for ten years until 1992. Since 1994 Keith has presented radio programmes for a ten-month stint with Classic Gold Radio and he is still presenting the late night *Keith Fordyce Show* for the BBC South West Region.

In addition to regular series, Keith has presented many 'one off' programmes. After some forty years as a presenter on radio and television he shows no signs of retirement - in 1996 and 1997 he was a compère and lecturer on the Cunard ships Q.E.2 and Cunard Countess.

Keith hasn't, however, only had a career with the media. Perhaps appropriately, for someone coming from 'Bomber County', from 1971 until 1988 he had a very enjoyable 'second string' when he created the Torbay Aircraft Museum. He says this was the happiest time of his life. A garden was created at the museum for the ladies to relax in whilst their men folk were admiring the aircraft. This was named the *Kenneth More Garden* in memory of the actor who was a regular visitor and made several films at the museum.

Keith and his wife Anne have lived in Devon since 1969. Until that year Keith had been commuting by train from London to Plymouth to present Westward Television's programme *Treasure Hunt*. He worked for that station until it lost its franchise after eighteen years and presented *Treasure Hunt* for fourteen of those years.

Anne and Keith have four daughters the eldest of these, Rebecca, was born in Wimbledon; the second, Kim, in Luxembourg; the third, Julie, in Watford and their youngest daughter, Sam, in Chesham! The children have long since flown the nest and Julie lives in Ocean Springs, Mississippi. Anne and Keith have seven grandchildren.

Keith says that he came to have a feel for Devon which he finds has much in common with Lincolnshire. Whenever they can he and his wife still visit his birthplace.

Freddie FRINTON

Freddie Frinton as plumber Fred Blackett in *Meet the Wife* and with Thora Hird in the comedy *The Bed.*

Freddie Hargate (alias Frinton) became famous for his cameo of a top-hatted drunk reeling about the stage in a state of semi-intoxication. His BBC television series *Meet the Wife* made him a household name all over the country as plumber Fred Blackett perpetually hen-pecked by his TV wife, Thora Hird. The audience figure of fifteen million was remarkable, especially for that time.

Freddie was born in 1915 and was the son of a Grimsby fisherman. He left school at the age of fourteen and started work in Forbes' fish curing factory in Riby. He would entertain his workmates by clowning around and he told the story of one such incident as follows : 'We used to have skate - those fish with great big flappers on either side; for a laugh I cut the middle out of one and fixed it over my head. I was just in the middle of an impromptu dance, making all the other chaps laugh, when the boss walked in…'   Freddie was eventually booked for a regular engagement playing to three 'houses' a night at the *Gloucester Arms*, Albion Street for £4 a week. By night he was cracking his jokes and singing such songs as 'Buddy Can You Spare A Dime,' and by day he was curing fish.

For a time Freddie worked alfresco on Cleethorpes seashore but his professional career really took off when he joined the Nibs Concert Party which used to tour pubs and clubs throughout Lincolnshire. He was spotted by comedian Tom Moss and immediately booked to play the Dame in pantomime in Southport. A number of pantomimes and revues followed until the Second World War when he served for eighteen months with an army searchlight unit before being transferred to *Stars in Battledress*.

After the war Freddie toured with George Black's *Strike A New Note* and finally his television break came as the 'drunk' in the Arthur Haynes show. His first appearance in a play was with Thora Hird at Blackpool in 1962 in *The Best Laid Schemes*. This was so successful that it was booked for two more summer seasons at Torquay and Bournemouth. The same team wrote *The Bed* for Thora and Freddie and the television series *Meet the Wife* evolved from this play.

Although Freddie Frinton was known as a 'drunk' he never touched beer. He said 'I've been playing the drunk for as long as I can remember. Men like him because they've either been him or have seen him'. In fact he was a quiet, home-loving soul who liked continental cooking.

Sadly Freddie Frinton died at the height of his television career on 16 October 1968. He had married his wife, Nora, whilst still in the Army and they had four children.

Yuri GALITZINE
(See photograph on back cover)

It comes as a surprise to find a Russian prince living in south Lincolnshire.

Prince Yuri Yurka Nikolaievitch Galitzine is the eldest son of Prince Nicholas Alexandrovitch Galitzine and Emma Lilian Fawcett-Hodgson. In 1916 his father was appointed Assistant Military Attaché in the Imperial Russian Embassy in London and was, therefore, in this country when the first Revolution erupted in April 1917. His mother came from a Westmoreland farming family.

After the fall of the Russian Monarchy in October 1917, Prince and Princess Nicholas Galitzine went to the United States and remained there for the remainder of the First World War. Prince Yuri was born in 1919 in Yokohama, Japan whilst his parents were returning to the United Kingdom.

For a time Prince Yuri lived with his family in Austria and France before they finally settled in England. His first language is German and second French. He didn't learn English until, at the age of eleven, he entered a preparatory school in Sussex. In 1932 Prince Yuri was awarded a scholarship to Stowe School and it was whilst at that school that he developed a particular interest in Ancient History. After leaving Stowe School in 1937, Prince Yuri became an apprentice in the glove factory owned by the French branch of the family at Millau, France. After twelve months he returned to London and became an apprentice with the Fairey Aviation Company working in the Experimental Workshops.

Prince Yuri spent three interesting months early in 1939 travelling through Germany, Austria, Czechoslovakia and Hungary. Sensing that war was imminent he returned to the U. K. and joined the army and soon after war was declared he was selected for officer training. He was commissioned in the Royal Northumberland Fusiliers and he eventually became General Staff Officer (Training) in Northern Ireland with the rank of Captain. He took part in the El Alamein and Tunis Campaigns and was then appointed liaison officer with the First Free French Division. He was made 'an honorary soldier of France' and later served as Psychological Warfare Officer in South East France, Holland and Western Germany.

After demobilisation in 1946 for a short time he was a feature writer for the *Sunday Express* and then joined Hunting Aviation Management Limited first as press officer and served in several other capacities including publicity manager and finally as personal assistant to the Chairman and Public Relations Officer for the Group. From 1949 until 1951 he was based in Africa and in 1952 he was seconded to serve as Chairman of the London Committee of the United Central Africa Association which had been formed to work for the federation of Rhodesia and Nyasaland. From 1953 until 1963 he served as a member of the Migration Council which had been set up to encourage emigration to the Commonwealth.

In 1954 Prince Yuri formed Galitzine and Partners and during the 1950s he enthusiastically participated in the collective life of the public relations profession. He served twice as a member of the International Public Relations Association and also as a member of the Professional Practices, Membership, Consultancy and International Committees. He was elected to a Fellowship of the Association in 1963. He was a founder member of the British Association of Industrial Editors and of the Society of Independent Public Relations Consultants. In the 1960s Prince Yuri was the author and publisher of three books on public relations.

For many years Prince Yuri was a Member of the Council of the Russian Refugee Aid Society and has served as Vice-Chairman and Chairman. He is now Vice President. He has always been interested in the history and genealogy of Russia in the seventeenth century. He is also interested in the medieval history of the East Midlands and is founder and Chairman of the Rutland Record Society and a member of the Northampton and Lincoln Record Societies as well as being a member of the Historical Houses Association, London Library, the Society of Genealogists, Life Vice-President of Men of the Stones. He is a collector of antiquarian books and prints.

Prince Yuri lives in South Lincolnshire and he has married four times. He has three daughters and two sons.

Montague Francis GLEW

Montague Francis Glew was born on 12th April 1893 at South Kelsey Hall and he was the second son of Walter and Grace Glew. He had an older brother, Aubrey Edmund, and his younger brother was named Leslie.

Walter and Grace Glew left South Kelsey *circa* 1905 and moved to Park Farm, Wittering. Francis (as he was usually known) learnt to fly at the Blackburn School, Hendon, together with Cyril Foggin, whose sister Rene, he was later to marry. He was granted his Royal Aero Club certificate on 4th February 1913, after flying a Blackburn monoplane for his test. The number of the certificate was 410, and it is still in the possession of his family.

Francis, Aubrey, Cyril and their friend Jack Burkitt (of Kingerby) worked as a team. They travelled up and down the country giving flying displays, including Market Rasen and Horncastle. Cyril and Francis bought their plane, a 1912 50hp Blackburn Monoplane (single seater), from Robert Blackburn and it was the seventh made by him. Crashes were a regular occurrence and a lot of time and money was spent in repairing the 'plane. Much use was made of the 'farmer's friend' - binder twine! It was eventually discovered that there was a hairline crack in the cylinder and when the engine reached a certain temperature it caused the 'plane to stall. In case of emergency while taking the 'plane to an engagement Francis acted as pilot and Cyril followed behind on a motorbike.

The flying display at Market Rasen was held on 10 and 11 July 1913, and was only five months after Francis obtained his certificate. His performance caused considerable interest and there was a comprehensive account in the *Market Rasen Mail* for 19 July 1913.

Adding to the excitement, apart from the 'grand display', was a crash on 11 July, this time caused by a broken petrol pipe. Although the 'plane received considerable damage to the struts, landing chassis, framework, engine and a broken propeller, Francis received no injuries. It meant, however, that the 'plane had to be repaired in 12 days, ready for a display at Horncastle.

The following advertisement appeared in the *Horncastle News and South Lindsey Advertiser* for Saturday 19 July 1913 :

A FLYING EXHIBITION
will be given (weather permitting) by
Mr M F Glew (of Hendon)
at Horncastle in the Crooks Field
Low Toynton Road,
on Wednesday and Thursday,
July 23 and 24.
Flying to commence about

3 o'clock until dusk
Admission 6d.   Reserved Inclosure 1/-
Motor Cars 2/6 including driver.
Public entrance through Mr English's Field, Green Lane.
Entrance for Motors and Traps through
Mr Read's Field, Low Toynton Road.

Flying Man to Visit Horncastle; - as will be seen from our advertisement columns, a flying exhibition will be given by Mr M F Glew (of Hendon) at Horncastle in the Crooks Field, Low Toynton Road, on Wednesday and Thursday, July 23rd and 24th. This is the first time Horncastle has ever been favoured with the visit of a flying man, and given good weather, we trust that the efforts of the promoters will be loyally supported. The flying will commence about 3 o'clock.   Entrance can be gained through Mr English's field, Green Lane. There is one sight peculiar to a flying exhibition and that is that people prefer to remain outside rather than to enter the field.   Not that they can witness the flights any better but they save the entrance money 6d in this case. 'A nod is as good as a wink to a blind horse', is an old but true saying.   We trust that as in other things, Horncastle will show us loyalty on the occasion of the flying man's visit.'

The following week the newspaper carried this account of the display :

Flying man at Horncastle - 'Unfortunate' aptly sums up Horncastle's initial visit of a flying man, Mr Montague F Glew of Hendon. Lincolnshire's only aviator had been engaged to give flying exhibitions in the Crooks Field, Low Toynton Road, Horncastle, on Wednesday and Thursday, but owing to the adverse weather the first day there was no flying, while on Thursday Mr Glew made a rather hurried descent at his second flight, and put his machine out of action. This was a great disappointment, not only to himself, but to the crowd of people, who had congregated to see him fly. At his first flight he ascended 500 feet and circled round the field in fine style before landing. At his second attempt Mr Glew went out for height, but owing to his engine, he was forced to descend rather sharply. The top left-hand longitudinal was damaged and though this in itself was slight it meant that the whole machine had to be dissembled to put the damage right. Further flights were out of the question, but a crowd of people took a keen interest in watching the machine being taken to pieces.   Mr Glew is a son of the late Mr Walter Glew of Wittering and formerly of South Kelsey, and nephew of Mr J. G. Glew of Market Rasen.   His machine is a 50hp Gnome-Blackburn of the military type.

At the outbreak of war in 1914 Francis was prevented from joining the Royal Flying Corps because of short-sightedness.   His elder brother, Aubrey and Cyril Foggin both joined the Royal Flying Corps. Aubrey was killed in 1916 but Cyril Foggin continued to fly throughout the war until 1918 when, after landing from patrol and returning to the officer's mess, he and three other officers were killed when the car in which they were travelling crashed into a tree.   Leslie,

Francis's younger brother served right through the war as a despatch rider.

After crashing his 'plane yet again in 1914, Francis put it into storage at his farm, where it remained until purchased for restoration by Richard Shuttleworth in 1938. The remains of the 'plane were found to be in a quite reasonable condition with the 50hp Gnome rotary engine in a dismantled state in a barrel in the granary. The Blackburn was partially restored by 1939, but not completed until 1946-7. On 25 September 1949 it was flown by Group Captain Allen Wheeler round three circuits at Farnborough Aerodrome during a Royal Aircraft Establishment 'At Home'. The plane is now kept at Old Warden Aerodrome at Biggleswade in Bedfordshire in the ownership of the Richard Ormond Shuttleworth Remembrance Trust. It is the oldest original British aeroplane capable of being flown.

Francis continued to farm at Park Farm Wittering, having married Rene Foggin. They had four children. Montague Francis Glew died in 1969 and Rene in 1979. The farmland over which Francis flew is now RAF Wittering.

Robert Samuel GODFREY

The presentation of an honorary degree to Robert Godfrey in 1952.
Left to right : the Subdean of Lincoln; the Archbishop of Canterbury; the Dean of Lincoln; Robert Godfrey; Sir Henry Dashwood, Registrar; the Bishop of Lincoln.

Although Robert Samuel Godfrey, who was appointed clerk of works at Lincoln Cathedral in 1919, is recorded in *Who's Who* as being the son of Samuel Godfrey and Elizabeth Keys and his date of birth was given as 23 August 1876, little is known of his early life and education. The same publication records that he was educated at public school before going up to University College, Oxford but there is no evidence for either of these statements.

On his birth certificate his father is described as a cottager and the family lived at Gedling, Nottinghamshire. However, of much greater importance is his contribution to the maintenance of the Cathedral. This is recorded at length in an obituary published in the

Lincolnshire Echo and extracts from this are reproduced below.

'One need look no further than Lincoln Cathedral to see a lasting memorial to Robert S. Godfrey. For it is largely due to Mr Godfrey's ingenuity and his untiring labours over many years when the entire fabric of the Minster was threatened with collapse that the Cathedral stands today as secure on its foundations as ever it has been. He it was who discovered in 1921 that the whole of the West Front and the towers were falling outward at the alarming rate of an inch every sixteen days and it was his brain that developed the instruments with which this steady disintegration was halted.

Godfrey saved further deterioration by injecting liquid cement under pressure and this method of grouting ancient masonry has since been copied in many famous buildings including St Paul's Cathedral and Durham Castle. Godfrey was ingenious and characteristically determined to overcome difficulties'.

Three years after the completion of the repair of the west front it was found that the south east corner of the Angel Choir was in a dangerous state and Godfrey remarked at the time that he would not have been surprised if that part of the Cathedral had collapsed at any moment.'

There is no doubt that Robert Godfrey lived for the Cathedral and his knowledge of the building was second to none but he owed much to his dedicated team and especially to Fred Higgins, who succeeded him as clerk of works.

Godfrey advised on the repair of many ancient and medieval buildings both at home and abroad and in 1929 he published a paper on the early history and various disasters and restorations in the past of Lincoln Cathedral. In 1931 he published a booklet entitled *Half-an-Hour at Lincoln Cathedral and the Special Repairs* and another entitled *The Romance of Lincoln Cathedral*.

In 1933 Robert Godrey was appointed CBE and in 1936 he was elected a Fellow of the Society of Antiquaries. In 1952 his work was recognised by the rare honour of the award of a Lambeth MA by the Archbishop of Canterbury.

Robert Samuel Godfrey CBE, MA, FSA, died on 30 March 1953.

Jabez GOOD

There is no doubt that Jabez Good was a remarkable man but he is little known now even in his native Burgh le Marsh. He was born in 1831 and for many years he was the local barber. Jabez taught himself woodcarving and his magnificent self-portrait won an award at the Workman's International Exhibition in London in 1870.

He also carved a bust of George II and a medallion portrait of Dr Wordsworth a former Bishop of Lincoln. One of his masterpieces can still be viewed today, the beautiful Eagle

Lectern at Burgh Church. Apparently this was carved using a penknife! As well as many beautiful works of art he built a whipping post, stocks and pillory to demonstrate how punishment was administered in earlier times. These were used for display purposes at various local events.

Jabez was also author of *A Glossary of or Collection of Words, Phrases, Place Names, Superstitions, etc., Current in East Lincolnshire*, which was published *circa* 1900. The words in the Glossary are those used by those who frequented his shop. Although many are true dialect others are actually slang words 'which were in common use in the County in the nineteenth century'. The book also includes 'A Valuable Cattle Table' from which 'the Weight of a Fat Pig or Bullock can be easily ascertained while living'. There is also a brief history of Burgh le Marsh.

Good was an avid collector and his barber's shop housed an interesting museum. In 1888 his collection of memorabilia was sold by auction. Amongst the items for sale were Jabez's carvings, Roman coins, some of which had been found locally and a pair of boots reputed to have belonged to Oliver Cromwell. Jabez was also a taxidermist, artist and signwriter. In fact it is surprising he ever found time to be a barber!

Jabez was involved in many local activities and at one time he served as the Parish Clerk. He designed the Triumphal Arches erected at the East and West end of Burgh for the Coronation celebrations of King George V and Queen Mary on June 22nd 1911. This must have been the last task in which he involved himself, as he died on 25 September 1911 aged 81. Although he is buried in Burgh Churchyard there is no headstone or memorial tablet to this remarkable local character.

The following verse, which it is said was on an envelope intended for delivery by the Post Office, sums up this remarkable man :

> Take this to Jabez whose surname is Good,
> A collector of bric a brac carver in wood,
> A numismatic cute in taxidermy famed,
> An artist he really is properly Named,
> A lover of virtue, a young oologist,
> And cutter of hair completeth the list,
> At the museum Burgh, this paragon dwells,
> In sight of the church and in sound of the bells.

Philip GOODRICH

Often when Bishop Philip Goodrich was visiting a church, if the bells were ringing to welcome him, he would insist on joining the ringers. No doubt the clergy treated this enthusiasm with a smile but it could delay the start of a service. This was especially true at Worcester Cathedral where he often made the long climb to the belfry. I am told that on one occasion the head verger was overheard saying to one of his colleagues, 'Grab the Bishop when he arrives and don't let him go up the tower or we'll be late again!'

Philip Harold Ernest Goodrich was born on 2 November 1929 at Pleasley Hill Nottinghamshire where his father was vicar. Five years later he, with his parents and two sisters, Joan and Margaret, moved to Corby Glen, Lincolnshire when his father was appointed Rector of Irnham with Corby. Whilst a schoolboy Philip was taught to ring on the four bells at Corby Glen by the sexton, Arthur Musson. He later came under the influence of the well-known and popular Bill Holmes of Edenham. Much to the amusement of his father, Philip would often imitate one of Bill's favourite expressions when trying to control the youngsters whom he was teaching – 'Remember the belfry is part of the church'.

After completing his schooling in Stamford, Philip went up to St John's College, Cambridge. His theological training was at Cuddesdon College, Oxford and he was ordained in 1954. That year he moved to St Andrews Church, Rugby, where he served his curacy until 1957, when he returned to Cambridge as chaplain of St John's.

It was at Cambridge that he met and later married Margaret Bennett, a historian and gifted teacher. In 1961 he returned to Lincolnshire with his wife and undertook the care of 14 parishes in the South Ormsby Group. This was a pioneer experiment in producing more effective pastoral care for small neighbouring rural parishes. In 1968 he was made Rector of St Peter and St Paul Church, Bromley and in 1973 he became Suffragan Bishop of Tonbridge, where he served until his move to Worcester in 1982.

Since the year 857 the Bishops of Worcester had lived at Hartlebury Castle but it was very expensive to run and Bishop Philip and his wife lived in only part of it. He dispensed with the chauffeur and greatly enjoyed helping, whenever he had the time, to look after the castle's moated garden.

Bishop Goodrich was a progressive, occasionally controversial bishop, and one of the most approachable and best-liked men in the Church of England. Affectionately known in Worcestershire as the 'people's bishop', he engaged with people wherever he went - whether he was working at home for deprived teenagers, children and their families as National Chairman of the Children's Society or visiting the powerless poor in Peru, he was always concerned for those at the bottom of the heap. During his time as Bishop of Worcester, from 1982 to 1996, he had his fair share of critics and his sometimes rather forthright language did not go down too well with the conservatives in the Church. But his critics were soon placated by his charm and his amicable modest approach. In the House of Lords he spoke on such subjects as the National Health Service, Bosnia and the Gulf War as well as subjects affecting the church's rôle in society.

Bishop Goodrich retired in 1996 and moved with his wife to Sutton St Nicholas in the Hereford Diocese. There he remained active, taking services in local churches and some confirmations. If the bells were ringing he would join the ringers and he was elected a vice-president of the Hereford Diocesan Guild of Church Bellringers. He took this very seriously as he did his membership of the local band of ringers at Sutton St Nicholas and attended practises whenever possible to help and encourage the learners. He was also able to continue his great love of gardening and particularly vegetable growing.

Bishop Philip Goodrich in the Ringing Chamber of St Matthias'
Church Malvern Link after dedicating two new treble bells in 1994

Bishop Goodrich once commented that, to him, life as a bishop was both a duty and a pleasure. He said, 'It's a fantastic job. Autonomy, travel, pastoral care, a roof over your head – you name it, it's got it. I can't understand why there aren't queues of people waiting to sign up'.

The Right Revd Philip Goodrich died on 22 January 2001 aged 71. His wife and four daughters survive him.

At a Service of Thanksgiving in Worcester Cathedral for the life of Bishop Philip the Venerable Frank Bentley, Archdeacon of Worcester referred to his 'impetuous enthusiasm' and his 'sheer joy of ministry and readiness to address social problems'. He also described him as 'never pompous or churchy' but said that he was 'always approachable and unpretentious'.

Richard William GOULDING

Whilst still at school, Richard Goulding became interested in natural history and started a collection of butterflies, moths and beetles which were all carefully catalogued and listed. At the age of sixteen the first article written by Goulding entitled 'Rhopalocerous Fauna in Louth' was published in the *Naturalists' World*.

Richard William Goulding was born on 23 November 1868 and he was the only son of J. W. Goulding who owned a bookshop and printing press in Mercer Row, Louth. He was educated at the National School in Westgate, Louth and went on to the King Edward VI Grammar School. In 1884 with fellow schoolboys H. W. Kew, E. Randall, H. Kendall, and W. L. Wells he formed what was to become the Louth Naturalists', Antiquarian and Literary Society which is still very active today.

On leaving school Goulding entered his father's business and he became interested in the documents, pamphlets and other papers which he found in his father's office. This encouraged him to investigate the Borough records which he eventually published as his first book *Louth Old Corporation Records*. In 1897 he wrote an article entitled 'Notes on the Lords of the Manor of Burwell' which was published in *Associated Architectural Society Reports and Papers* Volume XXIV.

In 1902 Goulding was offered the post of librarian to the Duke of Portland at Welbeck Abbey. As soon as he arrived at Welbeck he set about the enormous task of cataloguing the Duke's library. He became interested in the important collection of miniatures and when he had completed the library catalogue Goulding commenced a study of the miniatures and within ten years became an authority on miniature painting. His book, *The Welbeck Abbey Miniatures,* was published by the Walpole Society in 1916 and it is one of the most extensive monographs on miniatures in existence.

The Duke of Portland appointed Goulding his personal private secretary in addition to his duties as librarian. He also held the post of Assistant Secretary of the Lincolnshire Naturalists' Union for over thirty years and this heavy workload caused a breakdown in his health. In 1929 he returned to Louth and he died on 9 November in the same year. All his books, notes and memorabilia were presented to Louth Library and now form the Goulding Collection.

Richard Goulding was quiet and courteous but he could hold his own in intellectual circles. The Duke of Rutland considered him to be a remarkable man. He became widely recognised as a profound and learned authority upon English portraiture and costume. His knowledge and love of English literature and in particular of the writings of Charles Lamb made the library of Welbeck a familiar and happy retreat for him. He was also very knowledgeable in botanical studies.

GUTHLAC

Saint Guthlac was a hermit who was born *circa* 673 and died at Crowland on 11 April 714. Apparently his parents were members of the nobility. In his boyhood he had shown extraordinary signs of piety. After several years spent in warfare during which he never quite forgot his early training, he became filled with remorse and entered the monastery at Repton, Derbyshire. After two years of great penance and earnest application to all the duties of the monastic life he became fired with enthusiasm to emulate the wonderful penance of the Desert Fathers. For this purpose he retired with two companions to Crowland which was then a lonely island in the Lincolnshire fens. He spent fifteen years of rigid penance, fasting daily until sundown and then taking only coarse bread and water. Like St Anthony he was frequently attacked and severely maltreated by the Evil One, and on the other hand was the recipient of extraordinary graces and powers. The birds and the fishes became his familiar friends while the fame of his sanctity brought throngs of pilgrims to his cell. One of them, Bishop Hedda raised him to the priesthood and consecrated his humble chapel. Æthelbald, nephew of Penda, spent part of his exile with the saint.

During Holy Week of 714 Guthlac sickened and announced that he would die on the seventh day which he did joyfully. The anniversary (11 April) has always been kept as a feast. Many miracles were wrought at his tomb which soon became a centre of pilgrimage. After his death Guthlac appeared in a vision to Æthelbald and revealed to him that he would one day become king. The prophecy was verified in 716.

Æthelbald on becoming king proved himself a generous benefactor and he caused a large monastery to be built. Through the industry of the monks, the fens of Crowland became one of the richest places in England.

Geoffrey HADFIELD

Geoffrey Hadfield as a Seaborne Observer in 1944

In 1944 Geoff Hadfield was one of that select band of members of the Royal Observer Corps who volunteered to serve on board ship as Seaborne Observers during the Normandy landings. He was a Petty Officer Aircraft Identifier aboard the United States Navy Transport ship SS *Marine Raven*. The task of the Seaborne Observers was to recognise approaching aircraft and identify them as friend or foe to the gunners on the ships. He made two sailings as a Seaborne Observer. The first was from Swansea when 2,300 American troops were landed on Omaha Beach on D-Day + 2. On return the ship was sent to Belfast and three weeks later, on D-Day + 27, a further sailing was made with 2,800 troops on board and they were disembarked on Utah beach.

The foundation of the ROC goes back to 1918. Although too late to be of service in the First World War, the War Office agreed that it was essential to keep alive the art of air defence. After an experimental 'exercise' in Kent in 1924, observation posts were established in the Home Counties and the organisation of the Corps was formulated. Further expansion continued with No 11 Group based in Lincoln being formed in 1935. Towards the end of 1936 a network of 27 Posts was ready for use. It was at this time that Geoff joined the ROC and he recorded a total of 43 years' service which was recognised by the award of the British Empire Medal in 1975.

Geoffrey William Henry Hadfield was born in Alford on 24 July 1904 and was a member of a long established local family. He was the eldest son of Major James Henry Hadfield and his wife Sarah Elizabeth. Geoff was educated at the Church of England Boy's School in Parsons Lane apart from two years when he attended the Grammar School. Both his maternal grandfather, William Henry Northey, and father were successive headmasters at the Church of England School. William Northey came to Alford in 1862 and he married Sarah Bailey who was headmistress of the girls' school in 1877. Geoff's father was teaching at Wellingborough when William Northey died and he was appointed headmaster in 1900.

Geoff left school in 1921 and worked in various jobs, including three years as a motor engineer, before joining Marshall Sons & Co of Gainsborough in 1926. He left in the following year when he went to India as a tea planter and returned to Alford in 1932. During his time in India he served in the Surma Valley Light Horse from 1929 until 1931. On his return he set up a successful poultry farm on the outskirts of the town and he became a familiar figure riding his bicycle about the town.

After the war Geoff spent much of his time recording in detail the history of the town and compiled several booklets on that subject. These included a guidebook published by the town council. Geoff dealt with enquiries about the history of Alford and he meticulously answered many letters from home and abroad. He frequently acted as a guide for visitors to the town and he greatly enjoyed these tasks. Geoff acted as correspondent for Alford for the *Lincolnshire Standard*. He also helped with the Air Training Corps for a time after the war.

Geoff sustained serious injury to his left hand in the 1930s and in 1986 he was seriously injured when he was knocked down by a car in the town centre but within a year he had made a remarkable recovery. On the forty-fifth anniversary of D-Day, 6 June 1989, Alford Town Council presented Geoff with a certificate thanking him for his work as unofficial ambassador for Alford. Geoffrey Hadfield BEM died on 19 December 2001 aged 97.

Richard HAMMOND

Richard Hammond was born in Boston in 1829 but his parents moved to Gainsborough when he was two years old so his claim to have been 'the maker of the first pedal-and-crank bicycle in England' might well mean that Gainsborough can claim this honour.

Richard Hammond worked for his father in his coach-building business and, in the early 1860s, he became intrigued with the idea of building a velocipede. He abandoned his design for a three-wheeler in favour of a design for a two-wheeled machine. His first bicycle was ready for the road in January 1868 and it was made entirely of iron with three-foot wheels and after some practice he was able to ride it 'all over the town'. Although Hammond's machine was already much lighter than any foreign-produced machine, a second one with wooden wheels and iron tyres brought the weight down to 35 pounds.

Hammond arranged a demonstration ride over the fifty miles from Gainsborough to Boston and whilst he was consuming his breakfast in Lincoln a crowd of some 500 gathered to see this strange machine. Velocipede-riding became popular and races were held in Gainsborough and Boston with Hammond usually the winner.

Richard Hammond's claim to being the maker of the first pedal and crank bicycle in England could well be valid. The first French machine was brought over in November 1868 almost ten months after he had built his first machine. American machines had been imported earlier in the same year but after Hammond's machine was built.

Hammond also invented a dog cart which could carry two people and their luggage. From the evidence of trade directories he is known to have still been in business as a coachbuilder in 1892. After he died on 24 August 1901 at the age of 72 the business continued for several years under the direction of his widow. One of his machines is on exhibition in Gainsborough Old Hall.

John HASSALL
(See front cover for reproduction of *The Jolly Fisherman* poster)

John Hassall, the artist responsible for the famous painting 'Skegness is so Bracing' which is the first depiction of Skegness's mascot, *The Jolly Fisherman*, was actually born at Walmer, Kent on 21 May 1868. He was the eldest son of Lt Christopher Clark Hassall R.N. and his wife Louisa. His father was paralysed as a result of an accident and died in 1876 at the age of 38. John's mother took as her second husband General Sir William Purvis Wright. After attending school in Worthing John went on to Newton Abbot College, Devon where he received his first lessons in drawing. He then went on to Neuenheim College, Heidelberg where he said he spent three of the happiest years of his life.

It was intended that he would enter the Army but he failed the Sandhurst entrance examination twice. Despite his step-father's influence, he was unable to take a commission and he joined his brother Owen in Canada. It was a lonely life in Manitoba and John occupied his time by sketching and at an agricultural exhibition in the small town of Minnedosa about 140 miles west of Winnipeg he won three prizes for his pictures. This encouraged him to submit some sketches to the *Daily Graphic* which were published to his surprise in the issue dated 26 February 1890. On the strength of this success, John Hassall decided to return to England and become an artist and obtained an introduction to Sidney Cooper, R.A. only to be advised by this eminent Academician to give up the idea of becoming an artist.

Fortunately young John met Dudley Hardy who had exhibited at the Royal Academy and became a lifelong friend. It was Hardy's influence that led John to present himself to the Art School in Antwerp where he met Professor van Havermaet and his son Charles who spent six months in teaching him so that he was good enough to be accepted by the *Academia Julian* in Paris.

On his return to Antwerp he met and married Isabel Dingwall and they returned to England, living at 88 Kensington Park Gardens where he was to live for the remainder of his life. Isabel died in 1900 and in 1903 John Hassall married Constance Maud Brooke Webb and they had two children John and Christine. He became well-known for his advertising posters and produced around 700 at this time including perhaps his most famous 'Skegness is so bracing' poster for the Great Northern Railway. He started his own art school in 1905 in partnership with Charles van Havermaet which ran successfully for twenty years.

In 1901 Hassall was elected to membership of the Royal Institute of Painters in Water Colours. He was an illustrator of children's books and helped Baden-Powell design the uniform of the Boy Scouts. Hassall produced some 800 book covers and illustrated over 200 books which included the cover for Baden-Powell's 'Scouting for Boys'. In 1936 Skegness Urban District Council decided to show their appreciation of Hassall's inspiration in creating *The Jolly Fisherman* by making him a Freeman of the town. John Hassall died in 1948.

Martin Bladen HAWKE

Martin Bladen Hawke was born in 1860 the eldest surviving son of the Revd Edward Henry Julius Hawke, rector of Willingham by Stow, who ministered there for twenty years. The Rector married a young lady of 17 when he was aged 42 and baptised his own wife! In 1874 the Revd Edward Hawke inherited the Baronial title held by a cousin and he resigned the living of Willingham moving to Wighill Park near Tadcaster.

Martin was educated at various private schools in Newark and Slough before going to Eton where he proved his ability as a cricketer and athlete. He went up to Magdalene College, Cambridge, and played cricket for the University for three years, acting as captain during his final season. On graduating, Martin Hawke was invited to play for Yorkshire and in 1883 took over the captaincy, a post he held for more than twenty-five years even though he was not born in the county. At that time there was a strict rule that only natives of Yorkshire could play in the first team. It was probably relaxed in his case because of his family connections with the county and he may well be the only native-born Lincolnshire man to have played for Yorkshire.

At that time Yorkshire had never won the county championships but under Hawke's leadership their status gradually improved. At last, in 1893, Yorkshire won the county championship for the first time and whilst Hawke was captain they won the championship another seven times. Martin Hawke was not a great cricketer himself but he was able to inspire his players to give of their best and there can be no doubt he was responsible for the club's high standing in the cricketing world.

In the 1887-88 season he took part in an Australian tour but was called home to attend his father's funeral. He succeeded to the family title as the seventh Baron Hawke of Towton and led the England team in India, South Africa, West Indies, U.S.A., and South America.

After he ceased to play in 1910 Lord Hawke became president of Yorkshire CC and retained the post until his death. He served for many years as a committee member of the MCC and was president for five years during the First World War. He was several times chairman of the Test Match Selection Committee. Lord Hawke died in Edinburgh in 1938 aged 78.

Winifred HEATH

Winifred Heath was born in the Lickey Hills on Christmas Eve 1892. She became a much loved District Nurse based at Nettleham and after her retirement devoted most of her time to promoting the Lincolnshire Naturalists' Union and raising funds for that organisation mainly through the sale of dried flower arrangements. She also worked for the RSPCA, the Donkey Sanctuary, Lincolnshire Fieldpaths Committee and the Lincolnshire Branch of the Council for the Protection of Rural England.

Miss Heath had been orphaned at a very early age and was brought up by a strict spinster aunt. She became a student nurse at one of the London teaching hospitals and her sense of humour was never more in evidence than when she was describing the life of a student nurse in the early years of the twentieth century. After completing her training she went to India as a missionary nurse. Her descriptions of life in India at that time were always graphic and her love of children and animals was always apparent to those privileged to hear her stories.

After a very severe illness she had to return to this country and she became district nurse at Chesterton, Cambridgeshire before moving to Nettleham. She travelled all over the district by bicycle until she eventually acquired a small car.

'Heathie' as she was known was blunt, hardworking and dedicated to her calling. She very deviously and unobtrusively helped many of the needy and organised in many ways the sales and redistribution of jams and jumble. She was a member of the Lincolnshire Naturalists' Union and plant hunting was a joy to her. She knew all the local flowers, which she recorded. When she retired she botanised in Scotland and the mountains and the mountain flowers delighted her. Her retirement present was a visit to Switzerland which gave her great joy.

Bratoft Meadows was renamed by the Lincolnshire Naturalists' Trust Heath's Meadows in her honour. Amateur and professional botanists alike admire its rich neutral grassland flora, purple with green-winged orchids and yellow with cowslips, daintily laced with grasses. It is one of the best of its kind and 'Heathie' was honoured by this tribute. Each year it became a pilgrimage and a further inspiration. She continued up to the time of her death to motivate her friends to reaffirm their allegiance to their membership. Her RSPCA activities reflected her love of animals and her forthright condemnation of animal abuse was a byword. At heart she was a nurse and loved people. Her friends became the family she never had. Winifred Heath died in 1988.

Alex HENSHAW

Alex Adolphus Henshaw was born at Stratford-on-Avon on 7 November 1912 and his early education was at the King Edward VI Grammar School in Stratford - he remembers being taught in the same classroom as William Shakespeare! From 1922 until 1927 he continued his education at Lincoln School (now Lincoln Christ's Hospital School) and for some of this time he was taught in huts which had been erected during the first World War when the school had been used as a hospital. At the age of 12 Alex was awarded the Royal Life Saving Medal for saving a boy from drowning in the River Witham. His father Albert Henshaw established one of the earliest holiday camps in the country at the Trusville Holiday Estate near Mablethorpe

After leaving school, Alex joined his father's fertiliser business working at the firm's offices in Guildhall Street, Lincoln. He learnt to fly at the age of nineteen in 1932 with the Skegness and East Lincolnshire Aero Club making his first solo flight in April of the same year. His father bought Alex a Gypsy Moth G-AALN and only a year later he won the Siddeley Trophy in the King's Cup Air Race in a Comper Swift G-ACGL. Not surprisingly, he was the youngest pilot ever to achieve this. In the same year and in the same aircraft Alex won the 'Round the Houses Race' and, building on this foundation for the next fifteen years, he went on to write himself into aviation history, first as a sporting and racing pilot, and later as one of the outstanding test-pilots of World War II. Amongst his outstanding achievements was the record time in 1938 in the King's Cup Race - a record which still stands for a British machine.

The achievement for which he is best remembered is his flight in a specially prepared Mew Gull G-AEXF from Gravesend, Kent to Cape Town and back which broke all world records for solo or multi-crew flight, including that made by Flying Officer A. E. Clouston and Mrs Kirby-Green in the Comet Racer G-ACSS for the overall flight, there and back, by 33 hours. The previous fastest time for the outward flight had been set by Amy Johnson and for the return journey by H. L. Brook. Alex broke both these records by 57 hours. The outward flight took 392 hours and covered 6,300 miles. After a stay of 28 hours in Cape Town Alex set off on the return flight and, on 9 February 1939, four days ten hours and sixteen minutes after leaving Gravesend he landed at the airfield from which he had set out - there was only eleven minutes difference between the outward and homeward flights. To put this in perspective, bearing in mind how the advent of the jet engine revolutionised air travel, the fastest airliner in 1939 took over a week to fly from London to Cape Town, always providing the weather was favourable and that the pilot did not get lost! It is quite remarkable that Alex Henshaw's record for this solo flight still stands. Surely this is confirmation of a remarkable achievement which is regarded by aviation historians as one of the finest ever made and which was recognised in 1940 when Alex was awarded the Britannia Trophy for the most outstanding flight by a British subject.

On the outbreak of war in 1939 Alex applied to join the Royal Air Force but was invited to join Vickers at Weybridge as a test-pilot, which he did. After testing Wellingtons at Brooklands and Spitfires and Walruses at Southampton he joined Supermarine at their Castle Bromwich factory which manufactured Spitfires and Lancasters and nine months later was appointed chief test pilot. In total Alex flew 2,360 Seafires and Spitfires and the number of types of aircraft which he flew throughout his career is about 122. This most important war service was recognised by the award of an MBE in 1945 and further recognition came fifty years later in 1995 when Air Chief Marshal Sir Michael Graydon presented him with a Spitfire Trophy on behalf of the Battle of Britain Memorial Flight.

After the war Alex went to South Africa as a director of Miles Aircraft (S. A.) Ltd part of the General Mining and Finance Corporation, Johannesburg. In 1948 he returned with his family to England to build up the Golden Sands Holiday Estate at Mablethorpe. This became the largest holiday complex of its kind in Lincolnshire. He also managed farms in Huttoft, Anderby and Chapel St Leonards and the golf links at Sutton-on-Sea. Alex was awarded the Queen's Commendation for Bravery for his work during floods which devastated the east coast in 1953.

Although no longer living in the county, Alex maintains close links through the farms which he operates in conjunction with his son at Theddlethorpe, Mablethorpe, Sutton-on-Sea, Huttoft, Anderby and Chapel St Leonards.

In 1979 Alex Henshaw's book *Sigh for a Merlin* was published by John Murray and became a best seller. It was re-printed to mark the sixtieth anniversary of the Spitfire. His book *The Flight of the Mew Gull* was published in 1980.

Gervase HOLLES

　　Gervase Holles was born in Grimsby on 9 March 1606 and was the son of Frescheville and Elizabeth Holles. He was brought up by John Holles, the earl of Clare and admitted to the Middle Temple on 3 May 1629. In 1630 he succeeded to the family estate and married Dorothy Kirketon of Grimsby in the same year. Gervase occupied himself by collecting material for a history of Lincolnshire but moved to Mansfield in 1634 where his wife and daughter died soon after. His only son died in 1635 and later in the same year he decided to return to Grimsby. He was elected Mayor and on 26 March 1640 he was elected Member of Parliament for Grimsby.

　　Gervase Holles was a strong supporter of the Royalists and raised a regiment of foot at his own expense. In 1643 he was appointed governor of King's Lynn and he fought at the battles of Banbury, Brentford, Newark, Atherton, Bradford and Newbury. He was taken prisoner during the siege of Colchester and his estate was confiscated. In 1649 he was released from prison and allowed to go to France. He settled in Holland and was active in promoting the king's return to England. Charles II wished to create him a baronet but Holles refused this honour. After the Restoration he was made Master of Requests and in 1661 he was again elected MP for Grimsby. He continued to represent that town in Parliament until his death on 10 February 1674-75. He was buried at Mansfield.

　　The Parliamentarians destroyed much of Holles papers on the history of Lincolnshire but six volumes survive. The first volume was published by the Lincoln Record Society in 1911 as *Lincolnshire Church Notes* and was edited by Canon R. E. G. Cole. This volume consists of extracts from Harleian Manuscript 6829 in the British Museum and contains a description of Grimsby, Little Cotes and Humberstone as they were in 1634. The book also contains transcripts (in Latin) of documents relating to Clifton, Notts. but the most interesting and important part of the book is the record of monuments and coats-of-arms contained in some 290 Lincolnshire churches as they were immediately before the Civil War.

Ernest Terah HOOLEY

In the first volume of *Lost Lincolnshire Country Houses* (undated) Terence Leach stated that Terah Hooley owned Sudbrooke Holme and Temple Belwood for a brief period. Hooley was described as a swindler 'who after a life full of incident, went to prison'. I found this brief mention interesting and decided to investigate. As the result of a letter which was published in the *Derbyshire Evening Telegraph* I was sent a copy of *Hooley's Confessions*. I discovered that Hooley had also owned Tattershall Castle and the following is the account of Hooley's life which I was eventually able to piece together.

Ernest Terah Hooley was born at Radford, Nottingham in 1859, one of the eleven children of Robert and Martha Hooley. When Terah married Annie Maria Winlaw of Boston, Lincolnshire in 1881 at St Mary's church, Nottingham both he and his father described themselves as lace manufacturers. Terah Hooley was a non-smoker and teetotaller and apparently his only hobby was playing the harmonium at Long Eaton Baptist Church which had been founded by his grandfather, Robert Hooley. At the time of the 1891 census Terah and Annie Hooley had one son and four daughters. He still described himself as a lace manufacturer and he was then living at Risley Hall.

Terah Hooley developed considerable skill in the financial world and he was able to see an opportunity when it presented itself. From modest beginnings, in about fifteen years he became the most famous millionaire in England. He realised that the bicycle was becoming very popular and he floated the Swift, Singer and Raleigh companies which manufactured this new means of transport. The Dunlop Pneumatic Tyre Company manufactured rubber bicycle tyres and Hooley's purchase of this firm was his biggest coup.

Hooley said that 'he was the man who put the world on wheels' and

'I might never have become famous had it not been for the coming of the bicycle in 1894 which gave me the chance of handling big sums of money and taught me those daring methods of finance which, for a few years at least, brought me untold wealth'.

Hooley's principal home was Risley Hall in Derbyshire and the local Conservative party was persuaded to support him as their Parliamentary candidate. In 1896 he bought Papworth Hall, Cambridgeshire and got himself nominated as High Sheriff of the county. The other two candidates for the post were persuaded to withdraw and Hooley was appointed to the post.

It was widely expected that Hooley would receive a baronetcy at the time of Queen Victoria's diamond jubilee in 1897 but by then he had been declared bankrupt and the offer of a knighthood was withdrawn as was his Parliamentary candidature. He was also deprived of the post of High Sheriff.

In his *Confessions* Hooley wrote :

'... I might just as well be candid and admit now that I had made all possible preparations to weather the storm that was likely to burst about my head as a result of my bankruptcy. Some time previously both Papworth Hall and Risley Hall, and all their contents had been made over to my wife. In addition to this, there were mortgages on the two properties amounting to £70,000 and when I went smash the mortgagees rubbed their hands and said gleefully : 'Ah, we shall be all right!' They soon discovered their mistake. About a month before I filed my petition I had leased both places to friends who could be depended upon to let me have them back whenever I wanted them. Because there were tenants in possession neither Papworth or Risley could be sold'.

In 1900, whilst still an undischarged bankrupt, he negotiated the purchase of a concession from the Tsar of Russia to exploit the Siberian goldfields for £75,000. He sold the concession to a public company for a million pounds. He also acquired the Newfoundland pulp and timber operation for £3,000 and re-sold it for a million pounds!

In 1904 Hooley together with another 'financier' Henry John Lawson was tried at the Old Bailey for conspiring to defraud a publican named Paine who had invested £27,000 in Siberian Goldfields and received in return a piece of gold-bearing quartz. Hooley and Lawson were acquitted.

Hooley bought up estates and then sold off the land in small lots in order to make a very substantial profit. His acquisition of Tattershall Castle was by far his most important property in the county. He records this purchase in 1910 as follows :

'I bought from the Earl of Fortescue the famous Tattershall Estate, in Lincolnshire. The residence, Tattershall Castle, contains the finest carved mantelpieces in the United Kingdom.

Truth to tell, it was rather a bad deal. I cut up the land with a good profit, but the Castle itself proved to be a white elephant. No one would have it at any price, and, in despair of selling it, I worked an ingenious little ruse, which brought me an immediate reward.

A friend of mine in Fleet Street published a story in one of the papers to the effect that E. T. Hooley was going to sell the famous Tattershall mantelpieces to America.

It wasn't in the least true, but, nevertheless, it had the instant effect of causing an outcry in the Press about our historical carvings being sold for the benefit of get-rich-quick American millionaires. So the Marquis of Curson *[the Marquess Curzon of Kedleston]*, the late Foreign Secretary, promptly came forward in a spirit of public generosity and bought Tattershall Castle, lock, stock, and barrel and relieved me of a bad bargain'.

Although it is true that Hooley did try to purchase Tattershall himself, his offer was refused and he had to arrange for the property to be purchased by a third party. Before this could proceed Hooley's bank foreclosed on his mortgages. Hooley had, however, already arranged for the four fireplaces to be sold and, in fact, they had been removed from the castle. Fortunately it was possible for the fireplaces to be returned and reinstalled.

In 1912 Hooley was again tried at the Old Bailey. This time it was on a charge of false pretences in connection with the sale of the Thorney Hall estate in Nottinghamshire. After a trial lasting four days he was sentenced to imprisonment for twelve months. Hooley was released after serving nine months and led a quiet life for several years until he decided to take advantage of the Lancashire cotton boom. In 1920, he was charged with others for 'conspiring to cheat and defraud in the purchase of shares of Jubilee Cotton Mills Ltd and making certain written statements which they knew to be false'. The trial at the Old Bailey lasted five weeks and in passing sentence the Common Sergeant said that 'it was a gross swindle in which Hooley was the ringleader'. He was sentenced to three years imprisonment.

After his release Hooley continued to live at Risley Hall and he made a rather precarious living mainly by rearing and selling pigs. He indulged in some small-scale property dealings and tried to buy land from a farmer on the outskirts of Derby with the intention of selling it to Derby Borough Council at a profit as the town expanded. He was unable to raise the money to complete the purchase and the deal fell through. Eventually Risley Hall had to be sold and in 1939 at the age of eighty he was again declared bankrupt with liabilities of £898 and no assets.

A series of so called *Confessions* by Hooley, published by the *News of the World,* were reprinted in book form probably, in 1924. In this he said he bought property and businesses without the money to pay for them, sold for as much as he could, and got out with the profit. If a deal didn't come up to his expectations he simply did not complete the purchase. As he expressed it; 'I never "held the baby" as they say in the vernacular. Someone else had to do that.' His apparent generosity coupled with his appearance and personality enabled him to convince many people that an investment with him would bring them substantial profits.

Ironically, Hooley ended his days living at a guest house in Long Eaton where he died 1947 at the age of 88. His burial is recorded in the Parish Register for Risley All Saints as follows : Ernest Terah Hooley – buried 15th Feb 1947 aged 88 of 197, College St, Long Eaton formerly of Risley Hall.

SOURCES : Hooley, E. T. *Hooley's Confessions* (London, undated – *circa* 1925). I am grateful to Julian Burnside, Q.C. of Melbourne, Australia for information communicated and for reading the manuscript of this article. A number of others have contacted me and sent information for which I am most grateful. I am particularly grateful to Mrs Doreen Morley who sent me a copy of *Hooley's Confessions*.

Charles HUDSON

Lincolnshire is not noted for its mountains and there are not many hills of any note so it is a surprise to find in St James' Church, Skillington two windows commemorating the Matterhorn disaster of 1865 in which a former vicar, Revd Charles Hudson was killed.

Hudson was born in Ripon in 1828, the son of Joshua and Jane Hudson. He attended St Peter's School in York before going up to St John's College, Cambridge graduating BA in 1851. As well as being a scholar Hudson was a skilled oarsman. He was ordained deacon in 1853 and priest in 1854 shortly before going to the Crimea as a chaplain with the British forces. He remained in the Crimea for two years and then travelled in Turkey. On his return to England he took up a curacy at Bridgnorth before becoming vicar of Skillington in 1860. Hudson married Emily Mylne, the daughter of an Indian Army officer, in 1863.

The eleven years from 1854 to 1865 became known as the Golden Age of mountaineering. The Alpine Club was founded in 1857 and many of the founder members were clergymen. Amongst these one of the best known was the Revd Charles Hudson, who became the Club's secretary. It was said of him that he had 'climbed more mountains than he had preached sermons'!

By the 1860s the only major unconquered Alpine peak was the Matterhorn, which rises to a height of 14,691 feet. In 1865 several mountaineers decided that the time had come to scale this peak. The leader was Edward Whymper who, at the age of twenty-five, had already made six attempts on the Matterhorn. Two Swiss guides, Peter Taugwalder and his son, and Lord

Francis Douglas joined Whymper. Hudson was also about to begin his own attempt on the Matterhorn accompanied by nineteen-year-old Douglas Hadow and a Swiss guide, Michel Croz. Hudson was regarded as one of the ablest mountaineers in the world and had made an ascent of Mont Blanc by a new route from St Gervais in 1859. It was agreed that the two parties should combine. Although Hadow had climbed Mont Blanc and several minor peaks he was still a novice and Whymper only reluctantly agreed to take him on the attempt because he needed the experience of Hudson.

The party left Zermatt on 13 July 1865 and, after resting over-night on the Hornli Ridge, continued their ascent next morning reaching the summit soon after midday. During the afternoon, whilst descending, Douglas Hadow slipped and fell on to Michel Croz. The climbers were all roped together and the force of the impact knocked Croz over the ridge together with Charles Hudson and Lord Francis Douglas. Edward Whymper and his guide braced themselves but the rope snapped. The bodies of Hudson, Hadow and Croz were found next day and buried in the churchyard of Zermatt. The body of Lord Francis Douglas was never found.

The first window in Skillington church depicts Abraham's sacrifice against a background of mountains with a border that includes an ice-axe, a baton and a broken rope. In the chancel is another window with a depiction of the Matterhorn and above it the inscription 'He walked with God and was not, for God took him'. The windows were the gift of thirty-five Alpine explorers in memory of Revd Charles Hudson. Their names are inscribed on an adjacent tablet.

John HURT

There can be no doubt that John Hurt is one of this country's most distinguished actors and he has received international acclaim with films such as *The Elephant Man* and TV plays like *The Naked Civil Servant*. It is good to know that his most formative years were spent in Lincolnshire.

John Vincent Hurt was born on 22 January 1940 at Shirebrook, Derbyshire where his father was vicar. In 1945 his parents, the Revd Arnould Hurt and his wife, Phyllis, moved to Woodville, Staffordshire and John attended the local elementary school. He was very unhappy there and he transferred to the preparatory section of Ashby Grammar School. Prophetically, his form mistress said to John's older sister, Monica, 'Your little brother will one day be a great actor.' At the age of eight he was sent as a boarder to St Michael's School at Offord, Kent and at the age of fourteen he became a boarder at Lincoln School (now Lincoln Christ's Hospital School) where he remained for three years.

In 1953 Revd Arnould Hurt had been appointed vicar of St Aidan's, Cleethorpes and after leaving Lincoln School, John went on to study art at Grimsby College of Further Education. John had decided that he wanted to be an actor by the age of nine but his parents felt that this was too insecure a profession. At that time it was possible to obtain a teacher's diploma in art and he was persuaded that if he qualified as an art teacher he would always have a secure and respectable means of earning a living if the need arose. He did well at art school and won a scholarship to St Martin's College of Art in London.

After about a year John decided to leave St Martins and he obtained work with the Lincoln Repertory Company. With the help of a fellow member of the company he practised the four pieces required at the audition for entrance to the Royal Academy of Dramatic Art. He impressed the examiners and won a scholarship which paid for his first year at the Academy and Lindsey County Council paid for his second year.

John's first stage appearance was in a production at St Michael's School of Maerterlinck's *The Bluebird* in which he played the girl. He appeared in other productions at St Michael's and at Lincoln School where he played Lady Bracknell in *The Importance of Being Earnest.* John Grainger the Housemaster of School House was the director. He encouraged John's passion for the theatre and they became friends. During an interview with the headmaster at Lincoln School, when he was asked what he was going to do with his life, John replied 'I'd really like to be an actor'. The head said 'Well, you may be alright in school plays but you wouldn't stand a chance in the profession'.

Immediately after leaving RADA in 1962 John secured a part in the film *The Wild and the Willing* which was about University life. Most of it was filmed in Lincoln and the film's publicity man arranged a meeting between the head and John! One cannot help but feel rather sorry for the poor man.

Also in 1962 he made his stage début at the Arts Theatre, London. Since then he has made some 40 films and appeared in eleven stage plays and ten television productions including the series *Crime and Punishment.* John's career of almost 40 years has been extremely busy and he has never had to resort to teaching art to keep the wolf from the door!

He won BAFTA awards for *Midnight Express* in 1978 and for *The Elephant Man* in 1980 and other film titles which stand out are *A Man for All Seasons, 10 Rillington Place, Nineteen Eighty Four, Rob Roy* and *A Month in the Country* For his television appearance as Quentin Crisp in *The Naked Civil Servant* he won an Emmy Award. Another memorable television appearance was as Caligula in the series *I Claudius.*

In 1978 John Hurt made five films and in 1984 four films as well as appearing on stage and on television. Some idea of the stress which film-making creates was described by John in an interview. For his appearance in that remarkable film the *Elephant Man,* the make-up took seven hours to apply. This meant that he had to start at four a.m. finishing at ten at night. It then took two hours to remove the make-up. Although this is exceptional it does give some idea of the stresses and strains involved in film- making. Such a busy career has its cost. He married first at the age of 22 but separated eighteen months later. His second and third marriages also failed but he is making a fresh start with Sara Owens.

John has recently completed filming *Captain Corelli's Mandolin* in which he played Dr Iannis. He is hoping to be able to spend more time painting in the studio at his house in the Irish Republic. He has lived there for ten years not far from the Abbey where his brother is a monk.

Above : John Hurt aged 15 with his brother, sister and parents.

The three photographs below were taking during the filming of *The Wild and the Willing* in Lincoln

Above left: John relaxing between shots at Lincoln School
Above right: With John Grainger Housemaster at Lincoln School
Below: Five up and coming actors in the grounds of Lincoln Castle.
Left to right: David Sumner, Catherine Woodville, Ian McShane, Samantha Eggar and John Hurt.

See also photograph of John on the front cover of this book taken when
he was awarded an honorary degree by the University of Derby in January 2002.

In January 2002 John was awarded an honorary degree of Doctor of Letters by the University of Derby.

John has two wonderful sons, Alexander aged eleven and Nicholas aged eight. Long may he continue with his acting career.

FURTHER READING : Nathan, D. *John Hurt : An Actor's Progress.* (1986)

John HUSSEY

Sir John Hussey (who entered the House of Lords as Lord Hussey of Sleaford in 1529) was arguably the most important nobleman in Lincolnshire in the early sixteenth century and certainly the richest, with extensive estates across the whole of Kesteven. He was a particular friend of numerous Lincolnshire monastic houses and their abbots, often acting as their estate steward. He also had extensive Yorkshire associations and it seems likely that the Hussey family originated in that county before moving to Sleaford in the early fifteenth century.

He was born in 1466 and his father had been Lord Chief Justice of England and a prominent lawyer but Hussey's rise came about as a result of royal service: first to Henry VII's mother, Lady Margaret Beaufort, in whose household he served as a young man; then as a senior chamber servant and financial minister to Henry VII; and finally as a close associate (at least in the early part of his reign) of the young King Henry VIII. With such service came offices of power and profit, especially a stint as Master of the Wards under Henry VII.

A staunch friend of the Catholic church and opposed to the Reformation, he nevertheless went along with it publicly. Hussey was very close to Catherine of Aragon, both politically and religiously, while she was Queen and after the King divorced her and married Anne Boleyn - a move which angered and horrified him but which, outwardly, he accepted - he was appointed chamberlain to Princess Mary. Hussey's wife, an equally staunch supporter, was made one of her ladies-in-waiting.

In 1534 Hussey was involved in a half-baked conspiracy with a fellow elderly nobleman, Lord Darcy of Templehurst, designed to persuade the Emperor Charles V to invade England and save it for the Catholic faith. The plot came to nothing, but Lady Hussey was put in the Tower for a short time for supposedly treasonable remarks made while in Mary's service and it seems likely that Thomas Cromwell, Henry VIII's chief minister, had Lord Hussey marked as suspect from then onwards.

When the Lincolnshire Rising began in Louth and Horncastle in October 1536, Hussey, as the chief nobleman in the county and its Lord Lieutenant, should have organised resistance to it. Instead, he did nothing and even appeared to side with the rebels, at one point for example receiving a deputation of the Horncastle men at his house at Old Sleaford. His support was one of the rebels' main objectives and if he had unequivocally backed them the whole Reformation process in England might have been threatened. In fact, he sat on the fence, refusing to back either side, and then at the last moment fled to join the royal forces at Nottingham.

He was immediately arrested for complicity in the Rising but was spared, apparently after the intervention of the Duke of Norfolk. However, within weeks of being set free he was again in secret communication with the Imperial Ambassador in London and may have been acting as a contact between the latter and Lord Darcy during the Pilgrimage of Grace in Yorkshire. Once the Pilgrimage had been put down, he was re-arrested and tried for treason, probably as a result of new information about these contacts gathered by Norfolk and Cromwell. Hussey was beheaded at Lincoln at the beginning of July 1537.

SOURCE : I am grateful to Dr Simon Pawley for contributing this article.

Anthony JACKLIN

Sometimes a minor incident in our lives will change our entire future. This was certainly the case with Tony Jacklin. Like many young boys his ambition had been to make a career as a professional footballer but a knock on the ankle prevented him joining in a kick-about with his mates and he took a walk around the golf course in Scunthorpe instead. After enthusiastically discussing the game with his father, young Tony spent every spare moment at Scunthorpe Golf Club where he came to be regarded as part of the furniture. He learned by watching closely and three years later he became a member of the club. As they say, the rest is history.

Tony Jacklin was born at Bottesford, Scunthorpe in 1944 and is the son of Arthur and Doris Jacklin. He was educated at Doncaster Road Secondary Modern School. Tony's first job was in a local steelworks but this didn't allow much time for him to indulge in his obsession for golf so he was taken on by a local solicitor, Eric Kemp, who was prepared to let him have every afternoon off to practice the game. Perhaps Tony was particularly lucky as both Mr and Mrs Kemp were devotees of the game.

At the age of fourteen Tony beat all comers, including his father, in the Men's Open Day at Scunthorpe Golf Club and he repeated this success at neighbouring Elsham. He was a member of the British Boys team in 1960, Lincolnshire Junior Champion from 1959 to 1961 and Lincolnshire Open Champion in 1961. Tony turned professional when he moved to Potters Bar Golf Club to work with Bill Shankland in November 1961 at the age of seventeen.

Many successes came his way and he won a total of twenty-four tournaments world-wide including the British Open in 1969, the US Open in 1970, the Italian Open in 1973, the Scandinavian Open in 1973 and the German Open in 1979. He played in seven Ryder Cup matches in 1967 to 1979 and captained the European Ryder Cup team in 1983, 1985, 1987 and 1989.

In 1989 Tony was appointed director of golf at San Roque Club, Cadiz, Spain but, after several financial disasters, he moved to Scotland. He now lives in Lewisburg, West Virginia and works as a golf course designer. Tony also runs a wood engraving business.

For four seasons from 1969 to 1972 Tony Jacklin was the best-known name in international golf. The prestige which his success brought to this country was recognised when he was awarded an OBE in 1970 and his continuing services to sport brought him a CBE in 1990.

Tony's wife, Vivien, to whom he had been married for 23 years, died suddenly in 1988. They had three young children. He now lives with his second wife, Astrid and he says that after over 40 years as a professional golfer he no longer wants the pressures which that brought and his days as a serious competitor are over. However, no doubt he will still manage the occasional round!

George Wharton JAMES

George Wharton James was the son of John and Ann James of Gainsborough and was born on 17 September 1858. He was educated at the Queen Elizabeth Grammar School in Gainsborough and, in 1872 he was apprenticed to the local stationer and bookseller, Jasper Hannan.

Because George James was a sickly, asthmatic child he spent much time in his father's company. His fathers interests, which included the chapel, temperance and reading, were a considerable influence on him. Young George James was soon active in local Methodist and temperance circles and he frequently preached and lectured on the evils of alcohol, meat and tobacco. He became a Sunday School teacher and a local preacher and was deeply involved in organising temperance and self-improvement societies for young people in the town.

His father taught him the rudiments of music and by his twentieth year he was organist at the Gainsborough Congregational Church. He wrote a history of Gainsborough which was published in the *Gainsborough and Retford Times* in 89 instalments between May 1878 and September 1880 under the pseudonym *Gainsburghiensis*. This was followed by a history of Marshall's, the local engineering firm. In 1880 he married Emma Smith, a local grocer's daughter who had been a friend from childhood.

About six months after their marriage he emigrated to America where he was ordained as a local deacon by the Nevada Conference of the Methodist Episcopal Church and held various pastorships in Nevada and also in California. In addition to his ministry he undertook lecture tours. His wife had joined him in 1882 but in 1889 he was involved in divorce proceedings which led to him resigning both from his pastorship and from the Methodist Church. Physically and spiritually bruised by the accusations made against him he turned to the desert in search of health and wandered in the desert regions of California, living and sleeping rough and building up an enthusiasm and knowledge of the region which was to stand him in good stead in later years.

With his health restored he again became a popular and successful lecturer. In 1895 he married a Californian minister's widow and had a successful and happy second marriage.

James published several small volumes and a 457 page *Tourists Guide Book to Southern California* which went through at least five editions under various titles. These were the first of his enormous output of books and articles many of which were devoted to a very wide range of aspects of life in California and the American South-West. He was editor of the *Out West Magazine* and he founded and edited *The Basket* (devoted to Indian basketry) and was associated with *The Craftsman* (also devoted to Indian matters). He also founded and ran a small publishing house. Of all George Wharton James books *The Wonders of the Colorado Desert* which was published in 1906 is a classic and remains a definitive account of the history, inhabitants, plant and animal life of the Colorado Desert.

James was a strange, interesting and complex personality. He was a scholar and was awarded a doctorate by Santa Carla University probably in recognition of his research and literary contributions in the field of Californian history and art. His manuscripts are preserved in the Huntingdon Library and in the Museum of the South West, Los Angeles which also houses his photographic archive, his library and his collection of Indian and other artefacts from the American south-west.

George Wharton James is highly esteemed in the United States as a writer on the American South West and on Indian lore but he is virtually unknown in Lincolnshire. He died on 8 November 1923 at St Helena, California.

SOURCE : I acknowledge with gratitude the assistance of Jim English of Gainsborough in compiling this article.

Henry Law JAMES

When Henry Law James died in 1932 at Surfleet, he had been vicar of the parish for 34 years. Such was his popular reputation that bell-ringers throughout the county subscribed to add two more bells to the existing ten thus making them, at that time, the lightest peal of twelve bells in the country.

Law James was born in November 1868 at Cathedral Gardens, Gloucester, within the limits of the Roman city, a fact of which he was particularly proud. He was named after one of his godparents, Henry Law, who was Dean of Gloucester. Law James' brother, E. Bankes James, took their mother's maiden name. She was a descendant of Lady Mary Bankes who defended Corfe Castle which was under siege by the Roundheads in 1643 and again in 1645. Lady Mary is said to have baked mince pies in the shape of a cradle, and the James brothers would never eat mince pies unless the tradition was followed.

Law James was educated at Malvern College and went up to Gonville and Caius College, Cambridge in 1887, graduating with honours in the Natural Sciences. He was the University's fastest sprinter over 100 yards and was also a member of the football team. On one occasion after the University had been defeated by Arsenal he remarked ruefully that the opposing side had introduced a new technique - heading the ball!

He took Holy Orders and was ordained deacon in 1891 and priest in 1892, becoming curate at St. Martin's, Stamford at a salary of £20 per annum. He supplemented this by teaching chemistry at the Grammar School.

In 1897 the Bishop of Lincoln (Rt Revd Edward King) was looking for a successor to the Revd Hubert Parry, who had been vicar of Surfleet for some fifty years, and he offered Law James the living. After seeing the state of the church he turned the offer down, but the Bishop persisted and eventually Law James accepted at a salary of £120 per annum, of which £30 had to be paid to his predecessor until Parry's death in 1901. Law James preached his first sermon at Surfleet on Septuagesima, 28 February 1898.

There was no vicarage and Law James had to lodge with one of the churchwardens, John Richardson, until he was able to rent a cottage in the village. The church was in great disrepair and the chancel was used as a lumber room leaving only a side altar in the north aisle. The congregation was small and the parish poor but Law James decided to attempt to raise the money to restore the church. It is indicative of his popularity that within three years he had raised £2,000, a considerable sum for those days.

He was able to install new seating and choir stalls and to erect a new rood screen. In 1907 he had a new organ built. The bells were restored and augmented first to six and later to ten. During the Commonwealth the south window of the church was broken and never properly repaired. Law James decided to do this, and paid children small sums of money to search the churchyard for fragments of stained glass which he saved and eventually used to repair the window. The church clock was over 400 years old and had not worked for many years. Typically Law James was determined to repair it and he did, but in the process on one occasion it struck no fewer than 120 times!

Law James had many interests and a vast store of antiquarian knowledge, but despite this he was a devoted parish priest and won the love and gratitude of his parishioners. He possessed private means which he used generously in the interests of the parish. He was characterised by an assertive self-confidence, and if he decided a theory was correct or a procedure the only right one then in his opinion there was no more to be said on the matter. Sometimes he appeared to be impatient with those who did not agree with him and simply could not believe that his view could be questioned. Because of this his contemporaries appeared to be driven by sheer self-defence to a closer examination of their own theories and to go more deeply into the truths upon which these had been based.

As well as being a scholar he was interested in things mechanical. With Herbert Leverton he built a steam boat which was used to collect elderly parishioners on Sunday evenings to take them to church. It was also used to tow several boats on the annual Sunday School Feast. As well as carrying the Sunday School pupils and teachers, they took along the Whaplode Drove Prize Band. The steam boat was not particularly reliable and on one occasion Law James and Rupert Richardson, also of Surfleet, arrived at Bourne church covered from head to foot with soot!

In 1908 Law James purchased an acre of land for £100 and in 1913 built a vicarage at a cost of £1,900. He received grants totalling £700 and paid the balance himself. This was not an unusual procedure at that time. He had an upstairs study and visitors to the vicarage would have to sit through long, complicated and animated discussions between Law James and his brother. During the First World War James grew his own tobacco which was dried in the greenhouse and then soaked in rum and brown sugar. It was then rolled in tarred paper which produced wads like rolling pins. After smoking this the study ceiling ran like treacle!

For much of the information contained herein I am indebted to the late Charles Rawding of Surfleet who, after leaving school in 1914, became pageboy at the newly built vicarage. The duties of a 14-year old pageboy were hard, the hours long and the work varied to say the least. One of his duties each Monday morning was to collect bones from the butchers and these were boiled up in the copper to make soup for the poor. The pageboy had to clean the copper after the washing was done, and Charles admitted that at times the soup tasted of carbolic soap!

Law James always spent his holidays in North Wales for a month, but had a priest staying at the vicarage to carry on the daily services. Mr Rawding recalls one occasion when a visiting clergyman had to have a boiled egg just before midnight on the Saturday night so that he could celebrate Communion the next morning fasting.

When Law James first came to Surfleet he was a strong Protestant and all services were very anti-Catholic. Soon after his appointment he organised a Sunday School which was well attended, each child received a stamp for attending on Sunday mornings and if the child attended again in the afternoon the stamp was marked accordingly. In 1916 a 'National Mission of Hope and Repentance' held outdoor services in Surfleet led by the Revd. W. I. Rawson of Metheringham and the Revd. R. Bond from Holbeach Hurn. As a result, Law James was converted to the Anglo-Catholic tradition and altar frontals were converted into chasubles. He introduced acolytes and candles which on one occasion caused something of a sensation. This was at a choir festival when the Vicar of Wigtoft blew out all the candles and Law James relit them. This went on for some time until one of them gave way. It is not recorded which this was but Law James was noted for his strong personality!

His enthusiasm sometimes caused him to carry things to excess as on the occasion when the Bishop was visiting Surfleet and was met at the station by Law James dressed in full vestments. The Bishop was not amused and instructed Law James not to do it again.

After moving to Lincolnshire Law James became a great cyclist, and it was not unusual for him to turn up in knickerbockers and puttees after cycling some 100 miles in order to assist members of the Lincoln Diocesan Guild of Church Bellringers which he had been instrumental in founding in 1899.

His brother, Revd. E. Bankes James, became a master at Wykeham College and usually spent his vacations at the Vicarage bringing with him some of his pupils dressed in long belted coats and straw hats. Both brothers preached without notes and at times got carried away. It became the custom for one of the pupils to hold a finger up at the end of fifteen minutes to warn the preacher to draw to a close.

When Revd. E. Bankes James retired he came to live at Surfleet, and after his death in 1948 he was buried at the side of his brother, who had died in 1932, in Surfleet churchyard.

Elizabeth JENNINGS

The poetic works of Elizabeth Jennings relate to intensely personal matters in a plain spoken and objective style. Her verse frequently reflects her devout Roman Catholicism and her love of Italy.

Elizabeth Joan Jennings was born on 18 July 1926 in Boston and she was the daughter of Henry Cecil Jennings a local doctor. Her poem, *Childhood in Lincolnshire*, records the impression which the flat fenlands of the Holland District of the 'forgotten county' implanted in her mind during the six years before she left Lincolnshire.

At the age of six, Elizabeth's family moved to Oxford and, after leaving the High School there, she went up to Oxford University where she read English at St. Anne's College graduating in 1949 with an honours degree.

From 1950 to 1958, Jennings worked at the Oxford City Library. She then joined the publishers Chatto & Windus as a reader after which she worked independently as a free-lance writer and full-time poet based in her home in Oxford.

Elizabeth Jennings discovered poetry at the age of thirteen with Chesterton's *Battle of Lepanto* followed by Coleridge's *Rime of the Ancient Mariner*. She was also influenced by the odes of John Keats. As a young adolescent she was encouraged by her teachers and an uncle, who was himself a poet. It was at Oxford University, however, that she found her artistic niche. She 'found a most congenial kind of atmosphere in which a poet can write - friends who were themselves poets and who also seemed to be as interested in my work as they were in their own. Certainly I received ruthless criticism but I always felt that the people who criticized my work really wanted me to write better, really believed in and cared about me...'

Much later she became friendly with the 'angry young men' who were known as 'The Movement' and included Kingsley Amis, Robert Conquest, D. J. Enright, Thom Gunn, John Holloway, Philip Larkin and John Wain. Robert Conquest said that 'someone once described her association with us as comparable to that of a schoolmistress in a non-corridor train with a bunch of drunken marines - a slight slander on both sides.' It is unlikely that her work would have developed as it did had it not been for her exposure to the Oxford climate of the later 1940s and early 1950s.

Having already been published in *Oxford Poetry 1948*, Jennings found that her work suited the taste of Kingsley Amis and James Michie who were the new editors for 1949. Her first pamphlet, *Poems,* appeared in 1953 and earned her an Arts Council Award. This was followed by *A Way of Looking* in 1955 which won her a Somerset Maughan Award and this enabled her to visit Italy. In 1961, *Song for a Birth or Death,* marked a new development with its confessional tone and more savage view of love. Some of the best of her later poems concern her nervous breakdown and its aftermath. *Collected Poems 1967* was followed, in 1969, by *The Animals' Arrival*, *Lucidities* was published in 1970 and this was followed in 1972 by *Relationships*. A translation, which was first published in 1961, of the *Sonnets of Michelangelo* was revised in 1969. She has published poetry for children and *Let's Have some Poetry* was published in 1960 and *The Secret Brother and Other Poems for Children* was first published in 1966. In all a total of some twenty-five books of Jennings' poems have been published. Elizabeth Jennings has also contributed articles and reviews, as well as poetry, to the *Daily Telegraph*, *Encounter*, *New Statesman,* the *New Yorker, the Scotsman,* the *Spectator*, *Vogue* and other periodicals.

In addition to the awards mentioned above, Elizabeth Jennings received Arts Council bursaries in 1965 and 1968; the Richard Hillary Memorial Prize in 1966 for *The Mind has Mountains*; an Arts Council grant in 1972 and the W. H. Smith Award in 1987 for *Collected Poems*. She was appointed to a Fellowship of the Royal Society of Literature (FRSL) in 1961 and a Commander of the British Empire (CBE) in 1992.

The *Elizabeth Jennings Papers,* which consist of correspondence and manuscripts, have been deposited at the Roman Catholic Georgetown University, Washington D. C. U.S.A. Notable correspondents include many contemporary poets and writers such as John Betjeman, Charles Causley, Cecil Day-Lewis, Margaret Drabble, Roy Fuller, Laurie Lee, Peter Levi, Ruth Pitter, Anne Ridler, A. L. Rowse, Stephen Spender, Anthony Thwaite, and John Wain. Internationally acclaimed actors Sir John Gielgud and Alec Guinness are also represented by lengthy correspondence. Of special interest is the extensive correspondence from long-time friend, Dame Cicely Veronica Wedgwood, the well-respected historian and writer. Dating from 1969 to the end of 1971, the letters were sent when Jennings was going through a long period of depression. The collection also contains notebooks of first drafts of poems by Jennings dating from 1972 to 1983.

Elizabeth Jennings died on 26 October 2001 at Bampton, Oxfordshire.

Maurice JOHNSON

Maurice Johnson was the eldest son of Maurice and Jane Johnson. He was born at Ayscoughfee Hall in Spalding on 19 June 1688. Little is known of his early life except that he attended Spalding Grammar School. His father was a barrister and Maurice was called to the bar on 26 June 1710. However, he preferred to live mainly in Spalding and occupied himself in antiquarian pursuits. In 1709 Johnson founded the Spalding Gentlemen's Society of which he acted as secretary for thirty-five years and then became president. The Society, which is mainly concerned with the study of literature, is still very active.

In 1717 the revival of the Society of Antiquaries of London was largely due to Johnson's efforts. It was through his efforts that Dr William Stukeley (see page 84 of *Lincolnshire People*) became secretary to that Society and Johnson became the honorary librarian.

Johnson was a Justice of the Peace and Chairman of the South Holland Quarter Sessions and Deputy Recorder of Stamford. He was Steward of the Manor of Spalding for the Duke of Buccleuch, Steward of the Manors of Kirton-in-Holland and Crowland for the Earl of Exeter and of the Manor of Hitchin, Hertfordshire for James Bogdani. Johnson was also Recorder of Boston and Steward of the Manor of Holbeach and Whaplode Abbats.

In 1721 Johnson, with the Earl of Exeter and others, founded a similar Society to the Spalding Gentlemen's Society in Stamford but this was not successful. In 1745 Stukeley founded a similar Society which he called *The Brazen-nosed Society of Stamford*. In 1730, whilst Johnson was acting as counsel for the Dean and Chapter of Peterborough, he, with others, founded another literary society in that city but this was short-lived. In 1750 he attempted to set up yet another literary society in Boston but this was not a success.

According to Stukeley, it was Johnson who was responsible for preserving the remarkable triangular bridge at Crowland. He was a botanist and had a fine collection of plants. It was through him that such eminent men as the botanist Linnæus visited Spalding. He was also a numismatist and had a large collection of medals. He was the author of *A Dissertation on the Mint in Lincoln* which was published with other essays by him in the *Bibliotheca Topographica Brittannica* in 1790. He also compiled a history of coins from the time of Julius Cæsar to the reign of Queen Anne. Johnson collected seals, vases and crystals, armour, statues, charts, architectural plans and designs, stained glass and prints.

Johnson left a considerable collection of manuscripts which he indexed in 1750. These documents related chiefly to the law and history of Spalding, Boston, Stamford, Crowland, Peterborough and Hitchin.

Maurice Johnson died on 6 February 1755 and he was buried in the Johnson transept of Spalding Parish Church at the side of his wife who had died in the previous year. They had married in 1709 and they had had twenty-six children of whom sixteen had survived.

Wolley JOLLAND

When the Hon. John Byng was touring in Lincolnshire in 1791 accompanied by Colonel Albemarle Bertie he visited Louth and one of the curiosities he saw was the garden and hermitage constructed by the vicar of Louth, Wolley Jolland. He recorded this visit as follows :

> '[The garden] is almost cover'd with cloisters, seats, &c, all made of roots of trees, and moss, to correspond with an hermitage in the centre, finish'd with curious taste, and trouble; therein are several rooms, recesses and chapels, all lighted by an old stain'd glass (once in Tattershall Church); the ornamental parts are of fir cones; the tables of polish'd horse bones; with many inscriptions around, and upon the ground, from the scriptures. It is throughout the work of infinite labour, and highly curious; and so must the framer of it be, who was not at home; but his lady was, and she shew'd us her house'.

The following morning Byng and his companion attended Sunday service at the parish church of St James which he recorded as follows :

> '…When the minister appear'd, we were not a little surprised at the wildness of his eyes his sallow skin, and black flowing locks... His reading was vehement, and turgid, especially in the lessons, but when he came to his sermon where I expected declamation, he sunk into softness, and was inaudible, and unimpressive. The long service ended, (during which Coll B. sigh'd *piteously*) we…were then introduced to Mr J… a man seemingly eaten up by pride and particularity, with attempts at every knowledge and art. …Mr J., appears to be composed of as many curious, and odd materials, as his hermitage'.

Wolley Jolland was the fifth child and second son of George and Justina Jolland and he was born in Louth on 2 September 1745. His father was Warden of Louth from 1748 to 1749 and again from 1755-1756. He was elected Town Clerk in 1762 but he appears not to have attended meetings of the council. Although attempts were made to remove him he remained in office until his death.

Little is known of Wolley Jolland's early life but he may well have attended the Free

Grammar School in Louth. His obituary recorded that 'it is said his father intended him for the profession of the law, but, yielding to the inclination of his son, he finally educated him for the church'. For some time Wolley Jolland appears to have worked with his father as Deputy Town Clerk. On 14 June 1772 he was ordained deacon and became curate of Welton. On 19 December in the same year he married the daughter of William Weightman the rector of Yarburgh and on 26 July 1780 he was presented to the Vicarage of Louth.

Wolley Jolland appears to have been a somewhat eccentric, unworldly character. His readings in church would include comments : 'after the account of the Passion he would say 'here endeth this *dreadful* lesson'; after the story of Peter's denial ending with the words 'And when he thought thereon, he wept', he would add, *'as well he might';* and his comment on the 'darkness which may be felt' was *'a thick mist I take it'.*

The whole of Wolley Jolland's ministry of over fifty years was spent in Louth and he died on 16 August 1831 at the age of 85. An obituary in the *Stamford Mercury* stated that 'The amiable conduct of this gentleman endeared him to all classes; his charity drew forth the affection of the poor man – his kindness and urbanity endeared him to the more opulent classes'.

This brief account of this remarkable man has been condensed and adapted from a much more detailed account by Christopher Sturman in the *Report and Journal of the Georgian Group for 1987* entitled 'A Lincolnshire Hermit : Wolley Jolland (1741-1831)' pages 62-76)

Jonathan KERRIGAN

Jonathan Kerrigan became well known and something of a heartthrob for his rôle as Sam Colloby, the male nurse, in the BBC television series, *Casualty*. Young Kerrigan's first love, however, was not acting – like many a young lad he wanted to be a professional footballer. His father encouraged this ambition and took him and Paul Holland of Boston some 50 miles each way in all weathers to train at Mansfield! Jonathan played at county level and had trials for the English Schools Team, Nottingham Forest and Leicester City. At the age of fourteen he and Paul were signed up by Mansfield Town to play professionally for that club when he reached the qualifying age. Whilst Paul eventually played for Mansfield and has never looked back, an ankle injury made Jonathan decide to return to his second interest - acting.

Jonathan Richard Kerrigan is the youngest child of Patricia and Stanley Kerrigan. He was born in Lincoln on 14 October 1972 and has a brother, Jeremy, who works as an export manager, and sister, Louise, who works in insurance as a senior auditor. Jeremy is an enthusiastic actor in amateur dramatics but none of the other members of the Kerrigan family have ever had any interest in acting.

Jonathan's early education was at Fen Lane Primary School and later at North Kesteven School where he was greatly encouraged in his acting ambitions by drama teachers Helen Donnison and Keith Elms. Whilst still at school he was a founder member of the Imp Youth Theatre. The play *Alex,* which was written by the actors themselves, was performed by them at the National Theatre, London before Sir Ian McKellen, Timothy West and Prunella Scales and won the Lloyds Bank Challenge in 1991.   Later in the same year the Imp toured Australia with this play for three weeks.

Left to right : Jonathan, Sir Ian McKellen, Jane Asher and Keith Elms

In 1992 Jonathan went up to Bretton Hall College in the University of Leeds and graduated with a BA (Hons) in Theatre Arts in 1995.   Whilst at university he appeared in *Zoo Story* at the National Student Drama Festival in Scarborough and in many other productions including *A Midsummer Night's Dream* and *Equus*.   On television he has appeared in Byker Grove, *Peak Practice, Reach for the Moon, The Knock* and *Dinner of Herbs*.   After *Dinner of Herbs* Jonathan made a fifteen-minute film called *Talk* for the Disability Rights Commission. He played a young executive who woke one morning to find he is the only able-bodied person in a completely disability-friendly world.   He is the one who receives patronizing looks because he has all his limbs.   It is the wheelchair bound who are embarrassed to be seen with him.   This unusual and thought-provoking film was one of 900 entries for the Rushes Film Festival and it was judged to be the Best Overall Short Film.   Jonathan was particularly pleased with this as he would really prefer to be making films.   He has had interviews with casting directors in America but his present contracts have some time to run.

It was undoubtedly Jonathan's rôle in *Casualty* which gave him his big break and he has recently completed filming *Mersey Beat,* a ten-part television series which went out on BBC1 in July 2001.   He is contracted for another two series of this programme   Jonathan is now (January 2002) auditioning for a number of other television productions.

Jonathan always insists on doing his own stunts.   He takes the view that an audience is more sophisticated these days and can tell when a double is used for a stunt.   He admits that he enjoys the excitement which enables him to fulfil a boyhood fantasy of being an action hero. Notable stunts so far have been the spectacular backward fall from a balcony in *Casualty* and a twenty-foot jump in *Mersey Beat*.   One of the most frightening for the viewer as well as Jonathan was also in *Mersey Beat* when he rescued a young girl from a burning building and carried her on his back downstairs.   This was a real living, hot, fire and not achieved by some technical magic.

One of his most embarrassing television appearances, he says, was when he was asked to return to do another episode of *Byker Grover*. He had already bleached his hair ready to play Sam in *Casualty* and he was asked to dye it back to its natural colour with, according to Jonathan, disastrous results.

Jonathan comments on his acting career so far that he has been very lucky and from school he has had little respite from the gruelling life of a professional actor. But, of course, it is not just luck to have been in demand for such a variety of television plays. There is no doubt that, as a professional actor, Jonathan has exceptional ability.

Left : Jonathan with his parents and Claire Goose.
Right : As PC Steve Traynor in his latest series, *Mersey Beat*.
See also photograph on back cover of Jonathan as Sam Coloby in *Casualty*.

He lives in Bristol and, until recently, Claire Goose, who played the nurse Tina Seabrook in *Casualty*, shared the flat with him. Close by live Vince Pellegrino, with whom he shared a flat while filming *Casualty*, and Robert Gwilym who played Max in the same series.

Jonathan is a versatile musician and he is a proficient pianist as well as a competent keyboard and guitar player. If he had not become an actor he says he would have been a musician. He has a small studio at home in which he spends as much of his very limited spare time as possible. It was here that he composed the title music for *Mersey Beat*. His other interests are skiing, fencing, athletics and television documentaries.

Lincolnshire has produced a considerable number of actors and actresses over the years and it is good to know that this is still continuing. Long may Jonathan's career in the profession continue.

Hanserd KNOLLYS

Hanserd Knollys was born in 1598 at Cawkwell near Louth. He was the son of Richard Knollys who was vicar of Grimsby and he was taught by a tutor before entering the Free Grammar School at Grimsby. He then went up to St Catherine's College Cambridge graduating in 1627.

Knollys was appointed Master of the Free Grammar School at Gainsborough. Whilst at Cambridge he had come under the influence of the Puritans and Gainsborough was an important centre of the separatist movement. Knollys was ordained deacon in 1629 and licensed as a preacher in Humberstone parish church. In 1632 he married Anne Cheney of Wyberton and they were to have ten children.

After becoming disillusioned with the Church of England in 1636 Knollys offered his resignation to the Bishop of Lincoln. This was refused and, with the Bishop's encouragement, Knollys preached at a number of Wold and coastal villages including Wood Enderby, Fulletby and Wainfleet. He was arrested and found guilty by the Court of High Commission of nonconformity. Whilst awaiting sentence he escaped from gaol with the connivance of a sympathetic gaoler and set sail for America with his wife and some of their children.

Knollys was refused permission to preach in Boston but he settled in what is now Portsmouth, New Hampshire and founded a church at nearby Dover. As the result of a letter, which Knollys had written complaining of the government of Massachusetts, he was arrested on a charge of slander but after apologising to the governor he was allowed to move to Long Island. But he again ran into trouble and he and his family returned to England arriving on 24 December 1641. The decision to return to England may have been taken, in part, because of the arrest of Archbishop Laud for treason and the ascendancy of Puritanism.

Knollys was appointed Master of a school at Tower Hill, London but soon after he was chosen to be Master of Mary Axe Free School. He attended a nonconformist church and in 1645 founded his own Particular Baptist Church, assisting in writing a *Confession of Faith* for Baptist

Churches in London. His association with this church, which met at a number of places in London, continued up to his death in 1691.

In 1647 Knollys returned to Lincolnshire on his appointment as vicar of St Giles' church, Scartho. He left an assistant to look after the London congregation but for some ten years he travelled regularly between Lincolnshire and London. In 1656 Knollys' son, Cheney, was appointed vicar of Scartho and his father appears to have returned to London.

Throughout the Commonwealth period Knollys worked in London and promoted religious toleration. After the Restoration he was arrested for associating with a group of Baptists who had led an uprising against the monarchy. After release from prison he travelled to Holland with his wife and daughter and then moved to Germany where he remained for three years. During his stay in Germany Knollys wrote four books on Hebrew, Latin and Greek grammar which were published on his return to England in 1664.

Soon after his return plague broke out in London and during the two years when it raged many people moved into the countryside. Knollys remained with his church, as he did when the Great Fire of London broke out in 1666, ministering to the needs of his congregation.

In 1671 Knollys son, Cheney died and later in the same year his wife, Anne, also died. She is buried in Bunhill Fields, London. Knollys survived for another twenty years and is also buried in Bunhill Fields near to the graves of John Bunyan and the founder of the Quakers, George Fox.

Hanserd Knollys was a founding father of the Baptist church and wrote a number of books promoting religious tolerance. Perhaps his work influenced the founder of Methodism John Wesley who was born only twelve years after his death. Wesley's mother, Susannah, lived in London and could well have heard Knollys preach.

SOURCE : James, Muriel *Religious Liberty on Trial* (1997). I acknowledge with gratitude the assistance of Richard Ratcliffe, President of the Lincolnshire Family History Society who drew my attention to this source and sent me his lecture notes relating to Hanserd Knollys.

Thomas Edward LAWRENCE

Thomas Edward Lawrence was born at Tremadoc, Caernarvonshire in 1888 and brought up in Oxford. He was educated at Oxford High School and at Jesus and Magdalen Colleges, Oxford. From 1911 to 1914 he was an assistant in the British Museum's excavation of Carchemish on the Euphrates. In World War I he worked for Army Intelligence in North Africa from 1914 to 1916 but in that year he joined the Arab revolt against the Turks and was attached to the staff of the Hejaz Expeditionary Force. In 1918 he was transferred to General Allenby's staff and attended the Peace Conference in 1919 as one of the British Delegation, and, later, as an adviser on Arab affairs.

Lawrence refused both a knighthood and the Order of Merit but took a research fellowship at All Souls College, Oxford in 1919 and began writing his account of the Arabian campaign, *The Seven Pillars of Wisdom.* However, in 1922, in order to escape from his legendary fame, and in order to find peace of mind and the obscurity which he so desperately needed he enlisted in the recently-formed RAF as an aircraftsman under the name of 'John Hume Ross'. When his identity was discovered he transferred to the Royal Tank Corps in 1923 as 'T. E. Shaw'. In 1925 he transferred back to the Royal Air Force and was posted to Cranwell. In 1927 Lawrence changed his name by deed poll to Thomas Edward Shaw.

Lawrence was an early enthusiast of the fledgling aeroplane, which interest no doubt was heightened by the fact that his young brother Will served with the Royal Flying Corps and was killed in combat. Lawrence himself learned to fly whilst serving in the Middle East but, though he claimed to-have flown some 2,000 hours, he never qualified as a pilot.

The idea of such a famous war hero joining the forces as the equivalent of a private soldier unsettled a few politicians, but Lawrence had for some time known the Chief of the Air Staff Sir Hugh 'Boom' Trenchard, the founding father of the air force, and this friendship helped him to achieve his post-war ambition.

Lawrence's time at RAF Cranwell appears to have been a particularly happy period of his life and was recorded as such in a lesser known work *The Mint,* in which he chronicled his life as a recruit. He left instructions that this book was not to be published until the 1950s in order to protect those he mentioned therein and, in fact, it was not made available until 1955.

While at Cranwell Lawrence often visited Lincoln but he said

'The cathedral I did not like. Yet perhaps it's only because it succeeds too well. I do not think it disappoints so much as it chills. We come to it expecting to be cheered: and it tells us that we are no good at all'.

Lawrence often spent the night at a guest house on Steep Hill, Lincoln which was kept by an elderly lady who seemed to have looked after him in a rather autocratic manner. A plaque commemorating Lawrence's association with the building (now Brown's Pie Shop) was placed on the wall recently.

It was at Cranwell that Lawrence completed writing *The Mint* and towards the end of 1925 he was also preparing *The Seven Pillars of Wisdom* for the printer. At that time the rural roads of Lincolnshire were even more deserted than they are today and this gave Lawrence plenty of opportunity to ride his motorcycle. For years he had been an avid motorcyclist; British manufacturer George Brough had even designed and built several Brough Superiors for him. Twice a week he would ride on *Boanerges* his particular Brough at the time to Lincoln, Sleaford and Nottingham on a 'supply run' buying bacon, sausages, dripping and fresh eggs on behalf of his flight to supplement the mess and canteen food.

Lawrence was posted to India and on 7 December 1926 he left Cranwell leaving behind fond memories of his Lincolnshire posting. In a letter to a friend he said

' ...the RAF. is still my spiritual home, and I'm awfully sorry to leave Cranwell where I've had the best year I ever remember to have had'.

Before he left he presented a proof of the subscription edition of *The Seven Pillars of Wisdom* to the college library and in 1965 a library extension was named 'The Lawrence Room' and this houses, amongst other Lawrence memorabilia, his works, biographies and other books about him and a growing selection of newspaper articles featuring this enigmatic, multi-faceted man.

Lawrence was discharged from the RAF in 1935 at the age of 47 and was killed soon after in a motorcycling accident near his home in Dorset.   His published works are as follows :

Seven Pillars of Wisdom (1926); *Revolt in the Desert* (1927); *Oriental Assembly* (1929) *Crusader Castles* (1936) and *The Mint* (1955)

Terence R. LEACH

Terence Leach to whom I dedicated volume one in the series on *Lincolnshire People* was born in Dunholme in 1937.   He lived in that village which is near Lincoln for the whole of his life, except for National Service, and became interested in Lincolnshire history as a boy.

Terence joined the Historical Association while still at school. Whilst doing his National Service in the Royal Air Force he used to take his volumes of *Lincolnshire Notes and Queries* back to camp one at a time and so was able to read all twenty-four volumes from cover to cover! How many historians can claim to have equalled this feat?

After training as a teacher at Westminster College, Oxford he taught at Sincil Bank School in Lincoln before moving to the William Farr School at Welton where he specialised in history and religious education as well as serving as careers master for a time.

Terence was a dedicated member of the Lincolnshire Local History Society and of the Lincolnshire Architectural and Archæological Society and when the two amalgamated to form the Society for Lincolnshire History and Archaeology he served on its Executive Committee and was its Chairman for several years. He also chaired its Local History Committee and for many years organised its outings and tours as well as being a fertile source of subjects and lectures for the lecture programmes. Terence also initiated the Lincolnshire Portraits Survey for the Society. This may well have been the earliest survey of its type in the country.

Terence Leach was a member of many cultural and historical societies. Whilst training in Oxford he became interested in the history of Methodism in Lincolnshire. He was a founder member of the Lincolnshire Methodist History Society and became its vice-chairman. He also acted as its editor for several years. He served on the executive committee of the Tennyson Society and was a member of a number of other Lincolnshire based organisations. Terence was also a member of the Georgian and Victorian Societies and commented that he was 'really a Victorian born out of my time'.

Terence had a vast library of books and other material relating to the 'forgotten county' and would readily share his knowledge of Lincolnshire with others. He had the ability to talk in a popular way and so commanded a wide following for his weekly lectures at Dunholme and to a wider audience throughout Lincolnshire. His particular interests were in Lincolnshire families and their houses. It was Terence Leach who organised an annual lecture at Raithby in memory of Robert Carr Brackenbury (see *Lincolnshire People* page 18). He was particularly pleased when the restoration of the unique Methodist chapel built over a stable block at Carr's home was undertaken. It is in this chapel that the annual lecture is still delivered. Terence Leach also served as a churchwarden at Dunholme and had a wide interest and knowledge of English literature and the arts.

Terence's widow, Joyce, always supported him in all his interests and commented that she 'sometimes felt that I was married to local history as well as Terry'.

Terence Leach died on 16 April 1994.

Austin LEE

Austin Lee was a cleric who appears to have been particularly popular with his parishioners but at the same time he was a controversial figure. He set out to combat religious apathy but described the bishops as timid little men. He was the only son of a brilliant clergyman and was brought up at Claxby near Market Rasen although actually born at Keighley, Yorkshire in 1905. He was educated at Trinity College, Cambridge where he graduated BA in 1926. He entered Wells Theological College after graduating and his first curacy was at Kew where he served from 1928 until 1929. From 1931 until 1933 he was a chaplain in the Royal Navy.

Lee returned to Claxby as vicar in 1944 and for a time he considered resigning in order to contest a Parliamentary seat. Whilst at Claxby he issued a number of broadsheets which might well be likened to the political pamphlets of the eighteenth century. When Clement Attlee became Prime Minister in 1945 Austin Lee sent him an 'open letter' which was widely quoted in the Press. Referring to the appointment of a new bishop of Lincoln Lee said 'Names for this bishopric will be suggested to you. Among them will be men who have given offence to nobody, men who are colourless in their observances, inclining neither to the high or the low. Reject them all'. Austin went on to declare 'What was wanted for bishops were holy and humble men of heart who would attract men and women to the church by the power of love'. In 1948 Austin Lee left Claxby and accepted the living of St Stephen's, Hounslow where he remained until 1951.

Austin Lee became a feature writer with the *Daily Mail* and also the *Daily Mirror*. He was always a controversial figure and he had a number of provocative and controversial newspaper articles published. He gave up his living because he said, 'the Bishop dislikes me'. He alleged, 'that the church was full of humbug and bootlicking - appointments only go to those who can be guaranteed to give no offence'. He went to live in Galway, Ireland where he remained until returning to the priesthood in 1958 as curate in charge of West with East Allington and Sedgebrook moving to Carlton as Rector in 1959. In 1961 he became Rector of Willoughby with Sloothby and in 1963 became curate in charge of Mumby leaving Lincolnshire later that year to become vicar of Great and Little Paxton, Huntingdonshire.

In 1964 he produced a satirical leaflet in which he suggested that the 'shabby old fashioned parson' should be replaced by a musical prayer wheel! He had become somewhat bitter with congregations as well as bishops and he alleged that 'the average church congregation contains a galaxy of the meanest, most malicious back-biting, narrow-minded and bigoted members of the community'.

Under the pseudonyms of John Austwick and Julian Calendar he wrote a number of detective stories and he was a member of the National Crime Writers' Association. In 1959 he appeared in the B.B.C. television programme *Tonight* when he was interviewed concerning 'Miss Hogg' the heroine of a number of his detective stories. He also did some work on film scenarios and during his breaks between clerical appointments he worked in turn as a chef, barman and schoolmaster.

Life was never dull for Austin Lee and he deserves remembering as a very gifted and most colourful campaigning clergyman. He certainly earned the title conferred on him by the Press as a 'cleric with a broom'.

Austin Lee died in January 1965 and the funeral service took place in the chapel of Trinity College, Cambridge and his ashes were interred in the family grave at Claxby.

FURTHER READING : Lee, Austin *Round Many a Bend* (1954)

Arthur TOWLE (alias Arthur LUCAN)

Old Mother Riley was one of the most popular personalities of both stage and screen in the 1930s and 1940s. Arthur Towle, who created the Irish washerwoman, was born at Sibsey near Boston in 1885 and was the third child of Thomas and Lucy Towle. The family moved to Boston in 1891 when Thomas Towle became head groom at the *Peacock and Royal Hotel*. By 1893 Arthur had four brothers and two sisters.

Arthur became fascinated by the mock-Tudor style Shodfriars Hall which was close by his home. It not only housed bars, shops, a coal merchants and offices but also a theatre. In 1892 Arthur saw his first pantomime and he build his own model theatre staging productions for his own amusement.

At the age of eight Arthur was offered a job at Shodfriars Hall Theatre, sweeping the stage in the morning and selling programmes in the evening for two pence a week! Whilst

Arthur was still at school his father became seriously ill and died. Lucy had to find work in order to feed the large family and she took in washing from the *Peacock and Royal.* Arthur brought in laundry from the artistes at the theatre and he was to base the character for which he became so well known on his mother. His earliest stage appearance, at the age of ten, was in *Robinson Crusoe* at the Shodfriars Hall Theatre.

After leaving school at the age of fourteen, Arthur continued to work at the theatre selling programmes but made the most of his opportunities and learned a lot about the theatre. He decided to find work in Blackpool and left home without telling his mother. He worked for a few weeks busking on the beach and then as a singer on the pleasure steamers. He then joined a travelling show called *The Musical Cliftons.* This was a family run show and he was billed as Arthur Clifton taking part in comedy scenes as well as singing and dancing.

In 1909 *The Musical Cliftons* toured Ireland and Arthur enjoyed the travelling life. When he heard that the management of the *Queen's Theatre* in Dublin were hoping to stage a pantomime, Arthur went for interview saying that he had a script and had appeared in such a production in London. The manager was convinced and Arthur had to write a pantomime. He completed the task and the result, *Little Red Riding Hood,* was a tremendous success when it was performed at Christmas 1910. Arthur produced it and also played the Grandmother. Kitty McShane was understudy for the first performance but later took the title rôle.

When the pantomime season came to a close, Arthur joined the *White Coons Concert Party* in Carnoustie, Scotland writing a number of sketches for them. He was then offered a part in the revue, *The Honeymoon,* which opened in Huddersfield in November 1912. After 18 weeks the show closed and Arthur returned to Dublin. He proposed marriage to Kitty but her father disapproved and they decided to marry without her parents consent even though she was under age. The ceremony took place on 25 November 1913 and Kitty gave her age as nineteen when she was in fact sixteen.

It was now that the famous partnership was born and they were billed as *Lucan and McShane* with Arthur as an Irish washerwoman and Kitty as her teenage daughter. His stage name was taken from the name of the Dublin milk company, Lucan Dairy. Apparently he felt that this change of name made him more acceptable to the Irish!

The characterisation for which Arthur Lucan became famous came about when a fellow actor was indisposed and he was persuaded to take the part of Little Jack Horner's mother. After the birth of their son, Donald, in October 1915, it seemed probable that the act would have to cease but Kitty's parents offered to look after their grandson and Kitty and Arthur were able to carry on. At first the Irish washerwoman and her daughter were only seen in the provincial variety theatres and music halls but the impresario Dennis J. Clarke eventually discovered them. They were soon in demand by a much wider audience and in 1923 and 1924 they toured South Africa, New Zealand and Australia which was a great success. They continued to tour the Variety Halls but it was an appearance in the 1934 Royal Command Performance which established them at the top of the profession.

Arthur and Kitty were now able to buy a house in Wembley which they called Lucan Lodge and they were able to employ a chauffeur, gardener, maid, cook, cleaner and a butler. Their sketch *Bridget's Night Out* was included in a film called *Stars On Parade* which was released in 1936. This led to the offer of a part in a film entitled *Kathleen Mavoureen*. After appearing on stage in Blackpool and Manchester they made their first full-length film which was called simply *Old Mother Riley* and released in August 1937.

The film was very popular and it was followed by eighteen more, the last being made in 1952. On 13 August 1940 Arthur and Kitty made their first radio programme. This was a live production called *Old Mother Riley Comes to Town* and it was followed in November of the same year by an appearance in *Garrison Theatre*. In 1941 a Saturday night series called *Old Mother Riley Takes to the Air* commenced and from then until their final broadcast on 19 May 1950 in *Festival Music Hall* they made many broadcasts.

Unfortunately the success of Lucan and McShane was not entirely reflected in their marriage. Kitty spent their money almost as quickly as they made it and eventually she had an affair with Willer Neal who played Billy Bleach in several *Old Mother Riley* films. After forty years of marriage Kitty left Arthur to live with Neal. Eventually all three lived together in Lucan Lodge but after Kitty had arranged for all their possessions to be transferred to her she again left Arthur. The problems between them had meant that fewer engagements were coming their way. Arthur made a final film without Kitty and *Old Mother Riley Meets the Vampire* was released in July 1952.

Kitty caused a great deal of trouble for Arthur and the stress caused him to turn to drink. He continued to make regular stage appearances and he died whilst waiting to go on stage at the Tivoli in Hull on 17 May 1954.

In a comparatively short article it has been impossible to do justice to the career of Arthur Towle alias Arthur Lucan. I recommend anyone who would like to read the complete story to obtain a copy of Steve King's book *As long as I know it'll be quite alright: The life stories of Lucan and McShane* which was published in 1999. I am grateful to Steve for reading and correcting this article and for the photograph which is a still from the film *Old Mother Riley's Ghost*.

Henry Simpson LUNN

Henry Simpson Lunn was born in Horncastle in 1859 and was the son of a local tradesman and Methodist preacher. He attended Horncastle Grammar School and, in 1881, entered Headingley College, Leeds to prepare for the Methodist Ministry. After two years he moved to Trinity College, Dublin where he graduated with a degree in medicine. He was ordained in 1886.

Lunn began his business career whilst still at school by breeding mice and rearing poultry and game birds which he sold by advertising in the *Exchange and Mart*. By 1877 young Henry had branched out into the marketing of tennis court equipment. A Colonel Godfrey of

Cheltenham had sent him an idea for making metal markers which were manufactured by a local blacksmith. Henry also arranged for the manufacture of rackets, posts, nets, balls and a scoring device for fixing on the racket which Henry invented himself. He sold his business for £1000 to his father before entering Headingley College.

Henry's decision to join the Mutual Improvement Society appears to have been the catalyst which persuaded him to become a missionary. This Society had an ecumenical outlook with a membership of about a hundred made up of about equal numbers of Anglicans and Methodists. In July 1887 he married Ethel the eldest daughter of Canon Moore, rector of Middleton, County Cork and in the following October they sailed for the mission field in India.

Unfortunately the illness of Henry and their new-born son Arnold forced them to return to England in November 1888. Dr Lunn as he was usually known joined the West London Mission and he wrote a series of articles for the *Methodist Times* on 'A New Missionary Policy for India'. These articles were critical of the life style of some missionaries. An article entitled 'The Missionary Controversy' attracted some bitter and ill-founded criticism of Dr Lunn which led to him resigning from the Methodist ministry. In 1893 the Bishop of London offered him ordination in the Church of England but after long deliberation Lunn decided to refuse. He became chaplain to the Regent Street Polytechnic and lay representative to the Methodist Conference. He acted as reporter for the *Times*, the *Daily Chronicle*, the *Christian World* and a group of country papers. In 1891 he became editor of the *Review of the Churches* and continued this work until 1930. In 1892 Dr Lunn organised the first Grindelwald Conference which had as its aim Church re-union.

In 1893 he founded Co-operative Educational Tours and a number of tours to Europe, the Middle East and North Africa were arranged. A tour to Rome attracted 400 people. These tours were decidedly for the educated class and always had distinguished lecturers. In 1894 he arranged a cruise in the Mediterranean and, from October to April 1895, six consecutive cruises. As early as 1901 he used the new motor coaches for his 'Fortnightly Automobile Coaching Tours' which cost 15 guineas all-in from London to the continent. In 1902 Lunn set up the Public Schools Alpine Sports Club which played a major rôle in popularising Switzerland as a winter sports location. In the early years of the twentieth century Lunn was the first to organise round the world tours which cost £220! It was Henry Lunn who, in 1931, chartered the first holiday flight with twenty-four passengers leaving Croydon in the four-engined Hercules.

Through his organisation of trips from the United States to England he was invited to give a series of lectures at American Universities and he was asked to give the opening prayers in the Senate.

In the 1960s the travel organisation built up by Sir Henry Lunn was absorbed into the British Eagle Group and when Poly Travel was taken into the organisation the name was changed to Lunn Poly. The Polytechnic Touring Association, which became Poly Tours and later Poly Travel, had been founded in 1888 to provide holidays abroad at a reasonable cost for students and staff at the Regent Street Polytechnic in London.

Throughout his life Henry Lunn's main preoccupations were with church reunion and his work for peace. This work brought him into contact with archbishops, bishops, kings, princes and presidents and his work for peace was recognised in 1910 by the award of a knighthood. In the same year he stood for election to parliament for the borough of Boston but he was not elected and he was also unsuccessful when he stood for Brighton in 1923.

Sir Henry Lunn was a true exponent of the Protestant ethic of work and prayer and he wrote several books on religion including *Love of Jesus* and *Retreats for the Soul*. He also did much to popularise Lawn Tennis and he began the move for Alpine Sports and for Mediterranean cruises.

This remarkable man of whom Horncastle and Lincolnshire can be proud died in 1934.

FURTHER READING : Lunn, Henry *Nearing Harbour* (1934)

Halford John MACKINDER

Mackinder is known as the 'father of modern British geography' and is noted for his work as an educator and for his geopolitical conception of the world as divided into two camps, the ascendant Eurasian 'heartland' and the subordinate 'maritime lands'.

Halford John Mackinder was the son of a physician of Scottish descent and was born in Gainsborough on 15 February 1861. He was educated at Queen Elizabeth's Grammar School, Gainsborough and Epsom College before going up to Christ Church, Oxford in 1880. Mackinder studied natural sciences with a preference for biology. He graduated in 1883 and went on to obtain a degree in modern history before being called to the bar in 1886.

In 1887 Mackinder was appointed Reader in geography at Oxford University, the first such appointment in Britain. When, in 1899, the Royal Geographical Society established a School of Geography in Oxford Mackinder was appointed its first director. In the same year he made the first ascent of Mount Kenya, commenting that a geographer must also be 'an explorer and adventurer'.

Mackinder lectured for the Oxford extension movement, which had been formed to give educational opportunities to those unable to go up to university. This enabled him to travel widely throughout the country and particularly among the working men of the north of England. He became known for his enthusiasm for what he called the 'new geography' which he saw as building a bridge between the natural sciences and the humanities. His book *Britain and the British Seas,* which was published in 1902, is a recognised landmark in British geographical literature.

In 1892 Halford Mackinder was appointed principal of Reading College (later University) and in 1904 he was appointed director of the London School of Economics and Political Science in the University of London. In the same year he delivered a paper to the Royal Geographical Society on *The Geographical Pivot of History* in which he argued that interior Asia and eastern Europe (the heartland) had become the strategic centre of the 'World Island'. These views were set out in a book entitled *Democratic Ideals and Reality* which was published in 1919. Mackinder considered that the rôle of Britain and the United States was to preserve a balance between the powers contending for control of the heartland.

It is not possible here to set out in detail Mackinder's views, which were farsighted and were taken up by the German geopolitician, Karl Haushofer, to support his design for control of the World Island. During the Second World War it was suggested, in some quarters, that these views had inspired Hitler.

In 1924 Mackinder expounded his prophetic theory of the Atlantic Community that became reality after the Second World War as the North Atlantic Treaty Organisation (NATO).

In 1919 Mackinder was appointed British High Commissioner to southern Russia in an attempt to unify the White Russian forces and he was knighted in 1920. From 1920 until 1945 he was chairman of the Imperial Shipping Committee and from 1926 until 1931 he held a similar position in the Imperial Economic Committee.

Halford Mackinder entered Parliament in 1910 and retained his seat in the 1918 election but was defeated in 1922. He was appointed privy councillor in 1926 and amongst the honours he received were the Patron's Medal of the Royal Geographical Society and the Charles P. Day Medal of the America Society.

Sir Halford John Mackinder died on 6 March 1947 at Parkstone, Dorset.

John MACKWORTH

In 1412 Dr John Mackworth, Chancellor to Henry, Prince of Wales (later King Henry V) was appointed Dean of Lincoln. In 1404 he had been presented by King Henry IV to the stall of Empingham in Lincoln Cathedral and he was appointed to the Archdeaconry of Dorset in 1406 and to the Archdeaconry of Norfolk in 1408.

Whilst Dean of Lincoln under four bishops and for about twenty-five years, there were constant disputes between Mackworth and the canons and with the bishops of the see. After examining thirty-seven complaints made by the Canons against the Dean, Bishop Gray made an award in 1434 but this failed to bring order to the Cathedral.

Within a year of William Alnwick's translation from Norwich to Lincoln in 1436 he held a visitation to examine charges made by the Dean and Chapter one against the other. A total of forty-two charges were brought against the Dean. Amongst these grievances it was said that the Dean did not provide a substitute vicar when he was not in residence and that he did not provide food as the statutes required on certain days and for certain officials. It was said that the Dean in processions 'did not advance straight forward and in a direct line in due order from his own place in the choir, according to the custom of the Church, but across and not in a direct line, sometimes after the officiant [i.e. the priest conducting the service] of the Office, sometimes by his side, contrary to such custom'. It was alleged that the Dean's servants prevented the gatekeeper shutting the gates of the close at night and the Dean did nothing to correct this. It appears that the Dean appropriated money which had been paid to the Cathedral for the celebration of certain obits i.e. prayers for soul of the deceased.

A particularly serious allegation against the Dean was that at Chapter meetings he had with him members of his household 'armed with weapons of offence who sit there during the times of such Chapter meetings and assemblies to the great intimidation of the Chapter...'. According to the Canons, the Dean took away the 'Black Book' which records the customs of the Cathedral which should always be available for consultation.

Evidence was taken from every member of the Cathedral staff from the Dean himself down to the youngest chorister. Amongst those called the spokesman for the bellringers, John Rossyngton, complained that payment had not been made for ringing at obits. It was said that the Dean had instructed the Bellringers to stop ringing before the officiant at Vespers and Prime had been able to reach his stall and the Bishop gave instructions that in future the 'Cope Bell' should continue until all was ready. William Muston, vicar, complained that one John Bellringer kept a horrid dog in a kennel near 'Pele altare' in the nave. The vergers and bellringers complained that the Precentor did not feed them! It was also said that the Dean 'summoned persons to attend him at distant and unstatutable places, and told scandalous stories about the Canons to personages in high station'.

Both Dean and Canons agreed to abide by Bishop Alnwick's decision and he produced his *laudum* or award in 1439. To this day whenever a Canon or other dignitary is installed in Lincoln Cathedral he undertakes to 'inviolably observe the '*Laudum*' or Award of the Venerable Father in God, of pious memory, William Alnwick, sometime Bishop of Lincoln, and all the contents thereof...'.

The subsequent history of Dean Mackworth is unclear but Bishop Alnwick did have to ask him to answer charges brought against him in 1443 and 1444. In fact, the Dean was excommunicated but only five days later he was absolved by the Pope 'from any guilt of perjury which he may have incurred…'! However, it would seem that he continued to cause trouble

Bishop Alnwick died in 1449 and was buried in the place where he used to stand in processions. Dean Mackworth died two years later and a chantry was founded between the two easternmost pillars of the south side of the nave.

The death of the Dean did not entirely end this sad chapter in the history of the Cathedral. The Precentor continued to disregard the statutes and amongst other things, he was charged with violently attacking an acolyte.

About twenty-five years after the deaths of Bishop Alwnwick and Dean Mackworth, the value of the *Laudum* was recognised as a convenient collection of customs. The greater part was transcribed under the title *Constitutiones Ecclesie Lincoln super Laudum Dni W. Alnwyk Lincolniensis Episcopi.* .

FURTHER READING : Wooley, R. W. *The Award of William Alnwick* (1913)

John Gillespie MAGEE

John Gillespie Magee was born on 9 June 1922 in Shanghai. His father, also named John Gillespie Magee, came from Pittsburgh and went to China as a missionary in 1912. His mother, Faith Emeline Backhouse, was the daughter of the rector of Helmingham, Suffolk and went to China as a member of the Church Missionary Society. John and Faith married in 1921 and John junior was the first of their children.

John junior was educated first at the American School in Nanking and then, in 1931, he came to the UK and attended St Chad's Boarding School, Walmer, Kent. In 1935 he transferred to Rugby School and in 1939 he went to America to continue his education at Avon School, Connecticut.

John Magee had been writing poetry from an early age and, at the age of sixteen, he won the Rugby School Poetry prize. The same prize had been won 34 years earlier by Rupert Brooke who became John's idol. Whilst at Avon School, seventeen of his poems were published privately for circulation to his friends and family.

It was intended that John would go up to Yale University but, instead, he decided to join the Royal Canadian Air Force. After flying training in Canada he was posted to England and, after further training, he was posted to RAF Digby but he was actually based at RAF Wellingore which was a satellite of Digby. By the age of 19 he was a Section Leader of an operational Spitfire Squadron.

The poem for which he is best known, *High Flight*, which is reproduced below was written on 3 September 1941 three months before he was killed in a flying accident and he is buried at Scopwick.

HIGH FLIGHT

Oh, I have slipped the surly bonds of earth,
And danced the skies on laughter-silvered wings;
Sunward I've climbed and joined the tumbling mirth
Of sun-split clouds – and done a hundred things
You have not dreamed of - wheeled and soared and swung
High in the sunlit silence – Hov'ring there,
I've chased the shouting wind along and flung
My eager craft through footless halls of air.

Up, up the long, delirious, burning blue
I've topped the wind-swept heights with easy grace,
Where never lark, or even eagle, flew;
And, while with silent, lifting mind I've trod
The high untrespassed sanctity of space,
Put out my hand and touched the face of God.

High Flight was widely published and was quoted by President Reagan after the Challenger shuttlecraft disaster of 1986.

FURTHER READING : *John Magee : The Pilot Poet* (This England Press 1996)

Mike MALONEY

Mike Maloney was awarded an honorary doctorate by the University of Lincolnshire and Humberside at a degree congregation in July 2001. In a thirty year career as a newspaper photographer he has received 99 awards including one for a lifetime's exceptional achievement. However, he regards the doctorate as a very special honour and the greatest he has received. As he says 'there aren't many press photographers walking up and down Fleet Street who can put the word 'doctor' in front of their names'.

Mike is one of Lincoln's most loyal ambassadors and, as a professional journalist he has travelled worldwide meeting many famous (and infamous) people. He misses no opportunity of publicising his place of birth and, in particular, its magnificent Cathedral which Mike considers one of the finest buildings in the world.

He has a fund of stories and, of those which are printable, one is of a visit to the Kremlin in the company of the late Robert Maxwell. During dinner with Mikhail Gorbachev, who was then the leader of the Soviet Union and the second most powerful man in the world, Mike took the opportunity to present him with that remarkable good luck symbol, a Lincoln Imp tie-pin! Many others have been honoured by Mike in this way including President Ronald Reagan, Frank Sinatra, Max Bygraves, Shirley Bassey and Les Dawson. It is nice to know that, if they didn't before, through Mike they are now well aware of the location of Lincoln, England!

Mike was born in Lincoln in 1950 and educated at St Hugh's Roman Catholic School and St Peter and Paul's High School in the City. After leaving school he worked for a firm of industrial chemists but, after an unfortunate incident involving a mouthful of nitric acid, Mike decided against a career in chemistry. Instead he decided to continue his education at the People's College in Nottingham reading Chemistry, Physics and Maths and the Art College in Lincoln where he studied Art and Printing Technology. His introduction to the media world came when he started work in the printing department of the *Lincolnshire Chronicle*. From a very early age, he had developed an interest in photography and he received much good advice from the newspaper staff photographers which eventually led to his first photographic assignment - covering the 1967 St George's Day parade of the Boy Scouts at Lincoln Cathedral for which he was paid 10s 6d (£0.525p).

Mike desperately wanted to become a full-time photographer but a suitable job never came in Lincoln and he decided to take the plunge and move to London. At first he worked practically round the clock for the Fleet Street News Agency Service and he became well-known to all of the picture editors. He got on well with the personalities of the show business world and this soon led him to decide to work as a freelance. Mike's first big assignment and incidentally his introduction to the high life of caviar and champagne was to cover Noel Coward's birthday party at the Savoy.

This was the beginning of a punishing but very rewarding career during which he started work for the *Evening News* at 7.30 a.m. and, in the late afternoon, moving on to the *Daily Mirror* often working until 1.30 a.m. the next day. Mike kept up this routine for two years during which time he covered many of the major news stories of the 1970s. By now he had become so well-known in Fleet Street that, whilst still only twenty-four, he was offered and accepted a staff job at the *Daily Mirror*. Mike's first overseas trip was to North Africa to take shots of the filming of Zeferelli's picture based on the life of Christ. He followed this by joining Paul McCartney and his band *Wings* on an American tour. On their final night he was invited to dinner in Madison Square Gardens as the personal guest of McCartney. To his surprise and amazement he found that a companion had been arranged for him - Jackie Onassis. He has a love of sport which has led to some brilliant shots including a picture of Torvill and Dean in action which won first prize in the Ilford *Pictures of the Year* awards and *Photographer of the Year* award, a title he has won three times.

Mike with his wife, Michelle, and their fourteen year old son, Alexander,
after receiving the Freedom of the City of London in January 2002

Mike's dedication to his art has also brought its financial reward which has enabled him to indulge his two passions - cars and steam trains. In 1981 he was able to achieve one of his greatest ambitions and buy a Rolls-Royce Silver Shadow. His ownership of a Rolls led to a turning point in his career. Robert Maxwell arrived at the Mirror Building one morning in 1984 soon after he had bought the newspaper to find Mike's Rolls parked next to his own space and he demanded to meet the owner. The two got on so well that Mike found himself accompanying RM on many of his extensive tours.

Mike attained a unique personal relationship during the seven years he was Maxwell's personal photographer. RM, as he was usually known, always referred to Mike as 'Mr Snapper'. As well as accompanying RM to dinner with Gorbachev in the Kremlin he was present at the White House when Maxwell had an audience with President Reagan. He was present with the Queen and Maxwell in Scotland and Mike has recorded these and many more notable occasions during these seven eventful years in his book *Flash! Crash! Splash!* Although completely true, the book, which was published in 1996, reads more like a work of fiction. Maxwell was without doubt one of the most colourful and bizarre characters of this century.

The many awards which Mike has won have been in classes ranging from news and sport to Royalty and portraiture. Much of his success is due to his ability to charm people coupled with his undoubted technical skill which results in well thought-out and superbly executed prints. Many of his award winning photographs have become classics of the photographer's art and these include the shot which captured the Queen's excitement during the final stages of the Derby which, in 1978, won him the Martini *Royal Photographer of the Year* title and the Ilford *Photographer of the Year* award. A photograph of the Royal Family on the balcony of Buckingham Palace watching the fly past after the Trooping the Colour parade which also won an award really captures the excitement of the moment. A particularly exciting shot is of Shamu, the three-ton killer whale, taken at *Sea World* in Florida but there are so many and what does come across is Mike's ability to capture that fleeting moment which makes a picture great.

Mike has owned and tested many cameras during his career but he still has his first, a bakelite Kodak 127 which was given to him by his father for his tenth birthday. He writes a weekly feature page in *Amateur Photographer* and frequently appears on television as well as lecturing on P & O Cruises and whenever he can he publicises Lincoln and the county.

Philip MARSHALL

Although Dr Philip Marshall was born at Brighouse, Yorkshire in 1921 he is a 'yellow belly' by adoption having spent his early years at Alford. He is still fascinated by the outline of the Wolds and Miles Cross Hill just to the west of Alford. Hills seem to mean a lot to musicians and Dr Marshall calls to mind the influence of the Malverns on Elgar and the place of the Cotswolds in the musical life of Herbert Howells, whose work he particularly admires.

Marshall's first music lessons were on the fine organ at St Wilfrid's, Alford under the guidance of Frank Graves who was a strict teacher and hard taskmaster. On returning to Brighouse he came to the notice of the organist Whiteley Singleton who had been a pupil of Sir Edward Bairstow, a former organist at York Minster. Under Singleton's influence he was able to build on the solid foundation laid by Graves and came to realise what 'good' music should be.

After serving in the RASC during the war he became music master at Keighley Boys' Grammar School, Sub-Organist at Leeds Parish Church and organist at All Souls Church, Haley Hill, Halifax. At the Royal College of Organists he won the Limpus, Harding and Read Prizes, at Trinity College a fellowship diploma in composition, and at the Royal College of Music an associateship in voice training and class singing. He graduated Bachelor of Music at Durham University and was awarded a doctorate by the same University after a short period of study with Francis Jackson, who was Bairstow's successor at York Minster.

In 1951 Philip Marshall became organist at Boston 'Stump' and moved on after six years to become Organist and Master of the Choristers at Ripon Cathedral. He remained there until 1966 when he was appointed to a similar post at Lincoln Cathedral. When he decided to retire in 1986 he commented : 'twenty years in one place, in any capacity – musical or otherwise – is quite long enough'. This is a typical outspoken statement by this forthright man but, whilst most may agree in principle, his retirement was regretted by many.

He went on to say that 'many years ago, a few cathedral organists would vie with each other as to length of service, one who had served his cathedral for thirty-six years feeling slight resentment towards another who had served for thirty-eight years. In some instances it was a chosen and dedicated desire to 'die in office'.

Philip Marshall had no such desire - as he said 'the idea of bidding farewell in a crashing discord as he collapsed in a coronary convulsion is, for him, coarsely sentimental – and messy'. Far rather an obituary notice both heroic and touching in its simplicity -'Musician falls to death trying to rescue cat from tree', or in a secluded county churchyard, a simple stone engraved thereon 'Here lieth P. M. whose soul heaven snatched with his barley wine'.

Marshall played for his first church service at the age of twelve and, in all of his years of service to the church, he recalls the six spent at Boston as his happiest. After that his time at Ripon is recalled with great pleasure. Two events from his long career stand out above all others. The first was his involvement in the music for the Enthronement of Dr John Moorman as Lord Bishop of Ripon and the second the singing of the Lincoln Choir at High Mass in St Salvator's Cathedral, Bruges. This latter occasion was the highlight of the Choir's first overseas tour. The choir has, of course, made several tours since, but this event stands out in Philip Marshall's memory.

Other highlights of his time at Lincoln were the conducting of Elgar's *Dream of Gerontius* and J. S. Bach's *B minor Mass*. The visit of the late Herbert Howells to hear the first performance of a magnificent motet he had written for the Lincoln Choir was another memorable occasion.

The busy life of a cathedral organist leaves little time for composition, but Philip Marshall has composed music either when inspired to do so or at the request of the Dean and Chapter or other bodies. Such works include a cantata with the title *In Laudem Sancti Hugoniensis* composed for the 700th anniversary celebrations of the consecration of the Angel Choir which has been performed at Chingford and Neustadt as well as Lincoln. A setting of three Christmas Carols called *Visions of a King* was commissioned by the Lincoln Musical Society and two works were commissioned for the Inner London Education Authority String Orchestra. The first of these *Soliloquy and Fugue* was in memory of Herbert Howells being first performed at the Cathedral and later at County Hall, London. The second work was a *Concerto for Piano and Strings* which was performed in London in February 1988.

In retirement Dr Marshall says he does not miss his organ playing. He was happy enough to play the organ as an accompaniment to the Choir but he has no love for the organ as a solo instrument and any organ recitals he gave were under pressure. His musical interest has been in the Choir and his greatest joy at Lincoln was the daily rehearsals with boy Choristers from 8.30 to 9.30 each morning.

The good spirits, keen enthusiasm and loyalty of these youngsters helped to keep him young. The attainments of the Lincoln Choir during Philip Marshall's time at the Cathedral included regular broadcast for BBC Choral Evensong, five LP Records and four overseas tours is an obvious and justified source of pride to him.

Philip Marshall is an enthusiast of the steam locomotive and, in fact, built two miniature coal-fired engines. For him a train must have the smell of steam, real smoke and, above all, the atmosphere isn't right unless you get your hands dirty. Perhaps it was this interest which inspired him to compose that remarkable work, *The Spiritual Railway*, first performed by the Cathedral Choir on the platform of Lincoln Central Station when St Mark's closed.

He has a veneration for the cat in whose company he is always happy. Commenting on his retirement Philip Marshall said 'he is too old a dog to learn new tricks. He would prefer to be likened to that elegant animal, the cat, who could perform tricks, but does not see why he should, merely to conform to fashion and find favour with the few'.

Although Philip Marshall is shy and retiring he has presented musical evenings and his classes at the Lincoln Adult Education Centre were always very popular. He lives with his wife at Potterhanworth.

Raymond MAYS

Raymond Mays with his Brescia Bugatti 'Cordon Rouge' 1922

For thirty years Raymond Mays was a successful racing driver and just before the Second World War he broke many records on the old Brooklands circuit. He was born at Eastgate House, Bourne on 1 August 1899 and his father was a pioneer motorist. Young Raymond's interest in racing began at an early age. His father's Napier and Vauxhall cars were entered in local hill and speed trials and the mechanics from these motor car factories were always at the house preparing the cars for competitions. At the age of nine Raymond persuaded the engineers to let him ride with them on road tests.

At Oundle School he met Amherst Villiers who was later to work with him on many cars. It was Villiers who created the first supercharged Bentley and had much to do with the Napier-Campbell car in which Sir Malcolm Campbell broke the land speed record in 1927. After being commissioned in the Grenadier Guards in May 1918 and serving in France and Germany, Mays went up to Christ's College, Cambridge before joining the family wool business. Whilst at Cambridge he devoted every possible spare moment to motor racing and he had numerous successes with his Speed Model Hillman at Brooklands. He started competing in the Shelsey Walsh Hill Climb in 1921 and thereafter returned many times, often recording fastest times of the day or taking the record in his later cars - Bugatti, Mercedes, Invicta, Vauxhall and Riley.

In 1934 Raymond Mays with Humphrey Cook and Peter Berthon formed English Racing Automobiles Ltd and he was number one driver. The debut of the ERA racing car was to have been at the Isle of Man races in May 1934 but this had to be cancelled for further work on the springing. A little later Humphrey Cook and Raymond Mays set up class records at Brooklands and Mays won the Nuffield Trophy race at Donington Park which was the first road race ever held in England. From then on ERA. and Raymond Mays achieved world fame. In 1935 at the Nürnbergring before 400,000 spectators, a team of ERAs came first, second, fourth and fifth greatly to the displeasure of the Nazi backers of the German and Italian cars.

Raymond Mays with his ERA car *circa* 1978

After the Second World War, Mays twice won the British Hill Climb championship and was for many years holder of the Shelsey Walsh record in his own ERA. It was Raymond Mays who founded British Racing Motors in 1945 with the backing of many companies and individuals. His ambition was to restore Britain to Grand Prix racing with the most advanced engineering project in racing car design ever. The BRM sports car had a very chequered career initially and was only saved financially in 1952 by Sir Alfred Owen taking the project into the family engineering company as the Owen Racing Organisation with Mays as racing director. Success came in the late fifties and in the sixties when Graham Hill invariably qualified in one of the cars and led the team to the world championship in 1962. Later Jackie Stewart joined the team and helped keep BRM in the front rank for a few more years, finally ending in 1981.

In 1978 Raymond Mays devotion to the promotion of motor racing was recognised when he was made a Commander of the Order of the British Empire. He was a man of great personal charm who was devoted to the BRM car and its future. He was held in high esteem by all who knew him and was always interested in the careers of young and untried drivers who came to him for advice.

During his racing career Raymond Mays always carried with him in the pockets of his overalls a number of lucky charms. These included a small black cat given to him by Bebe Daniels the film and radio star, and a black wooden doll which he had been given by the musical comedy actress Jose Collins. He also had a small ladybird sewn on his overalls and never raced unless he wore something coloured blue.

Away from racing he had many friends in the theatrical world - among them Ivor Novello and Noel Coward. Raymond Mays, CBE died on 6 January 1980.

FURTHER READING : Mays, R. and Roberts, P. *B. R. M.* (1962). McGregor, Michael *Raymond Mays of Bourne* (1996)

I am grateful to Bourne Civic Society for permission to use the two photographs.

John MERRYWEATHER

Few people today will realise that the Observatory Tower at Lincoln Castle was built as recently as the early nineteenth century. Even fewer will have heard of the man responsible, John Merryweather. Apparently Merryweather was keen on astronomy and had the tower built so that he could spend the night stargazing! Although there is no record of him discovering any new heavenly bodies, he did spot at least one earthly body attempting to escape over the wall.

In 1799 Merryweather was appointed Keeper of Lincoln Prison, which was then housed in the Castle. From the evidence of some sources he does not appear to have been very popular and he was charged with brutality to a female prisoner but was acquitted. He is said to have been a devious man who was over-concerned with obtaining preference for himself and his friends, and possibly too familiar with the female felons in his care. A prisoner at the Castle in 1820 said that 'Our governor was a genius in his way. He was not an educated man, but he had the reputation of being an adept in astronomy'.

During the thirty years Merryweather was at the Prison, the number of prisoners rose from single figures to more than eighty at any one time. The majority of these were transportees and one of the duties of the Gaoler was to see them safely on board ship. Merryweather usually undertook that duty himself and, when the prison was visited by James Nield whose *Report on English Prisons* was published in 1802, he found the prison to be 'well regulated' and the gaoler 'intelligent, active and humane'. When Merryweather had illiterate condemned prisoners in his charge, he placed other prisoners in the cell who could read the Bible or Prayer Book to the person about to be executed.

When the Crown Court was built in 1824, prisoner labour was used and the following is an extract from Merryweather's report :

> 'From 15 to 20 of the prisoners are employed under my direction and the assistance of a Turnkey, in working a stone quarry, levelling or forming the ground, cutting stone, serving masons and assisting generally in doing any labour required about the building or premises.
>
> But as labour so performed by them is not capable of being valued, the amount of their earnings is not ascertained, and all they receive for it is an extra diet – one and a half pounds of good beef without bone, weekly.'

As well as being a stargazer Merryweather kept poultry and on 16 October 1828 he recorded :

> 'Have this day sent away all the poultry I have been in the habit of keeping pursuant to an Order at the last Gaol Sessions - with the exception of a Peacock for whom I have not yet been able to find a satisfactory asylum for a very old pet'.

For his time John Merryweather appears to have been a compassionate gaoler and, so far as he was able, he cared for his charges and did all he could to help them. When he retired in 1830 he went to live on Steep Hill, Lincoln. He was born in 1768 and died in 1861 at the age of 93 and is buried in Eastgate Cemetery, Lincoln.

Austin Vernon MITCHELL

Austin Mitchell has been Member of Parliament for Grimsby since 1983 so he is well on the way to being accepted for naturalisation (or perhaps nationalisation) as an Honorary Lincolnshire Yellowbelly. Unfortunately, he was actually born over the border in Baildon, Yorkshire on 19 September 1934.

After attending the Woodbottom Council School he went on to Bingley Grammar School before going up to Manchester University. He graduated with a BA and went on to earn an MA before going up to Nuffield College, Oxford to research for a DPhil. From 1959 until 1963 he worked as a lecturer in History at the University of Otago, Dunedin, New Zealand. He then moved on as Senior Lecturer in Politics at the University of Canterbury, Christchurch, New Zealand where he remained until 1967. He returned to England to take up an appointment as official fellow of Nuffield College until he commenced a career in television in 1969. He had already had twelve months experience of television when he was presenter of New Zealand's equivalent of *Panorama*.

Austin worked as a journalist with Yorkshire Television from 1969 until 1977 with a break from 1972 to 1973 when he presented the BBC *Current Affairs* programme. His full-time television career had to be put on hold when he was elected to Parliament but he presented *Target for Sky TV* from 1989 until 1998 and he is a regular member of such programmes as BBC's *Any Questions?*

In parliament he was opposition frontbench spokesman on Trade and Industry from 1987 until 1989. He was a Member of the Agriculture Select Committee and took the chair of the All Party Media Group.

During a very busy life he has found time to write nineteen books most of which are on New Zealand and British Politics although he has also written books on Yorkshire-related subjects. As a candidate for naturalisation perhaps he will eventually find time to investigate that elusive element of Lincolnshire life - Yellow Belly Humour!

When Austin is able to escape from London he lives at Sowerby Bridge with his wife, Linda and youngest son, Jonathon. His other three children all daughters have long since flown the nest. The Mitchell's home is not far from that of his friend Richard Whiteley. Both Austin and Richard originate from Baildon and both worked as journalists on Yorkshire Television's news programme *Calendar*. In his autobiography Richard tells the story of Austin's launch into politics as follows :

The telephone rang on Austin's desk and was answered by his secretary. The message left for him read 'Ring East Mid. Lab Party. Reg. Org'.

On his return from lunch the following telephone conversation took place :

'Labour party – Hello.'
'Hello. Is Reg there please?'
'Reg…Reg who? We don't have a Reg.'
'Yes you do. It's Austin Mitchell. I was told to ring Reg at that number - Reg. Org.'
'I think you need to speak to Mr Bridges, our Regional Organiser.'

Austin Mitchell has a very outgoing personality, perhaps some would say flamboyant and this has stood him in good stead. As Richard Whiteley comments 'he loved dressing up or dressing down, prancing around in the snow in underpants, in and out of the newly arrived phenonomen of sauna baths.'

Austin lists his recreation as 'worritting'!

Ras Prince MONOLULU

Although Monolulu was not a native of Lincolnshire he certainly touched the lives of many Yellow Bellies - and others. For this he has earned a place in this book. He is best known as a racing tipster but his colourful dress, sense of humour and ability as a raconteur brightened the lives of many who met him on the racecourses of Britain and the Continent and in the markets of London and the Provinces for some fifty years.

According to his biography, Monolulu was born in Addis Ababa, Ethiopia presumably in about 1880. Before he was twelve years of age he ran away to the coast and was taken to see one of the ships in the harbour at Djibouti. Many sailors deserted and young Monolulu was 'persuaded' to join the ship as a cabin boy. Perhaps he did not take much persuading to go to sea. When asked to give his name in order that the necessary papers could be completed he said he was Ras Prince Monolulu. Nowhere has he recorded his real name and this self-imposed title stuck with him for the remainder of his life.

Eventually he found his way to New York at a time when America was being swept by dozens of religious movements. He joined the crusade led by the founder of the Salvation Army, General William Booth, but this was not for him and he soon left and took up with several other Missions. As he says 'anything and everything so long as I could eat.' On one of the Missions he became friendly with a Scotsman and he was persuaded to be baptised into the Christian Church as Peter Mackay!

The life of an evangelical preacher soon palled and he became the cook's assistant on board a steamer plying between New York and Connecticut again becoming Ras Prince Monolulu! In 1902 he joined the cattle boat, *Minnetonka* which was due to sail for England. On landing at Tilbury he made his way to London and found work as a sculleryman, perhaps appropriately, at the Eccentrics Club.   His next venture was an appearance in the chorus of a negro show, *In Dahomey*, on the stage of the Shaftesbury Theatre.   After the show finished he took to singing in the streets but this didn't pay well enough and he decided to walk to Epsom where he met an Irishman who was selling tips on the racecourse.   They worked in partnership for nine months with Monolulu drawing the crowds whilst the Irishman sold the tips.

During the winter months, when there was no flat racing, he worked in the London Markets but clearly he had found his feet and looked forward to the first meeting of the flat racing season at Lincoln in March.   He became a well-known figure at racecourses up and down the country.   He was accepted by the racing fraternity and was known to all the leading owners and trainers – including royalty.   He eventually travelled throughout the continent and even visited Russia with an American Negro theatre show.   He was received as a Prince by the Tsar!

Monolulu's cry 'I gotta Horse' became familiar at racecourses up and down the country. He told the following story of the way in which this became his battle cry :

'A character called Gypsy Daniels in the early days of the twentieth century went around the racecourses begging people to repent before it was too late, and telling them how he had been saved.   He began to be quite a nuisance to me, because he told his story well and always gathered a crowd round him, a crowd that I wanted round me.   I stood near him on Epsom Downs on Derby Day, and he had an audience that was too large for my liking.   He was taking all the customers away from the tipsters.   My prospective clients were too interested in him and something had to be done about it.

Then my big chance came.   Gypsy Daniels, with his arms raised high, and his fingers pointing aloft, cried, 'I've got Heaven!   I've got Heaven!'   Quickly edging myself into the crowd, I made the people roar when I mimicked him, with my arms aloft and my fingers pointing to the sky and bawled, as loud as I could :

'And I gotta Horse!   I gotta Horse!'

My crowd came back.   The prospect of backing the winner of the Derby was more appealing on that day, than the more remote chance of having an early glimpse of the next world'.

Although it is 40 years since Lincoln's race course on the Carholme closed and 37 years since the Prince died many people can still remember his colourful figure standing on the Cornhill in Lincoln offering the name of the winner of the Lincolnshire Handicap for a shilling or two.

According to a contemporary newspaper report Monolulu married Miss Nellie Adkins in August 1931 but this is not mentioned in his autobiography.   Something of the affection with which he was held is confirmed by the fact that in Maple Street, London there is a hostelry named *The Prince Monolulu.*

Prince Monolulu died in London in 1965 aged 84.   It is interesting to note that 'Ras' is the Ethiopian for 'Prince'.   Before he was emperor Haile Selassie was called Ras Tafari Makonnen. Hence the term 'Rastafarian'.

FURTHER READING : White, Sidney H. *I Gotta Horse : The Autobiography of Ras, Prince Monolulu* (1950)

Thomas Wimberley MOSSMAN

Thomas Wimberley Mossman was born at Skipton, Yorkshire in 1826 and was brought up by a maiden aunt.   He was a studious, solitary boy very fond of reading, particularly history. He attended Peel Grammar School in the Isle of Man and then went up to St Edmund Hall, Oxford where he became interested in the Oxford Movement.

After Mossman graduated BA in 1849 he was ordained and served his first curacy at Donington-on-Bain where his uncle, the Revd Conrad Makings Wimberley, was rector.   He moved to Panton in 1852 and became vicar of Ranby in 1854.   His final move was to become vicar of West Torrington and rector of East Torrington in 1859.   After settling into his new parishes he founded the Brotherhood of the Holy Redeemer for the benefit of poor students who wished to enter Holy Orders.   The students became known locally as 'Mossman Monks' because of the monastic type of dress they wore.   In 1867 they visited Lincoln and attracted considerable attention in their 'outlandish garb, cassocks, beads, and crosses'.   One had his head shaved and called himself Father Augustine.   The Bishop of Lincoln seems to have refused to ordain Mossman's students but a number were received into Holy Orders in other dioceses.   The Brotherhood eventually moved to Newcastle.   Mossman was not involved in the move and the Brotherhood soon collapsed.

Thomas Mossman was a great writer and corresponded with Cardinal Newman, Gladstone and Pope Leo XIII.   He also conducted considerable correspondence with the press. Mossman wrote a number of learned books including a *History of the Early Christian Church* and received a grant of £100 from the Civil List 'in aid of his labours for literature and ecclesiastical history'.   Mossman's two-volume novel *Mr Gray and his Neighbours*, which he wrote under the pseudonym 'Peter Piper, Esq.' was published in 1877.   This caused considerable comment and the incumbent of Biscathorpe alleged that he had been caricatured.   The book was withdrawn from Lincoln Library.

Although he had the reputation of being inclined towards Roman Catholicism he officiated at the burial in 1880 of the daughter of Free Methodist parents and invited the Methodist Minister into the church to give an address.   This was a very rare occurrence at that time but Mossman insisted that nonconformists should be treated as Brethren of Christ and dissenters should be granted the right of burial 'as an act of Christian love'.   In a letter published in the *Non-conformist* in July 1881 he suggested that Archbishops and Bishops should send Christian greetings to every Presbyterian, Congregationalist, Baptist and Methodist Minister, giving them permission to officiate in any church.

Mossman was a great champion of the poor and opposed the means test. He said to the 'working men of Lincolnshire be up and doing and may God bless you in your long effort to raise your down-trodden class'. He was an extremely complex character and became a national figure for his support of the extreme ritualistic party. Mossman became a member of the Order of Corporate Reunion and an advertisement appeared in the *Lincolnshire Chronicle* which stated that an Ordination would be held in the Parish of St Martins in the Fields London on 3 October 1882 by the Right Revd Thomas Wimberley Mossman DD Catholic Bishop of Selby, Rector of Torrington and Prelate of the Order of Christian Reunion. The Bishop of Lincoln, not surprisingly, was extremely concerned, commenting that Mossman had 'caused yourself to be consecrated…Bishop' and had 'ordained a deacon…without the knowledge or consent of the Bishop…'

During Mossman's last illness Cardinal Manning travelled to West Torrington and received him into the Roman Catholic Church. Mossman died on 6 July 1885 and on the afternoon of his funeral at four o'clock several acolytes carrying tapers, censers and holy water led a procession of priests in front of the coffin which was covered with flowers and crosses. This coffin was followed by a procession of all the villagers and there was a great deal of interest in the funeral of a Roman Catholic in a Church of England building. The service was conducted by Canon Dwyer, a Roman Catholic priest from Market Rasen, and was attended by a large number of robed Anglican clergy.

There is no doubt that Mossman was a man of great public conscience who spent his life seeking true Christianity. His grave at West Torrington is marked by a large cross.

FURTHER READING : Anson, Peter *Bishops at Large* (1967)

Max NOTTINGHAM
(See photograph back cover)

In 1968 a new broadcasting phenomena began – the phone-in. This was introduced by BBC Radio Nottingham but other radio stations quickly adopted this cheap and popular idea. For some listeners calling the local radio station became almost a full-time occupation. The best known serial caller is Max Nottingham of Lincoln. With between 150 and 300 calls a year to radio stations in the Midlands and the North he can easily claim to hold the record for the sport. His record for the number of calls in a year is actually 311 calls, which were made in 1995.

Max is also a prolific writer of 'Letters to the Editor' with an average of six hundred a year to newspapers throughout the length and breadth of the country. Most of those who write 'Letters to the Editor' or take part in radio 'phone ins' specialise in a particular subject but Max's subjects for both media range widely. Although the majority of his letters deal with local issues, he also writes on a wide variety of national subjects. Similarly his phone calls are a mix of jokes and more thoughtful and philosophical subjects.

Max reads the *Lincolnshire Echo* and *Mirror* at home but he is also to be found almost daily in Lincoln Central Library where he scans through many newspapers. This keeps him extremely well- informed and he is able to note possible subjects for the media. He feels that this hobby is a means of self-expression and regards English as a wonderful language. Clearly he loves talking and writing. He occasionally indulges in humorous verse and has published a booklet entitled *Shafts of Wit and Tinkling Bells.*

Max was born on 28 July 1933 in Gainsborough and was the youngest of Frank and Sarah Nottingham's eleven sons and two daughters. His education was at several elementary schools and it amuses him when in some circles, because of the knowledge that he has gained through his hobby, it is assumed that he is a university graduate. He comments that perhaps over the years, whilst taking part in programmes broadcast by the BBC, his native Lincolnshire accent has become rather 'posh'.

Max's family moved to Scunthorpe and then to Leadenham towards the end of the Second World War and finally to Lincoln in 1962. After National Service in the REME he worked on a farm for a time but most of his working life was spent in the offices of several Lincoln firms.

Max has appeared on BBC TV's *Look North* programme and he was filmed answering calls from listeners to Radio Lincolnshire's phone in programme. He has appeared on Ned Sherrin's Radio 4 *Loose Ends* programme but possibly his most memorable experience was presenting a phone-in where the callers were all professional presenters! The tables were turned on Max when he was featured in an article on 'Serial Callers' in the *Sunday Observer Magazine* dated 6 March 1994. He has also been featured in the *Lincolnshire Echo* and *Yorkshire Post.*

Unfortunately, the early morning and evening 'phone-in programmes which were such a popular and useful feature on Lincolnshire's local radio no longer exist. However, Max is still to be heard whenever the opportunity presents itself and, of course, letters from him regularly appear in both local and the national press. Long may he continue to inform and entertain us in his own inimitable way.

Max still lives in Lincoln's West End.

James S. PADLEY

During the course of a long and active life, James Sandby Padley was instrumental in changing the face of Lincolnshire by planning, constructing and improving roads and waterways, building more than fifty bridges and surveying estates with a view to their improvement.

Padley came to Lincolnshire in 1819 as assistant to Captain Stevens of the Royal Engineers who carried out the first Ordnance Survey of the county. This was directly due to the initiative and influence of the members of the Burton Hunt. In the Preface to *Fens and Floods of Mid-Lincolnshire* Padley records that, in 1819 and 1820, he surveyed 'nearly the whole of the main roads' within an area 'in the form of a square extending from Wragby to Southwell and from Dunsby Lane to Spital'.

It was, no doubt, during his work for the Ordnance Survey that Padley became acquainted with Charles Chaplin, MP for Lincolnshire of whom it was said that 'he could himself return no fewer than seven members to Parliament, since to vote the way the Squire ordered was the whole duty of the good tenant'. When his Ordnance Survey work was finished Padley undertook a survey of the Chaplin estates at Tathwell, Temple Bruer and Blankney Fen, a task which he accomplished so well that the formidable Squire recommended him as successor to William Hayward in the post of Surveyor of the County Bridges for the Division of Lindsey. To this office were shortly added those of Surveyor of Sewers for the Lincoln District and of turnpike roads for the same area. For the next sixty years or so he was actively engaged in the execution of these duties, in addition to which he had a considerable private practice. He undertook work for Lincoln Corporation and other public bodies.

Padley found time for historical research and literary work. On Friday, 5 August 1881, less than a fortnight before his death, he recorded in his diary :

> 'Took Palmer's Cab at 7 o'clock and went to Washingborough, called on Mr Marshall, Royal Oak Inn, drove down into Heighington Fen to see the place where the Antient Boat was found made out of an oak tree to record in my History'.

On 13 August he wrote the Preface to the book for which he will long be honoured, *Fens and Floods of Mid-Lincolnshire.* This most valuable work contains a wealth of first-hand material which would otherwise have been lost, relating to the great flood of 1795 as well as much historical matter regarding drains, duck decoys, inland navigation, swan-marks, manorial customs and many other subjects.

Thirty years earlier Padley had published *Selections from the Antient Monastic, Ecclesiastical and Domestic edifices of Lincolnshire*, which contained 21 plates of measured drawings of old buildings in Lincoln as well as Somerton Castle, Tupholme Abbey and Temple Bruer. A large collection of his papers, including maps and estate plans, is preserved in the Lincolnshire Archives.

J. S. Padley died on 18 August 1881 at Hildred's Hotel Skegness during a summer holiday with his family. He was aged 89 and the following tribute was paid to him :

'The deceased gentleman's career was a most successful one, marked by those characteristics which indicate the possession of great natural ability, indomitable perseverance, uprightness of life, and such geniality of manner that every one with whom he was associated both respected him and valued his friendship…During his long life we believe that he never made an enemy.'

For most of the nineteenth century, Padley had been a familiar and respected figure throughout Lincolnshire. Today, despite the fact that he was one of the pioneers of the Ordnance Survey in three counties and that much of his engineering work in the way of bridges, roads, sluices and drains still survive, he is largely forgotten. However, his lasting monument is the four (20 inches to 1 mile) plans of Lincoln, dated 1842, 1851, 1868 and, in conjunction with James Thropp, 1883.

Montague Russell PAGE

Russell Page was born on 1 November 1906 and was the second son of three children of Harold Ethelbert Page a solicitor who lived in Greetwell House, Greetwell Road, Lincoln.

In his book *The Education of a Gardener* he writes :

'I started to understand about plants by handling them. It was on one summer holiday when I was perhaps fourteen that, bored with the riding and jumping competitions at a local agricultural show, I wandered off to the flower tent. There in an atmosphere hot and heavy with the smell of trampled grass, people, animals and flowers, my attention was caught by a tiny plant of *Campanula pulla* with three deep purple bells, huge in comparison with its frail leaves and the minute pot in which it grew. It was mine for a shilling and opened a new world for me'.

From this small beginning young Russell spent all his pocket money on plants and his holidays were spent cycling around the countryside collecting leaf-mould, grit, sand and gravel for his own small garden. His passion for plants and gardens became well-known for miles around Lincoln and he met an elderly lady who lived near Lincoln Cathedral and shared his enthusiasm for flowers. Half the tiles in the hallway of her house had been taken up and re-placed with a chequer board of primula seedlings! The drawing-room had ivy around the windows, walls and ceiling.

Russell Page learned about plants and gardens in the best possible way - by trial and error. At the age of seventeen he was given the means to make his first rock garden and friends began to invite him to design their gardens for them.

From 1918 until 1924 he attended Charterhouse School in Surrey but returned to his parents' home during the vacations to continue his gardening. His professional career as a landscape gardener was founded when, in 1929, he designed and built a rock garden at North

Luffenham, Rutland for which he was paid one pound a day.

Whilst he was at Charterhouse School Gertrude Jekyll, who was in her eighties, still gardened close by and Russell described her as '... a dumpy figure in a heavy gardener's apron, her vitality shining from a face half concealed by two pairs of spectacles and a battered and yellowed straw hat.'

In 1927 Page went on to the Slade School in London to study art under Professor Tonks. After graduating he continued his artistic studies in Paris where he met his lifelong friend, Andre de Vilmorin. Whilst in France he took every opportunity to visit gardens, undertaking small gardening jobs to pay his upkeep including the reorganization of the garden of a chateau near Melun and another at Boussy Saint-Antoine.

In 1932 Page returned to England to work in the office of landscape architect, Richard Sudell. It was at this time that he first worked at Longleat and this association was to continue for most of Page's life.

From 1934 until 1938 Russell Page wrote articles for the magazine *Landscape and Gardening*. In 1935 Page began an association with landscape architect Geoffrey Jellicoe which lasted until 1939. During this time their work include Royal Lodge, Windsor Great Park; Ditchley Park, Oxfordshire; a chess-board garden for Holme House, Regent's Park; planting guide for the development of the village of Broadway, in the Cotswolds and Charterhouse School.

In 1935 Page met the French decorator, Stephane Boudin at Ditchley Park, and this was the start of a collaboration which was to last for the remainder of his life. The following year Page commenced work at Leeds Castle and this was yet another project which was to last for the remainder of his life. From 1937 until 1939 Page was a lecturer in landscape architecture at the University of Reading but in 1940 he was recruited by the Political Warfare Department of the Foreign Service to control broadcasting to France and to organize the French Service for the BBC. In 1942 he was promoted to the Political Intelligence Department of the Foreign Office. In conjunction with Sir David Bowes-Lyon and Sir John Wheeler-Bennet, he worked with the United States government in setting up foreign-language broadcasting services. In 1943 he was sent to work in Cairo and in 1945 he was given the rank of lieutenant-colonel and posted to Ceylon. Later that year Page was demobilized and was able to return to London and in 1947 he married Lida Gurdjieff the daughter of the mystic George Gurdjieff. Their only child, David was born in 1948 and they were divorced in 1954.

Russell Page was in great demand as a Garden designer especially on the French Riviera but he also designed a garden for Mohammed Sultan at Guizeh, Egypt, for the Duchess of Talleyrand and at the Creux de Genthod, Switzerland. In 1950 Page worked for King Leopold of the Belgians at Waterloo and at the Moulin des Dames, Chantilly.

Page returned to England to direct and design the Festival Gardens, Battersea Park, for which he was awarded an OBE. From 1951 until 1954 Page worked on the landscaping of the gardens of the Supreme Headquarters of the Allied Powers in Europe (SHAPE) near Paris.

In 1953 Russell Page began work on the grounds of the Duke and Duchess of Windsor at Gif-sur-Yvette, France. Page's work was now recognised world-wide and he carried out many prestigious projects too numerous to mention here In 1962 he left France to live in London and his autobiography, *The Education of a Gardener,* was published later that year. Page continued to design gardens throughout the world including the United States and he was asked by the government of Venezuela to design parks and advise on conservation. He carried out projects in Chile as well.

Many details of Russell Page's life and career are sketchy because most of his files which were kept in London were destroyed during the war. Late in life he began to collect his plans and papers and these are now preserved in Belgium.

Trying to record Page's projects is a bewildering task - suffice it to say that he was exceptionally versatile and for the greater part of his career his work was on the grand scale. Montague Russell Page died in London on 4 January 1985.

Nicholas PARSONS

Most people know Nicholas Parsons from his famous comedy partnerships with Arthur Haynes in the 1960s and later with Benny Hill in the 1970s. He was the presenter of the television quiz show *Sale of the Century* which ran from 1971 to 1984 and is the host and chairman of the long running radio comedy show, *Just a Minute.* These have helped to make him known to a wide public and he has had a very long and varied career in show business.

Nicholas has appeared in one of the *Dr Who* series on television and a number of musicals in the West End including *Charlie Girl, Into the Woods* and, more recently, *The Rocky Horror Show.* He also has a number of films to his credit including *Brothers-in-Law, Carlton Browne of the FO* and *Don't Raise the Bridge, Lower the River.* However, his greatest success has been in comedy plays in the West End. When he was starring in *Boeing Boeing* in 1967 he turned down the opportunity to play Broadway preferring to stay in this country with his wife and two children, Suzy and Justin. He is a brilliant impersonator, a talent which he put to good use in such shows as *Listen to This Space* and other radio variety programmes.

Nicholas Parsons was born in Grantham on 10 October 1928 and is the son of Dr Paul Parsons, a medical practitioner. After kindergarten at Grantham and Kesteven High School he moved on to King's School, Grantham but was only there for one term before being sent as a boarder to Tenterden Hall, Hendon, a preparatory school in North London. His parents also moved to London at this time. He was not happy at Tenterden Hall and eventually both he and his brother moved to Colet Court, the preparatory school for St Paul's Cathedral.

When war broke out in 1939 the school was evacuated to Berkshire but Nicholas remained in London transferring to Clark's College in Finchley. He always wanted to be an actor but, to please his family, in 1940 he went to Glasgow to begin an engineering apprenticeship on Clydebank. He also went to Glasgow University but never finished his

Top left : A recording of *Much Binding in the Marsh* in 1954 with (from left to right) Kenneth Horne, Dora Bryan, Richard Murdoch and Sam Costa.

Top right : Arthur Haynes as his famous tramp character with the Reverend Nicholas Parsons.

Bottom left : Nicholas with Dora Bryan and Cyd Charisse when they appeared on Denis Norden's afternoon programme in 1986

Bottom right : Nicholas in 1972 with his children Suzy and Justin then aged thirteen and eleven.

degree although he did complete his apprenticeship. Whilst at University he joined the Drama Group, the Debating Society and also played Rugby for the University - even achieving an East v. West Scottish trial game.

Nicholas appeared in repertory from 1949 to 1951 at Bromley in Kent and was regularly in cabaret from 1951 to 1965 in London's West End. He also worked as 'straight man' in partnership with Eric Barker from 1952 to 1955 and was resident comedian at the famous Windmill Theatre for eight months in 1952.

Nicholas Parsons was made Variety Club *Radio Personality of the Year* in 1967 for his satirical show *Listen to this Space.* He was entered in the *Guinness Book of Records* for delivering the longest after dinner humorous speech in 1976. This was to help raise funds for the children's charity Action Research. He was Rector of St Andrew's University from 1988 until 1991 and was awarded an honorary Doctorate of Laws by that University.

Nicholas works a lot for children's charities and is a past president of the Lord's Taverners. He is also a governor of the National Society for the Prevention of Cruelty to Children. He is Barker of the Variety Club of Great Britain and devotes much of his time to other charities. It is a long way from his first professional job in show business as a Carroll Levis Discovery doing impersonations. It is to be hoped that he will be able to continue for several years more as chairman of *Just a Minute,* which is still running on Radio Four after thirty-five years, and with his work for charity.

It has been very difficult in a short article to give a comprehensive account of the long and varied career of Nicholas Parsons. I urge the reader to obtain a copy of his autobiography *The Straight Man : My life in Comedy* which was published in 1994.

Frank PICK

Frank Pick was born in Spalding in 1878 and trained as a solicitor. He entered the service of the North Eastern Railway after qualifying and four years later, in 1906, he joined London Underground Electric Railways working first on traffic development and publicity becoming commercial manager in 1912. During these early years he arranged for Underground posters to be designed by leading artists such as Frank Taylor and Gregory Brown. In his concern for the appearance of Underground publicity, Pick commissioned Edward Johnston to introduce a completely new design for the lettering used by the Underground Company. This was introduced in the summer of 1916 and has remained in use to the present day for all signs, notices and posters. It is in fact the very hallmark of London Transport and Johnston also redesigned the familiar bull's eye device used for station names.

Pick became assistant to the general manager and rose quickly becoming vice-chairman in 1933. It was his vision which transformed London Transport into a model, unified, modern system noted for quiet and orderly design and the buildings and appurtenances form a harmonious and functional pattern that blends in well with the urban landscape.

Stations offered a great challenge but the earliest designs in the fashionable *art nouveau* style with sombre dark elevations soon palled. Pick was determined to find an entirely new style and in the summer of 1930 accompanied by Dr Charles H. Holden, he visited north-west Europe. Influenced by this visit, Holden produced a design for the new Sudbury Town station which was of a clean, undemonstrative and functional style which set the fashion for a classic series of stations.

Pick's efforts came to a climax in the new works of the 'thirties and by 1940 the familiar pattern was complete. No detail was forgotten and even such accessories as door handles and clocks received attention. The general pattern of orderly grace was extended to staff quarters, signal cabin interiors and other places beyond the public eye.

Frank Pick was a founder member of the Design and Industries Association and he was able to employ the best artistic and design talent of the day. Inspired and guided by him artists, architects, industrial designers and typographers gave of their best. Amongst them were the architect Charles Holden, the sculptors Eric Gill and Jacob Epstein, and graphic artists such as Edward McKnight Kauffer.

Frank Pick died in 1941.

FURTHER READING : Jackson A. A. and Groome D F *Rails through the Clay* (1962)

Isaac PITMAN

Not many people will realise that Isaac Pitman, the inventor of the well-known shorthand system, spent several years working as a schoolteacher in Barton-on-Humber.

Pitman was born in Trowbridge, Wiltshire on 4 January 1813 and left school at the age of thirteen and worked long hours as a clerk in a textile mill. He would wake up at 4 a.m. every morning in order to study and resumed his studies in the evening after work. So that he could pronounce words correctly he read *Walker's Dictionary* through and made a note of about 2,000 words with the symbols of their pronunciation. This aroused in him an interest in phonography. He says that, 'with that instinctive love of knowledge common to all boys', he started to learn shorthand, again borrowing the relevant books from the library.

When he was 18 years old his father decided he should become a teacher. After five months at Training College he became Master of the British School at Barton-on-Humber. The Trustees managed the school in co-operation with the Teachers' Association who had appointed Pitman.

There were 120 boys, and Pitman is known to have made a favourable impression among them. As a disciplinarian he was almost a martinet, but he made little use of the cane, preferring to give detention after school hours to incorrigible boys although this might upset his own arrangements. Outside school he was an active believer in mental and moral improvement for the inhabitants of the town. He gave lectures on astronomy which became very popular. He also became secretary of the Temperance Society for whom he wrote a special tract which he delivered to every householder in Barton.

In 1835 he became a Methodist preacher for the Barton Circuit. In connection with this work he wrote out the 'Plan' of Ministers in minute copperplate letters, neatly executed. In the course of his work for the circuit he visited villages around Barton. It is known that he conducted services in the Methodist Chapel at Ulceby in 1835. There he saw a new *Comprehensive Bible*. Comparing this with his own copy of the Bible he detected 38 errors in the older edition. Listing these carefully he sent them to the publishers of the new *Comprehensive Bible*. The very next coach which arrived in Barton brought him a copy of the new Bible with a request from its publishers that he correct it thoroughly. The magnitude of his task can be imagined when it is known that there were 500,000 marginal references alone.

The young schoolmaster tackled the job systematically. Estimating the amount of revision he could accomplish daily he decided that he could complete the work in three years and, in spite of many hindrances, he finished it before that time. Although the work involved 5,000 hours of the closest mental and physical application he refused to take any payment for it as he said, 'the work has been a great satisfaction and benefit to me.' He added, 'but now I want to give my whole attention to my Phonetic Shorthand...'

He had tried to teach Phonography to his boys, but found the several systems available all unsatisfactory in some way. The obvious solution to his problem, to him, was to compile his own system. So we can really claim that Pitman's Shorthand was born in Lincolnshire, although Isaac had left the county before he had gone far with the work. In 1835, at Brigg, he married a Mrs. Holgate, a lady of good birth and education who was the widow of a Barton solicitor. For family reasons he then left Barton, in 1836, to live in Wotton-under-Edge, Gloucestershire, but during tours in later years to popularise his system of Shorthand, he again visited Barton in 1841.

There are memorial tablets to Isaac Pitman in Bath, Trowbridge, Wotton, and even in New York. There is a plaque on the house in Barton where he lived for four years, which records the fact that it was there that he began to invent his Shorthand.

FURTHER READING : Baker Alfred : *The Life of Sir Isaac Pitman* (1908)

William Arthur POUCHER

William Arthur, the son of John and Rachel Poucher, was born in Horncastle on 22 November 1891. His father was a clerk employed by Roberts & Son, corn and seed merchants, and his mother was the daughter of Charles Dixon, the manager of the local gas works. In his youth he wanted to become a professional concert pianist, but this was not possible, and after leaving the Grammar School he was apprenticed to Carlton & Sons, chemists. He then trained at the Pharmaceutical Society's College in Bath, where he obtained a Ph.D. Walter, as he preferred to be known, considered becoming a doctor, and went to Charing Cross Hospital, but left to become a pharmacist in the Royal Army Medical Corps and served throughout the first world war, mainly at a Casualty Clearing Station.

After the war he married Hilda Coombes, and joined a manufacturing chemist in Cheltenham as Chief Chemist. He later set up as a consultant to the perfumery and cosmetic industries in London, until one of his clients, Yardley, persuaded him to join them as Chief Perfumer, and he remained with them until he was 65. He specialised in the synthesis of flower perfumes, and in 1923 published *Perfumes, Cosmetics and Soaps* which is still regarded as the definitive work. There have been many editions and the book is still in print and used by perfumers all over the world. In 1952 he was elected the first Honorary Member of the Society of Cosmetic Chemists of Great Britain, and in 1954 was the first European recipient of the gold medal of the U. S. Society of Cosmetic Chemists for 'his outstanding contribution to the art and science of cosmetics'. He later achieved some notoriety, particularly after appearing on a television chat show, for his habit of wearing make-up. When questioned he commented, 'It's up to every man to make the best of his appearance'.

A visit to the Lake District after the first world war so impressed him that it sparked off a lifelong love of mountains and a passion for photographing them, and this interest in photography and mountain country finally developed into a second career, as author and landscape photographer. He was a perfectionist and would sometimes wait days for the optimum lighting conditions for a single shot. His first work as a mountain photographer was *Lakeland Through the Lens* published by Chapman & Hall in 1940. This was followed by a further twenty books in black and white. He then compiled four guide books, which were published by Constable, to the Lakes, Peaks and Pennines. He was also the author of eleven books of colour photographs, the last being *The Magic of the Highlands* in 1987. Even in his 90s he was prepared to travel in a helicopter for the first time to take aerial pictures of the Alps. He was elected a Fellow of the Royal Photographic Society in 1942 and an Honorary Fellow in 1975.

In 1983 the British Mountaineering Council gave a dinner in his honour and presented him with an engraved crystal goblet 'in recognition of his great service to the sport'. At the age of 92 he drove to Wales, gave a vigorous and witty speech, then drove off again back to the Lakes.

This Horncastle man of many parts lived life to the full and died in a nursing home in his beloved Lake District on 5 August 1988 at the age of 97.

Abraham de la PRYME

Abraham de la Pryme was the son of Huguenot parents from Ypres in Flanders who had settled in England. He was born at Hatfield in the Isle of Axholme in 1672. His father appears to have been involved in the drainage of the fens at Hatfield Chase and he and his wife were married at Sandtoft chapel on 3 April 1670.

Pryme was educated at Hatfield by the Revd William Eratt minister of the parish and began keeping a diary before he was twelve. On 2 May 1690 he was admitted pensioner at St John's College, Cambridge and held a scholarship there from 7 November 1690 to 6 November 1694 graduating BA in January 1694. He was then ordained deacon in the Church of England and on 29 June 1695 he became curate of Broughton near Brigg. He was interested in natural history and antiquarian study and contributed eight papers, relating to the counties of Lincoln and York, to volumes xxii and xxiii of the *Philosophical Transactions* of the Royal Society. With a view to writing the history of Hatfield Chase he returned to his native place in November 1697 and dwelt there until September 1698 when he took priest's orders and accepted the post of curate and divinity reader at the church of Holy Trinity, Hull. Here he constructed a 'copious analytical index of all the ancient records of the corporation' and compiled a history which has formed the basis of all subsequent works on the borough.

De la Pryme was possessed of properties in Lincolnshire and at Hatfield but his expensive tastes exhausted his income. Through the favour of the Duke of Devonshire he was appointed, on 1 September 1701, to the vicarage of Thorne. While visiting the sick he 'caught the new distemper and fever' and after an illness of a few days died on 12 or 13 June 1704 and he was buried in Hatfield church. He had been elected to a Fellowship of the Royal Society on 18 March 1702.

De la Pryme's diary, which he kept throughout his life and contains much interesting and useful material, was published by the Surtees Society in 1870. His 'History of Winterton' was published in *Archæologia* volume Xl. His poem on the hermitage at Lindholme is printed in Peck's *Description of Bawtry*. Many of his manuscripts are now in the British Library and among them are his 'History of Hatfield and the Chase' and some of his collections on Hull.

Nesta ROBERTS

Nesta Roberts first decided that she wanted to join the staff of the *Guardian* at the age of nineteen when a 1200-word sketch, the first of many written, by her was accepted for publication and appeared on the back page of that newspaper. It was, however, to be many years before she achieved her ambition.

Nesta Mary Roberts was born on 10 January 1913 in Barry, Glamorganshire where her father was a marine engineer. She was educated at St Winifred's School, Llanfairfechan in

North Wales and her first book, which was published in 1937, was an account of the first fifty years of that school.

It was expected that she would go on to Cardiff University to read English but her mother objected and, in any case, Nesta had other ideas. She had set her heart on being a writer, so journalism was an option. Two local weekly papers interviewed her and both editors expressed their concern that they employed young men and had only got one lavatory! Despite this problem, after writing a test essay on 'Bank Holiday at the Seaside' and assuring the editor that she had her School Certificate, she was taken on for two years as an unpaid pupil by *The Barry and District News and Vale of Glamorgan Gazette.*

Nesta remained with that newspaper for a further two years and was paid 8s a week. She then replied to an advertisement in the *Daily Telegraph* for a woman reporter to work on the *Louth and North Lincolnshire Advertiser.* She applied and was successful. Nesta worked in Louth for about a year before moving on to work for the *Grimsby Evening Telegraph* where she remained during most of World War II. Ever since first coming to Louth she has regarded the town as her home.

After the end of the war she moved on to the *Nottingham Journal.* At the same time she was still writing 1200-word sketches for the *Guardian* and one of these caught the attention of the then editor, A. P. Wadsworth, who was somewhat taken aback when he found the piece had been written by a woman! However, it was this incident which led to an offer of employment by the paper. Whilst achieving her long-standing ambition she also became the Guardian's first woman reporter.

With the *Guardian,* she had a varied but immensely enjoyable career working at various times as a feature writer, dramatic critic, news editor and health and welfare correspondent. She wrote several books based on her experiences in the last post. The first, *Everybody's Business*, had as its subject the Mental Health Act 1959 and was published in 1960. In 1967 she wrote a history of *Cheadle Royal Hospital* to mark its bicentenary and in the same year her book on *Mental Health and Mental Illness* was published. Nesta's experiences as a Health Correspondent also inspired her to write *To Tell the Truth* (1966), *Our Future Selves* (1970) and *A Doctor in Practice* (1974).

In the late 1960s Nesta was appointed the *Guardian's* Paris correspondent. and she developed a sympathy with France and the French. She left the staff of the Guardian in 1972 but continued to write as a freelance for the paper from places as varied as Italy and Soviet Russia.

In 1976 her book, *The Face of France,* was published. This records a journey through France following in the footsteps of two nineteenth-century orphaned children. *In Search of a Quiet Holiday* appeared in 1960 and *The Companion Guide to Normandy* in 1980. The popularity of this book led to the publication of a second edition in 1986. She contributed several chapters to the *Collin's Guide to France* which was edited by John Ardagh and published in 1985. Nesta supplied the text to a book entitled *Derbyshire Photographs* by Andy Williams which was published in 1984.   She has also written short stories and a play for the BBC.

Nesta Roberts has had a long and most interesting life. It was a great pleasure to meet her.

John SHEPPEY

Dr John Sheppey was appointed Dean of Lincoln Cathedral in 1388 and was the immediate predecessor of the notorious and better known John Mackworth (see page 102). Sheppey was, in fact, little better in his conduct and at a visitation by Bishop John Buckingham in 1393 many acts of violence were recorded.

Little is known of Sheppey before he came to Lincoln except that he had been Chancellor of Lichfield. It was said of him that 'he showed neither moderation nor complaisance but used opprobrious and insulting language towards [the Chapter]...' It was said that he accepted bribes so that misdeeds should go unpunished but the most startling accusation was that he wasted the goods of the Church in

> 'voluptuous expenses in dances in the campanile ... in pictures, play-actors and the like, and that he was in the habit of attending at the wakes and shows held on the commons outside the city, and set up wrestling matches in the close and palace, and at St Giles' Hospital at which he acted as umpire, and offered a 'cat-o'-mountain' as a prize to the best wrestler'.

Among the Dean's numerous domestics and retainers was one Robert Pakynton who, on 27 December 1393, while Vespers was being sung 'of malice prepense, violently and atrociously assaulted a certain servant of Master Peter of Dalton the Treasurer of the Church, Thomas by name, causing no small effusion of blood' and the cathedral had to be reconsecrated. The feud between the Dean's household and the servants of the Church became more bitter and on New Year's Day 1394 Simon the Bellringer, who was walking by the north porch after Vespers, was attacked by seven of the Dean's household who were lying in wait for him. Pakynton was the leader of the attackers and they were described as 'sons of Belial not having the fear of God before their eyes'   Simon ran back to the Cathedral but was prevented from entering by the Dean's men who were armed with swords and daggers. He was severely beaten and wounded in the head but it is not recorded whether he survived the attack.

Bishop Buckingham was at Stow Park and he was informed of this incident in the morning. He hurried back to his Palace at Lincoln and he immediately called for a report. As a result he declared the Cathedral polluted and ordered that Divine Service was not to be celebrated. The attackers were summoned to appear before the Bishop but they ignored this and they, together with the Dean, were excommunicated.   The Cathedral remained under interdict and no services were celebrated until mid-January when, after an appeal led by the Sub-Dean, the Cathedral was reconciled. The Archbishop of Canterbury on 18 February ordered that the delinquents should humbly petition the Bishop to rescind the excommunication and that twenty marks should be paid to him.

Before he would release them from excommunication, the Bishop ordered that the four leading delinquents should walk at the head of a procession to the Cathedral with bare feet and 'naked heads' each devoutly carrying a wax taper, that of Pakynton, as the most guilty of them, weighing one pound with the other three weighing half a pound each. This was to be repeated on Ascension Day and at Pentecost. All but Pakynton carried this penance out and he was again excommunicated. After about nine months on 13 December 1394 the Sheriff of Lincoln was ordered by King Richard II, presumably at the request of the Bishop, to '... seize the body of Pakynton and bring him to justice'. Eventually Pakynton was received back into the Church after swearing to abide by its mandates and after carrying out his penance which he did.

The evidence clearly shows that Dean Sheppey was as difficult as possible in his dealings with the Bishop and the Chapter. He clearly encouraged Pakynton in his misdeeds.

Dean John Sheppey died in 1411 and was buried in Lincoln Cathedral

SOURCES : This account is a very much edited version of that which appears in the *Associated Architectural Societies Reports and Papers* Vol. 18 pages 96-102.   The record of the King's involvement can be found in the *Calendars of Patent Rolls 1391-6* pages, 216, 410 and 429.

Hawley SMART

Hawley Smart was the son of Captain George John Smart and was named in honour of Sir Joseph Hawley the third baronet, who was the his father's brother-in-law. George Smart managed the Lincolnshire estates of Sir Joseph and Tumby Lawn near Kirkby-on-Bain was built for him.

Sir Joseph Hawley kept a stud of racehorses at his seat in Leybourne Grange in Kent and four of them won the Derby. Racing was Sir Joseph's passion and absorbing hobby and it could well be that his nephew, Hawley Smart, came under his uncle's influence whilst visiting him.

Hawley Smart was born at Dover in 1833 and, in 1883, he married Alice Ellen daughter of John Smart of Budleigh Salterton, Devon. His career provided the background to his many novels. He served in the Crimea and was at the fall of Sebastopol. He then went to India where he served during the Mutiny. He left the army in 1864 and probably resided at Tumby with his father who died in 1871. Hawley suffered losses on the turf and turned to novel writing. The opening scenes of his first novel, *Breezie Langton,* appears to be set at Doddington Hall. Lincolnshire features in a number of his novels and *Saddle and Sabre* which was published in 1888 is set partly at 'North Leach nestling at the foot of one of the long undulations of the Lincolnshire Wolds', and chapter four entitled 'Lincoln Spring' is set at the Lincoln Races.

Hawley Smart regularly produced two or more novels a year and his total output appears to have been 38. His last was called *A Racing Rubber* and was published in 1895 after his death. His wife wrote the Preface and she says that attempts had been made to persuade her to change the title of the book by 'the Nonconformist Conscience [which] would seem to imply that horse racing is in itself a crime'. She had refused saying that her husband had been working on the last chapters of the novel 'at the time of his sudden and unlooked for death' and she would not 'presume to change, or in any way touch the work of one, whose absolute knowledge of his subjects, a knowledge gained not by hearsay, but acquired by practical experience of both soldiering and racing, when the latter certainly, stood higher in general estimation that at present, had made him a favourite with the reading public for nearly forty years'.

It seems that Mrs Smart had been accused of 'assisting' Hawley with the novels but she vehemently denied this saying that she had acted merely as her husband's secretary and had assisted 'in the merely mechanical work of writing from dictation, numbering and arranging of chapters, proof correcting, etc'. She added that her husband 'wrote of what he knew; had studied racing from those palmy days when Sir Joseph Hawley's two year olds almost swept the board; had learnt at least practical soldiering in the trenches before Sebastopol, and again in India in '57 and '58'.

The late Terence Leach commented 'it is interesting to compare Smart's racing stories with those of Dick Francis. There are as many villains, perhaps, but Smart always has a country house or landed gentry background. To my surprise I have found many of them very readable'.

Hawley Smart died at Budleigh Salterton, Devon in 1893.

SOURCES : This article is based on articles published in the *Newsletters* of the Society for Lincolnshire History and Archaeology Nos. 27, 28 and 51.

Edith SMITH

In 1915 Grantham was the first place in the British Isles to have women police. Before that date there was a voluntary society of women in Grantham who helped the Police in cases concerning females. These volunteers were needed because Belton Park near Grantham was used as a training camp and, at the outbreak of the First World War in 1914, 14,000 soldiers were stationed there. This attracted large numbers of prostitutes into Grantham with brothels opening and women roaming the camp at night. The sudden increase in the population of the area created considerable public order problems. As it happened, a staff officer at the Belton camp was brother-in-law of Margaret Damer Dawson, who was leader of the so-called Women Police Service. This led to the arrival of Mary Allen and Ellen Harburn who proceeded to patrol the streets of Grantham and the area surrounding the camp.

At first they worked on sufferance under the Chief Constable and Provost Marshal and were funded by a local ladies' committee. Very soon they proved themselves and were publicly praised by the camp's commanding officer, Brigadier-General Hammersley. In May 1915 Mary Allen and Ellen Harburn were sent to Hull and an ex-midwife, Mrs Edith Smith who was a widow with one son, and a Miss Teed replaced them. Edith was described by Dorothy Peto, who was later to become head of the Metropolitan Woman Police, as 'a woman of outstanding personality, fearless, motherly and adaptable'. Edith had taken Peto on her first patrols in Hyde Park, London early in 1915 when she had gone to London to gain some experience. In Grantham she quickly commenced the work of cleaning up the streets, theatres and picture houses, of prostitution.

In November 1915 a meeting was called and attended by a number of prominent local ladies. It was chaired by the Bishop of Grantham and attended by Margaret Damer Dawson and Lady Nott Power, who was patron of the Women Police Society. The bishop said that the women police deserved support from public funds. He said that the work of 'keeping young girls from temptation and evil...must [be done] by those who, because of their position in life would have tact, delicacy, firmness and promptitude'. The Chief Constable agreed that women police should get official status 'for their arduous and unenviable duties'. Miss Teed had already resigned and on the 29 November 1915 Edith Smith was sworn in and became the first professional woman police officer in Great Britain.

Although women were now known as 'official' police officers they were never given the power of arrest. This was because the Home Office ruled that the appointment of women as constables was illegal. They said that women could not be officers because of their physique! As Edith commented a year later, her new status and authority was a tremendous help in her work and she earned the respect of her superiors. A summary of cases handled by Constable Smith in 1916 includes ten prostitutes who were 'proceeded against and convicted', as were two disorderly houses and one fortune-teller. Two landladies were prosecuted under the Defence of the Realm Act. She also reported ten dirty houses to the sanitary authorities and dealt with 24 'illegitimate baby cases'. At a conference of the Women Workers Union in December 1916 she said 'A large portion of the police work is of a sordid character but even then it has its interesting side - the study of human nature at its worst'.

Her report for 1917 listed 383 cases of which fifty were described as 'rescue cases handed to [the social] worker', forty were 'respectable women helped in court affairs' and another forty were 'foolish girls warned'. Three local girls were returned to their parents, ten girls were placed in homes and soldiers' wives were visited. In all thirty types of case are listed.

Clearly Edith Smith was a dedicated lady and the right person for this work. She used the front room of her home in Rutland Street, Grantham as a consulting room and the hours she worked were long. In May 1917 a pay rise brought her income up to £2.10s a week which made her better paid than the oldest constable of the force who received only £1.7s. 6d. It was said that this was due to the fact 'that Mrs Smith did more work and it was of a different class'. She got no days off, no overtime and was not entitled to a pension. Perhaps her devotion to her work eventually took its toll as she resigned in late 1917 due to ill health. She became matron of a nursing home and eventually committed suicide.

SOURCES : Lock, Joan 'Grantham's other 'first'' in *Police Review* 6 June 1966. Information supplied by Grantham Museum.

A. E. (Ted) SMITH

Ted Smith's work for nature conservation has been recognised by many honours and awards. Recently he was appointed an Officer of the Order of the Golden Ark, an Order which was established in 1971 by Prince Bernhard of The Netherlands to give recognition to people dedicated to the conservation of nature worldwide. Amongst those who received the Order at the same time as Ted were conservationists from Spain, Norway, the Netherlands, India, Indonesia, Russia and Sri Lanka. This international award follows the honorary Doctorate awarded by the University of Lincolnshire and Humberside in 1998 and his appointment as a Commander of the British Empire (CBE) in 2000.

Ted Smith with Prince Bernhard after receiving the insignia of an Officer of the Order of the Golden Ark

As an amateur naturalist Ted Smith was drawn into the conservation movement in its early stages, first as co-founder with Tom Baker (see page 7) in founding the Lincolnshire Naturalists' Trust (now the Lincolnshire Wildlife Trust) in 1948. He was the first Honorary Secretary of the Trust and served from 1948 until 1968. The Trust's office was at Ted's house in Willoughby until 1965 when, as a result of Ted's negotiations and influence, the Manor House in Alford became the headquarters. In 1968 Ted became Chairman of the Trust and served in that office until 1999 when he became President which post he still holds. Later, he helped to secure the conversion of the Society for Promotion of Nature Reserves which was founded by Charles Rothschild in 1912 into the National Association of County Trusts. This enabled Ted to promote the formation and development of Trusts throughout the country. He became Honorary

Secretary of the SPNR in 1960 and its first full-time General Secretary in 1974. When he retired at the end of 1978 he continued for some years as Special Advisor and then as a Vice-President.

Arthur Edward Smith was born on 24 August 1920 at Alford. After leaving Queen Elizabeth's Grammar School in Alford he went up to Leeds University in 1939 and graduated with a BA in 1942 and was awarded an MA in 1943 followed by a Diploma in Education in 1944. He was Senior English Master at Leeds Grammar School from 1944 until 1946 and filled a similar post at Paston Grammar School, North Walsham, until he was appointed Resident Tutor in Lindsey by the Department of Adult Education, University of Nottingham. He remained in that post until 1974 when he was appointed General Secretary of the Royal Society for Nature Conservation.

In recognition of his early service to voluntary nature conservation he was appointed to the Order of the British Empire (OBE) in 1963 and he was the first recipient of the Christopher Cadbury Medal 'for services to the advancement of nature conservation in the British Islands'. Nationally he also served on the Nature Conservancy Council (now English Nature) for twenty-two years during which period he was Chairman of the Committee for England. Ted was a Council member of the National Trust for eight years and of the Royal Society for the Protection of Birds for five years. He was a member of the conservation advisory committee of the World Wide Fund for Nature for eight years.

Ted's concern for the environment and the changes affecting it, and his ability to explain that concern to others, has been backed by a broad vision of what can be achieved. His preparation of reports and papers reflect a thoroughness and attention to detail vital in the campaign to convince individuals, organisations and government of the critical importance of nature conservation in the British countryside. He has been able to create opportunities to make progress, often in difficult conditions.

As a keen ornithologist he was the author with the late Dick Cornwallis of *The Birds of Lincolnshire* which was published in 1955. An address which he delivered as the President of the Lincolnshire Naturalists' Union in 1969 was updated and published in 1999, whilst he was President for a second term, in *The Lincolnshire Naturalist* under the title *Nature Reserves in Lincolnshire : their functions and value.* He edited the *Lincolnshire Red Data Book,* which was published in 1988, and lists endangered plants and animals. This was the first publication of its kind in the country. *Nature in Lincolnshire : towards a biodiversity strategy,* which was published in 1996, points the way for the future.

Ted himself puts great emphasis on the support he has had from his family. He says 'My wife Mary and I have shared a common interest and endeavour. Her unfailing support and her skill and understanding as naturalist, gardener, botanical artist and craftsman – to say nothing of her devotion to home and family – have been an integral part of whatever contribution we may have made to the appreciation and conservation of nature. Moreover our daughters have spontaneously shared our interest and played their full part.'

Ted and Mary's elder daughter, Alison, is Head of the Department of Metabolic Biology in the John Innes Institute and a Visiting Professor at the University of East Anglia. Their younger daughter, Helen who has two children, is a Consultant Biologist.

Long may Ted continue to encourage the campaign for nature conservation and care for the environment both locally and nationally.

SOURCES : I am grateful to David Robinson OBE who followed Ted as Honorary Secretary of the Lincolnshire Trust and Resident Tutor for Nottingham University, and to Stuart Crooks, Director of the Lincolnshire Wildlife Trust, for their assistance in compiling this article.

Freddie STOCKDALE

Pavilion Opera, based in Lincolnshire, has staged over 1800 performances in 23 countries and in a variety of venues which, as well as many country houses in this country, have included the British Embassies in Paris, Tokyo, The Hague, Washington, Algiers, Amman and Karachi. It all started when Freddie Stockdale built a Pavilion in the garden of his house at Thorpe Tilney near Lincoln. It was designed by the architect Francis Johnson, with windows by John Piper, as a private opera experiment. The first performance in 1981 was *Cosi Fan Tutte* with six singers and a pianist.

This initial experiment became a full time business and in his book, *Figaro Here, Figaro There,* which was published in 1991, Freddie gives a witty and revealing diary of a year in the life of this remarkable company. Freddie is general manager and there are around 40 evening performances each year in an assortment of venues worldwide. The Pavilion Opera Educational Trust was founded recently to stage free performances in state schools for children aged from 9 to 11. Over 13,000 children have seen programmes which emphasise the ancillary subjects in opera including history, poetry, geography, model making and the reporting of the plots as in a modern newspaper. Ruskington, Metheringham, North Hykeham and Gainsborough Primary Schools were visited in 2001.

Frederick Minshull Stockdale was born on 20 May 1947 at his parents farm at Hoddington, Hampshire. After preparatory school at Ludgrove he continued his education at Eton College and then went up to Jesus College, Cambridge to read law. After graduating in 1970 he bought Thorpe Tilney Hall near Lincoln where he grew corn and onions as well as building on his mother's Guernsey herd which was sold in 1984.

As well as farming and acting as general manager of the opera company, Freddie has served his adopted home county in many ways. He was an Independent County Councillor for four years, a member of the committee responsible to the National Trust for Tattershall Castle for 15 years, a Trustee of Lincolnshire Old Churches Trust for 20 years, a member of the Trent Regional Health Authority for six years and a member of the Nurses and Midwives Whitley Council for four years. He fought the Lincoln seat as a Democratic Labour candidate at the General Election in 1979 and in the 1983 General Election he again fought the Lincoln seat but as a Social Democrat.

Surprisingly, for such a busy person, Freddie has written eleven books including five crime thrillers under the pseudonym John Gano.

Freddie's book, *Figaro Here, Figaro There,* gives a fascinating account of the trials and tribulations of managing an opera company. These include problems associated with temperamental singers and eccentric owners of country houses. I recommend this book as essential reading for the opera enthusiast. Freddie lives at Thorpe Tilney Hall with his second wife Adele Mason, who is an opera singer. He has four sons and a daughter from his two marriages.

Thomas SULLY

Thomas Sully was the son of a strolling player and he was born in Horncastle on 5 November 1783. His parents emigrated to America in 1792 and settled in Charleston, South Carolina. Young Thomas's natural skill as an artist was encouraged during his formative years and he became well known locally as a portrait painter of considerable talent. He became a naturalised American citizen and some of the local people paid for him to travel to England for a year to study.

In London he was a pupil of Benjamin West and was greatly influenced by the portrait painter Sir Thomas Lawrence. On his return to America he set up his own studio in Richmond, Virginia and rapidly became a well-known and successful portrait painter. After three years he was able to save enough money for another trip to Europe where he continued his studies under such famous painters as West and Lawrence. During this time he painted a portrait of Queen Victoria now in the possession of the St George's Society of Philadelphia.

On his return to the United States he opened a new studio in Philadelphia and the rich and famous came to have their portrait painted. Lafayette, Jefferson and Washington sat for him but he later widened his interests and amongst his most famous paintings is *Washington Crossing the Delaware* which now hangs in the Boston Museum of Fine Arts. Sully only made one more visit to England, in 1837 but his paintings were regularly exhibited by the Royal Academy and the British Institution between 1820 and 1840.

Although his parents were actors and little is known about them, his brother-in-law M.

Belfons was an émigré French miniaturist and his brother Lawrence was also a painter. When he died in 1872 Thomas Sully left some 2000 portraits and 500 other pictures.

John SUTTON

Although John Matthias Dobson Sutton was born in Cleethorpes on 9 July 1932, that was only because his mother went into St. Hugh's Nursing Home there for his birth. He is a native of Alford and says 'one has to put 'place of birth' on so many forms these days and I would so much rather have been able to put 'Alford' than 'Cleethorpes'!'

His father was secretary at Alford Brewery then owned by Colonel Jay. Until the age of eight John attended the Council School and then moved on to Alford Grammar School and for the whole of his time there had the well-respected H. J. H. Dyer as his headmaster (see page 41). He says he only really made his mark at school in one way. He and two other sixth formers caused a huge explosion while messing about in the otherwise unoccupied laboratory.

He left after taking Higher School Certificate in 1949 to work as the first ever cadet to be employed by the Grimsby Borough Police. Within two weeks he was moved to the CID and shortly afterwards, as they were short of detectives, he was put in charge of the CID Office through which every crime, complaint or incident was channelled. John says that he has always been grateful for that police experience, as in those 15 months he saw aspects of life he did not know existed and he benefited greatly later on from the understanding it gave him.

He was called up for two years National Service in 1950 and trained as a pilot. He found he was enjoying flying so much that he stayed on and eventually was offered a permanent commission. On his first squadron he qualified as an instrument flying examiner and since those duties were in addition to normal flying training he was able to log flying hours more rapidly than most. He was also given management responsibility quite early on which he enjoyed and which led to greater opportunities. So much so that, rather unusually in flying posts, he had been a flight commander three times by the age of 28. Although he continued to fly for the next 30 years and commanded two squadrons, promotions inevitably meant more time behind a desk and less in the cockpit. Promotions came quite quickly for John as he was a Group Captain at 38 and an Air Vice-Marshal before his 45th birthday.

The majority of John's staff appointments were in London. They were all quite demanding but were at least at the centre of events working either directly for the Heads of the three Services or for the Chief of the Defence Staff. But in between these appointments, John was able to return to work more closely with flying units, first as Commandant of the Central Flying School at Cranwell and secondly as Deputy to the Commander-in-Chief, RAF Germany.

John's last appointment in London, in 1982, was as Assistant Chief of Defence Staff (Commitments) which involved a number of responsibilities worldwide and, as opposed to his previous posts there, gave him an opportunity to travel. One of his responsibilities was to work out appropriate force levels in the Falklands, the war there just having finished. It was decided to build a new airfield which could quickly absorb substantial reinforcements, thus enabling the forces on the spot to be reduced to a minimum. John has memories of standing with a shepherd on a totally deserted moor and it seemed the ideal spot for the new airfield. A year later he stood on the same spot but by then was standing on a partially completed runway. Just a further year on he travelled by 747 which landed on the new 3,000 yard runway and taxied up to normal airport buildings with hangars and accommodation.

Wing Commander John Sutton, Officer
Commanding No. 14 Squadron RAF Germany

In January 1986 John was promoted to the rank of Air Marshal, knighted, and appointed Commander-in-Chief of Royal Air Force Support Command. The Command's responsibilities were for all the RAF's training, its deep engineering and wholesale supply. This involved a workforce of some 47,000 on some 200 units with a budget of about £740 million. Occasionally, John was able to fly in the Command's various types of aircraft, particularly the Hawk and the Gazelle helicopter, the availability of the latter being a great boon for visits, as it could be positioned outside his office.

After three and a half years as C-in-C and 39 years service, Sir John retired and the following year was sworn in as Lieutenant-Governor and Commander-in-Chief of Jersey. Jersey is self-governing but under the Crown and hence a Governor is appointed by Her Majesty to ensure that what is rather vaguely described as 'good government' is carried out. Thus while the work is mainly representational it extends beyond that and includes specific responsibilities such as immigration - as entry into Jersey is entry into the UK. Somewhat to his surprise, Sir John found that he was associated with clergy appointments.

Jersey Governors do not normally feature in the international media nor are they usually booed in the Royal Square. Sir John managed both when he was obliged to remove the Deputy Bailiff from office. The Bailiff in the Channel Islands is the President of the Parliament and Head of the Judiciary so sacking his deputy is pretty serious stuff. The fuss was caused by selective reporting in the local press coupled with some local politicians seeking personal visibility. However it soon became clear to everyone that it was a straightforward case of the person concerned falling down on the job, in spite of repeated warnings. Once this was realised, the mood completely changed and flowers were delivered to Government House by the van-load accompanied by a great many apologetic letters.

His Excellency Air Marshal Sir John Sutton and Lady Sutton preparing to receive
guests at a Reception to mark the Queen's Birthday at Government House, Jersey in 1992

After five years in Jersey -which he describes as the icing on the cake - Sir John came home to retirement which he did not find easy. It was nice to have more time for family, house, garden and golf but he missed the challenges he had enjoyed for so many years. So for four years he took on the voluntary job of Chairman of the Council at University College, Northampton. He says that one of his duties there was to award honorary degrees. Rather odd, he comments, for someone who has never been an academic.

Sir John was awarded the Queen's Commendation for Valuable Service in the Air in 1967 and was appointed a Companion of the Order of the Bath in 1980. He was created a Knight Commander of the Order of the Bath in 1986 and a Knight of the Order of St John of Jerusalem in 1991.

Thomas SUTTON

Thomas Sutton was born in 1532 at Knaith, a hamlet about three miles south of Gainsborough. His father, Richard Sutton, was a member of a long established Lincolnshire family and lived at the manor house which they had leased from the D'Arcy family.

Little is known of Thomas's early life but he is believed to have been educated at Eton before going up to Cambridge University. It is known that by the age of 26 he had become a professional soldier and was involved in the rebellion of the Catholic nobility of 1569 in northern England. On 28 February 1570 Sutton was appointed Master of the Ordnance for northern England and commanded one of the batteries at the siege of Edinburgh Castle in May 1573. During his service in the North, he obtained from the Crown and the Bishop of Durham leases of land which were known to be rich in coal. He moved to London in about 1580 and, by lending money to the nobility on the security of their estates, he was able to amass a great fortune.

He married a rich widow, Elizabeth Dudley, which made him the richest commoner in England.

Thomas Sutton's contribution towards the cost of the defence of the country in 1588, which was the year of the Spanish Armada, was the largest made by any private individual. In May 1611 he purchased Howard House which had been built on the site of a fourteenth century Carthusian monastery which was dissolved by Henry VIII. The monastery had been inhabited by monks from La Grand Chartreuse near Grenoble, France. Sutton converted the house which still retained parts of the monastery into a home for 80 pensioners and a school for 40 needy scholars. Chartreuse became anglicised to Charterhouse, the name by which the school is known.

When Sutton died on 12 December in the same year he left instructions that the bulk of his fortune was to be used for the foundation and endowment of Charterhouse. He left £500 each to Magdalen and Jesus Colleges at Cambridge and the income from his property in Lincolnshire was left for the benefit of 20 poor citizens of Lincoln.

Thomas Sutton died at Hackney and two years after his death his body was reburied in a tomb in the chapel of Charterhouse. The school moved to Godalming in 1927 but the London foundation remains as a residence for deserving pensioners.

Bernie TAUPIN

Many of us can still remember Elton John singing *Candle in the Wind* at the funeral of Princess Diana. It was a very moving occasion and I wonder how many readers realise that the song was written by Bernie Taupin who is a true Lincolnshire Yellowbelly.

Bernie's father, Robert, originated from a French family, and although he was born in London, he was educated at a boarding school in Dijon. It was intended that Robert should be a lawyer but, because of ill health, he decided on a career in agriculture. After training in Scotland he managed a farm in Kirton-in-Holland and then became stock manager for the Haverholme Estate at Ewerby. Bernie's mother, Daphne Cort, came from a background of Anglican clergymen and schoolmasters. Robert and Daphne married in 1947 and their first son Tony was born in 1948. Bernie was born in 1950 and a third son, Kit, was born eleven years later.

In 1960 Robert decided to become a smallholder and chicken farmer on his own account. The family moved to Maltkiln Farm which was in the centre of Owmby-by-Spital. The farmhouse was large and rambling and eventually they moved into a new bungalow. The old house was unlived in and it made a marvellous place for the two older boys to play all kinds of games. Bernie became infatuated with the American West and set up a museum of the Alamo in one of the rooms.

Their maternal grandfather had a great influence on the impressionable boys. It was he who encouraged their interest in nature, teaching them to recognise plants, birds and butterflies. He also instilled in them a love of English literature and Tony and Bernie played games based on Scott's *Lochinvar* and Macaulay's epic tale of Horatius instead of the usual Cowboys and Indians or Cops and Robbers. There is little doubt that grandfather Cort was responsible for Bernie's ambitions as a poet and storywriter and, after he died, Bernie wrote *To a Grandfather* which clearly confirms this. At the age of ten he wrote an account of the fall of the Alamo which he sent to a publisher. He was almost as thrilled by the letter of rejection as he would have been had it been accepted for publication!

One of Bernie's early heroes was Joe Brown (see page 19) the cockney guitarist who was, in fact, born at Swarby which is only about ten miles from his own birthplace Although Bernie joined Joe's fan club he had no idea that they were fellow yellow bellies! In the early 60s the television programme, *Ready Steady Go*, which was presented by another Lincolnshire native, Keith Fordyce (see page 52), brought to Bernie new icons. His great love was for songs with a cowboy theme and the American West.

The time eventually came when Bernie had to consider life beyond Market Rasen Secondary Modern School. He decided that he would like to be a journalist with a local newspaper. He obtained a job with the *Lincolnshire Chronicle* but not as the chief reporter he craved for – he was a printer's apprentice in the machine room at the Lincoln printing works.

After a disagreement with the foreman, Bernie joined the ranks of the unemployed until he was offered a job on a chicken farm. The long hours with very little time off even at weekends and the unpleasant nature of the work soon found Bernie again out of work.

Bernie had been writing poems from time to time as the mood took him and some two months after leaving the chicken farm he saw an advertisement from Liberty Records in the *New Musical Express* inviting writers to contact them. He decided to send in samples of his work but never posted the letter. However, his mother found it and put it in the post. Little did she know what this would lead to. He was invited to an interview which resulted in a number of lyrics finding their way to Reginald Kenneth Dwight who had also replied to the same advertisement!

Seventeen-year-old Bernie teamed up with twenty-year-old Reginald Dwight, who eventually changed his name to Elton John, and for the first few years of the partnership, Bernie lodged with the Dwights. Reg occasionally came up to Lincolnshire to stay with Bernie and his parents. He recorded one of these visits in his diary as follows 'Saturday 29 March 1969 – Watched the Grand National and then went to see Owmby Utd win 2 – 1. Went to RAF Waddington tonight'. An album, *Empty Sky*, was produced for the then recently formed DJM Record Company. In 1970 recordings were issued under the label of Music of America (MCA). However, Elton John's real début was at the *Troubador* in Los Angeles and from then on it has been an almost continuous success story. A particularly successful period was between 1972 and 1976 with sixteen songs all written by Bernie in the top 20. Amongst the songs of this period was *Saturday Night's Alright for Fighting* which was inspired by Bernie's recollection of the time when it was not unusual for rockers from Market Rasen and Caistor, after leaving the *Aston Arms* at closing time, to amuse themselves by fighting each other. A number of other

Top left : Tony and Bernie with their parents at Owmby.

Top right : Tony and Bernie with Grandfather Cort.

Bottom left : Bernie and Elton at Boston Glyderdrome in 1973

Bottom right : The eightieth birthday party for Mrs Taupin at Bernie's ranch in Los Angeles.
Left to right : Laura (Tony's daughter), Kit with daughter Rachel,
Mrs Taupin, Tony, Vincent (Tony's son). Bernie is at the front.

See also page 174

lyrics have a Lincolnshire background and these include *When I was Tealby Abbey, First Episode at Hainton, Rowston Manor, Flatters* and *Brothers Together.*

After he became well known Bernie bought a cottage, Piglet-in-the-Wild, at Tealby to provide a retreat from the hurly-burly of London and show business. In 1972 he married Maxine at Holy Rood Catholic Church in Market Rasen and, although Elton was best man, he was never invited to visit the cottage because of the publicity this would inevitably attract. Interestingly, the photographer at the wedding was Mike Maloney (see page 107) who had been working at the *Lincolnshire Chronicle* at the same time as Bernie.

Bernie has never sought the limelight and prefers to work alone. His surname 'Taupin' is derived from the French *une taupe* meaning a mole. Perhaps this is appropriate for someone who has always preferred to avoid publicity and be the underground worker.

The partnership between Bernie and Elton has lasted for over thirty years, except for a three-year break in the late 70s when Elton was going through a very difficult time in his personal life. The two reunited in 1980 and Bernie has provided the lyrics for almost 600 songs, some of which were for other artists but the vast majority have been performed by Elton John. Bernie says that it usually takes him about half an hour at the most to write a song. If he finds that he is not getting anywhere after that period then he just throws it away. Amongst the best known are *Goodbye Yellow Brick Road, Daniel* and, of course, *Candle in the Wind.* This last song was originally a tribute to Marilyn Monroe. The lyrics were rewritten by Bernie for Elton to sing at Princes Diana's funeral and the proceeds from the record sales are given to the Elton John AIDS Foundation. Elton is on record as saying that without Bernie there would be no Elton and perhaps the same is true in reverse. The two met at a crucial time in their lives and have complemented each other.

Bernie has always had an enthusiasm for American country music and the album recorded by Elton John, *Tumbleweed Connection,* was dedicated to American culture and the wild, wild West. In the mid 1990s Bernie returned to this theme and formed the group *Farm Dogs.* In 1996 an album *Last Stand in Open Country* was released and the album, *Immigrant Sons* was released in 1998. These albums were recorded at Bernie's studio in the Santa Ynez Valley where he runs a ranch.

Bernie has lived in California for twenty years and is now an American citizen. His mother, who has recently celebrated her eightieth birthday, and his younger brother also live in America.

SOURCES AND ACKNOWLEDGEMENTS : I am grateful to Bernie's brother Tony for his assistance in compiling this account and for allowing me to use photographs from his collection. I recommend as further reading Bernie's autobiography *A Cradle of Haloes* (1988) and Phil Norman's autobiography of *Elton John* published in 1991.

Arthur THISTLEWOOD

Many people have heard of the Cato Street conspiracy but few have heard of Arthur Thistlewood. He was born at Tupholme near Bardney in 1770 the son of William Thistlewood who was a stockbreeder and farmer. It was intended that Arthur should be a land surveyor but he never followed that business. He was influenced by the works of Thomas Paine (see *Lincolnshire People* pages 76-77) and travelled to America and France shortly before the downfall of Robespierre. It was, no doubt, in France that he developed the opinions which remained with him for the remainder of his life.

On his return to England in 1794 he made no secret of the fact that he was 'firmly persuaded that the first duty of a patriot was to massacre the government and overturn all existing institutions'. He was appointed ensign in the West Riding militia in 1798 and he obtained a lieutenant's commission in the Lincolnshire Regiment.

On 24 January 1804 he married Jane Worsley and resided in Bawtry and later in Lincoln. His wife died on 30 April 1808 and Thistlewood left Lincoln to escape his creditors and eventually settled in London. He became a member of the Spencean Society which aimed at revolutionising all society in the interests of the poor. In 1814 he went to Paris where he lived for some time. On his return to England, together with James Watson, he organised a public meeting on 2 December 1816 at Spa Fields, London. The intention was to start a revolution with the immediate intention of occupying the Tower of London and the Bank of England. Thistlewood had visited the guardrooms and barracks of the Tower on numerous occasions and he was convinced it would be an easy conquest. However, informers had told the government of the plot and a reward was offered for the capture of Thistlewood and Watson. Thistlewood was eventually arrested as he prepared to sail to America but Watson had already left the country.

Thistlewood was tried for high treason but found not guilty. This narrow escape did not deter him and on St Bartholomew's Fair, 6 September, he led an attack on the Post Office and the Bank of England which was to be blown up. Another attempt was arranged for 12 October but the authorities were forewarned and no attacks actually took place. Thistlewood then seems to have proposed the assassination of the Prince of Wales and Privy Council and, in particular, the Home Secretary, Lord Sidmouth. He had written a number of letters to Sidmouth and he was arrested and charged with breaching the peace and sentenced to twelve months imprisonment.

Thistlewood and Watson organised public meetings at Kennington on 21 August 1819 and at Smithfield on 30 October. Although every effort was made to keep the arrangements for these and other meetings secret, the authorities were aware of every movement and were well prepared. Thistlewood and his associates then realised that any moves towards anarchy in London would be unsuccessful and set their sights on the North. Little support was forthcoming from this quarter and Thistlewood returned to his old plan of assassination. However, Thistlewood's plans were reported to the Home Office by one of the committee of thirteen which had been set up by the revolutionaries.

A plot to assassinate the Cabinet was formulated and the government allowed this to mature. Thistlewood's final plan was to assassinate the ministers at dinner, attack one of the leading banks, set fire to public buildings, seize the Tower of London and Mansion House and set up a provisional government. It was intended that a proclamation would announce the appointment of a provisional government and the calling together of a convention of representatives. The death of George III on 29 January 1820 was regarded as favourable to the plot. A Cabinet dinner at the Earl of Harrowby's house in London, which was announced in the *Times,* was regarded as the ideal occasion on which to make the attempted assassination.

The twenty-five conspirators met on 23 February in a loft over a stable in Cato Street where arms, bombs and hand grenades had been stored. Most of the assassins were arrested as they were setting out for Lord Harrowby's house. However, there was a struggle and Thistlewood killed a police officer thus escaping capture. He was caught on the following day and imprisoned in the Tower of London. After a trial for high treason lasting three days he was found guilty and hung at Newgate, together with four other conspirators, on 1 May 1820.

Pishey THOMPSON

In 1820 Pishey Thompson's monumental work on the history of Boston was published. It had the lengthy title *Collections for a Topographical and Historical Account of Boston and the Hundred of Skirbeck in the County of Lincoln.* A second edition was published in 1865 but this time with the simpler title *The History and Antiquities of Boston.*

Pishey Thompson was born at Freiston on 18 June 1785, the only son of John Thompson a grazier and his wife, Mary Evison. Pishey's mother died in 1789 shortly after the birth of her third daughter and his father died three years later leaving Pishey an orphan at the age of seven.

Pishey commenced his education at the age of six at Boston Grammar School but after his father's death he was sent to school at Wragby for four years, and then transferred for two years to a school at Freiston and finally to a school in Skirbeck. At the age of sixteen he returned as an assistant teacher to the school at Freiston run by Mr Adams.

In June 1804 Pishey Thompson became a clerk at Sneath and Son's Bank in Boston and he began collecting material for a history of Boston. In 1807 he married Jane Tonge and they set up home with her sister and brother-in-law Mr and Mrs Charles Wright. A year later the Thompsons' opened a bookshop and lived on the premises. The business was not a success and two years later it closed. Fortunately Pishey was still employed by the Bank. Four years later the Bank failed but he was able to find employment as chief clerk with the firm of Claypon & Co.

In August 1818 Jane Thompson sailed for America to visit relations and on 11 October 1819 Pishey joined her. He immediately applied for American citizenship which was granted on 27 December 1819. Before leaving Boston he had arranged for his history of Boston to be published.

Pishey Thompson kept a store and bookshop in Pennsylvania Avenue, Washington but this business failed in 1833. He then became an accountant with the U.S. Senate and in 1836 he became cashier with the Patriotic Bank of Washington. Five years later he was forced through ill health to give up this appointment and the Thompsons' returned to England to live again with the Wrights.

This was a particularly unhappy time for Pishey Thompson. He could not find work and, in 1843, he opened a bookshop in Boston with the help of a loan of £300 from his brother-in-law. The bookshop closed after only five weeks!

Later in 1843 an offer of employment from a Dr Bartlett of New York decided Pishey Thompson and his wife to return to America. Although Dr Bartlett's offer fell through he was successful in finding employment as a reporter for the U.S. Senate and in the following year he was writing regularly for the *National Intelligencer*.

In 1845 Pishey Thompson was appointed European correspondent for the *National Intelligencer* and he and his wife left America for the last time. They settled in Stoke Newington, London and they remained there for the remainder of their lives.

Jane Thompson died in 1851 and Pishey Thompson died on 25 September 1862. A brass plaque to his memory was placed in the Lady Chapel of St Botolph's Church, Boston.

Henry THOROLD

There is no doubt that Henry Thorold deserves remembering as one of Lincolnshire's characters. Indeed, perhaps he should be included in any gallery of this country's personages of the last fifty years. He maintained the tradition of clergyman-squire at Marston, which had been the home of the Thorold family since the fourteenth century, but, as patron of the living, he would never have dreamt of appointing himself incumbent. He was once described as 'having a profile like George III's and a stomach like George IV's…knows Lincolnshire backwards and all the families that ever were, they being to a man his relations.'

Henry Croyland Thorold was born on 4 June 1921. His father was Chaplain-General to the armed forces and Henry's lifelong passion for architecture sprang from his father's associations with the cathedrals of Cologne, Chester and Salisbury, with the Royal Military Chapel at Sandhurst and then with St Paul's, Westminster Abbey and Southwark.

After prep school at Summer Fields, Thorold was educated at Eton and then went up to Christ Church, Oxford before preparing for ordination at Cuddesdon Theological College. He was ordained into the Scottish Episcopal Church during the Second World War, becoming personal chaplain to the Bishop of Brechin. In 1946 he became a naval chaplain, serving in the cruiser *HMS Leander* and then in the depot ship *HMS Forth* where he surprised his fellow officers by taking the ratings to admire the glories of Maltese architecture. From 1949 to 1968 he was chaplain and also a housemaster at Lancing College where he tended to treat the boys as undergraduates and entertained them (by rota) to lunch or dinner. He took them on outings, by Rolls-Royce, to cathedrals and museums or to Glyndebourne. He was formal in class and very particular about correct pronunciation.

After retirement, he became chaplain at Summer Fields and spent his time between Oxford and Marston until, in 1975, he took up permanent residence at Marston where he remained for the rest of his life.

In 1970 Thorold was appointed a Trustee of the Lincolnshire Old Churches Trust when Lord Ancaster asked him to form the Special Committee to undertake fund-raising and give the Trust a new start. The Trust was founded in 1952 to raise funds for repairs to ancient parish churches and encourage their continued use. He became chairman in 1983 and remained in that post until he became ill and reluctantly resigned in 1998 when he was appointed an Honorary Vice President. Thorold had a particular gift for inspiring local families to adopt and look after neglected churches which might otherwise become ruinous. Although never an incumbent, he held services in many remote Lincolnshire churches and his declamatory style of preaching with long pauses were famous and kept the congregation on the edge of their seats. He was a great believer in the dignity of worship and was firmly of the 1662 persuasion.

Henry Thorold became a prolific author, writing the Shell guides to Lincolnshire, Durham, Derbyshire, Staffordshire and Nottinghamshire. He also wrote the *Collins Guide to Cathedrals, Abbeys and Priories* and *Lincolnshire Churches Revisited* with a foreword by The Prince of Wales. His masterpiece was *The Ruined Abbeys of England, Wales and Scotland* which was published in 1993. A long awaited study of *Lincolnshire Houses* was completed shortly before his death. The manuscripts for his books were written in longhand with a pad resting on his knee. For his writings he was awarded a Lambeth Degree.

Thorold acquired a splendid 1951 Bentley Mark VI Mulliner in which he visited many churches and country houses in Lincolnshire and further afield. At Marston no television, radio or newspaper was to be found and the house was said to be one of the coldest in Europe as the constant stream of visitors both young and old found to their cost.

The Revd Henry Croyland Thorold, clergyman and antiquary, died on 1 February 2000 aged 78.

Michael TIPPETT

Michael Tippett was, with Benjamin Britten, one of the most significant of English composers to come to maturity during the Second World War. He was older than Britten by nine years and took longer to mature. Although he wrote much music in the early 1930s it was not until the *Concerto for Double String Orchestra* of 1939 that he began to make a major reputation. This was clinched with the performance of *A Child of Our Time* in 1944.

Michael Kemp Tippett was born in London on 2 January 1905. His father was a lawyer and his mother, who had trained as a nurse, was a supporter of worthy causes. None of his family was musical and neither of his parents could understand or support his early musical ambitions.

At the age of nine Michael was sent to a preparatory school in Dorset and then to Fettes College, Edinburgh. He was unhappy there and he transferred to Stamford Grammar School where he was much happier. His parents, Henry and Isabel Tippett, because of financial difficulties had left London to live at an hotel they owned at Cannes in the South of France. Michael spent most of his vacations there and became fluent in French as a result. It was at this time he discovered the restorative powers of marmalade, a solace which remained with him for the remainder of his life!

Whilst at Stamford, Michael had piano lessons with Mrs Frances Tinkler who had taught Sir Malcolm Sargent (see *Lincolnshire People* page 81). At the age of fourteen he was taken to an orchestral concert in Leicester conducted by Sir Malcolm and appropriately this set him on the path towards a career as a composer. Apparently the headmaster at Stamford Grammar School, when he heard of young Michael's chosen career, commented that he would never earn enough to afford a boiled egg let alone a boiled shirt.

Michael taught himself composition using a book by Charles Stanford. However, it was a chance encounter with a professional musician which persuaded his parents at last to agree to pay for Michael to study at the Royal College of Music: they made it a condition that his object would be to become a Doctor of Music. He was accepted and his first acquaintance with the world of professional music began in 1923.

Michael Tippett studied composition at the RCM with Charles Wood, piano with Aubin Raynar and conducting with Malcolm Sargent and Adrian Boult. After a concert of his own work left him dissatisfied he returned to the college for further study with R. O. Morris. He gained further musical experience by working among unemployed ironstone miners in Yorkshire. In 1932 he returned to London on appointment as conductor of the Morley College Orchestra which had been formed to help out-of-work musicians. He also conducted choirs associated with the Labour Party. Tippett's play *The War Ramp* was based on the conflict of political idealism and pacifism. His *Song of Liberty* reflected his dismay at the darkening European scene.

Tippett joined the Peace Pledge Union in 1940 and registered as a conscientious objector. Three years later he was sentenced to three months imprisonment for refusing to undertake non-combatant military duties, work on a farm, or a hospital, or teach in a civil defence establishment. Whilst he was in Wormwood Scrubs, Benjamin Britten and Peter Pears visited to give a recital with Tippett turning the pages for Britten.

A Child of Our Time, which was composed in the early years of the Second World War, and has as its theme the horrors and social consequences of war, was published in 1944. This was the first of Tippett's works to attract attention and praise outside England and it is regarded as his masterpiece.

After the war he limited his other work in order to spend more time on composition. However, he started to give talks on the BBC Third Programme and World Service in order to earn a modest secondary income. In 1951 he decided to resign from Morley College and he moved to Wadhurst, Sussex where his mother joined him (his father having died in 1944).

Amongst Tippett's major works were five operas notably *The Midsummer Marriage* which was premiered at Covent Garden in 1955. The *Ritual Dances* from this work quickly became a popular concert item. In 1963 a BBC performance of the *Midsummer Marriage* conducted by Norman Del Mar brought much acclaim. A recording conducted by Colin Davis in 1971 made it a bestseller in Britain and the USA. His chamber music and especially his string quartets have also been well received. From 1969 until 1974 Tippett was director of the Bath Musical festival.

In 1959 he was appointed CBE and in 1966 he received a Knighthood. In 1979 he became a Companion of Honour. The Royal Academy and Royal College of Music had already made him an Honorary Fellow and between 1964 and 1977 he received Honorary Doctorates from fourteen British Universities and many other honours followed.

Sir Michael Tippett, who was unmarried, died on 8 January 1998 at the age of 93.

FURTHER READING : Kemp, Ian, *Tippett : The Composer and his Music (1984).*

Richard TODD

For over forty years Richard Todd, who has lived in south Lincolnshire for many years, was one of the best-known British actors not only in this country but worldwide. His association with the county has long since earned him acceptance as an honorary 'yellow-belly'.

Richard Andrew Palethorpe-Todd was born on 11 June 1919 in Dublin and he is the son of Major A. W. P. Todd whose family had lived and farmed in County Tyrone for many years. His mother, Marvilla Rose Agar-Daly (usually known as Vill) came from County Kerry. When Richard was six months old he and his mother joined his father who was a doctor in India with the British Army. In 1922 his father retired and they lived for a time at Richard's grandparents house at Toome in County Antrim but it was soon decided to leave Ireland for Holsworthy,

Devon. At the age of twelve Richard entered Shrewsbury School but, unfortunately, soon after he became ill with rheumatic fever and periocarditis. Through sheer will power he made a very good recovery but it was not until the age of fourteen that he returned to School. It had been decided that this should be at Wimborne Grammar School and his father bought a practice in the town which enabled Richard to live at home.

At the age of sixteen Richard played the part of a lady surprised in her bedroom and also a vicar in a school production of John Galsworthy's *Escape*. Richard had already taken part in play-reading sessions and had attended a professional production of *The Tempest* in connection with his School Certificate studies. This fired an ambition to be a dramatist. Through the influence of his grandmother the Italia Conti Stage School in London accepted him. Italia Conti insisted that, if he was to write plays, he must have a complete grounding in every aspect of theatrical work. During his time at the school he appeared in crowd scenes in two Will Hay films and had small parts in other films including *A Yank at Oxford*. He also played leading rôles for two seasons in Conti's production of *Where the Rainbow Ends*. As a result Richard's ambition moved away from writing to acting.

Richard auditioned and was accepted for the 1937 season with the Regent's Park Open Air Theatre Company playing small parts and understudying some leading rôles. In 1938 he joined the newly formed Welsh Players which presented a new play each week and this gave him a good grounding in stagecraft. In early 1939 the Welsh Players disbanded and in August Richard joined another new venture, the Dundee Repertory Theatre. On 3 September war was declared and Richard immediately volunteered but was not called up until July 1940. He served with distinction in the King's Own Yorkshire Light Infantry and the Parachute Regiment until demobilisation in 1946.

Richard returned to work with the Dundee 'rep' for eighteen months until he successfully auditioned for a part in the film *For Them that Trespass.* This opportunity came because his agent before the war, Robert Leonard, had become casting director for The Associated British Film Corporation. He remembered Richard and invited him for a screen test.

After this breakthrough, Richard starred in many notable films some under the directorship of such great Hollywood directors as Alfred Hitchcock and King Vidor. However, he feels that he owes most to Vincent Sherman who, in 1949, directed *The Hasty Heart* for which Richard won a Golden Globe Award as the Most Promising Male Actor and for which he was also nominated for an Oscar as the Best Actor in a Leading Rôle. He has made almost sixty films and this includes a number based on the Second World War such as *The Dam Busters* made in 1954 and *The Longest Day* (1962). Other notable films were *Robin Hood* (1952), *Rob Roy* (1953) and *The Virgin Queen* (1955).

Richard eventually began to feel typecast as the 'stiff upper lip' English officer and in the sixties he returned to the theatre. He is particularly remembered for stage appearances in *An Ideal Husband* (1965-66 and 1997), *Dear Octopus* (1967), *This Happy Breed* (1980) and *Brideshead Revisited* (1995).

Top left : Richard Todd's first film, For Them That Trespass

Top right : Richard in Stagefright with Jane Wyman, Alistair Sim and Sybil Thorndike

One of Richard's most famous rôles : Wing Commander Guy Gibson V.C.

Dairy farmer Todd with his children Peter and Fiona.

In 1970 Richard with Duncan Weldon and Paul Elliott formed Triumph Theatre Productions with the object of revolutionising provincial theatre in Britain and also exporting British theatre. It became one of the biggest theatre production companies in the world and plays were being presented in America, Canada and Australia, in fact all over the English-speaking world. Richard feels that many theatres in this country have remained open largely because of Triumph productions. In the late 1970s Richard resigned his directorship so that he could devote more time to his acting career but he occasionally took part in productions.

Until his father broke the mould, the Todd family had farmed in Ireland so it is not surprising that, in the late 1950s, Richard established a dairy farm and market garden on his Haileywood estate in Oxfordshire. After seven years Richard decided to sell the estate and he and his family lived for a time at Bampton Grange, Oxfordshire before moving to Maidenwell Manor, near Louth. Eventually he decided that south Lincolnshire would be an ideal base and, in the mid-1970s, he purchased Elm House, Market Deeping. This was always intended as a temporary home and when the Old Rectory at Little Ponton near Grantham came on the market this became the family home.

Richard Todd has had a long and distinguished career in acting in all its aspects. His contribution to the profession was recognised when, in 1993, he was appointed to the Order of the British Empire (OBE).

It has been very difficult in a short article to do justice to Richard Todd's exceptional career and I found his two-volume autobiography fascinating reading. May I conclude by recommending *Caught in the Act* (1986) and *In Camera* (1989) as a fascinating account of the life of a leading actor.

Cornelius VERMUYDEN

Cornelius Vermuyden was an engineer who introduced Dutch land reclamation methods into England and it is he who can be credited with much of the drainage of the Lincolnshire Fens.

Vermuyden was born in 1595 at St Martin's Dyke in the island of Tholen in the Netherlands. In 1621 he was employed by Charles I to repair a breach in the bank of the Thames at Dagenham. This was successfully accomplished and the king employed him to drain Hatfield Chase and the Isle of Axholme in 1626. This venture was jointly financed by Dutch and English capitalists. It was a controversial undertaking not only for the engineering techniques used but also because it employed Dutch instead of English workmen. The island of Sandtoft was chosen for the establishment of a base on which to house the Dutch workmen and this was stockaded to protect them from the local inhabitants who hunted and fished in the fens. Some 200 houses housing about 1000 workers were built. A Calvinist chapel was also built and this stood until 1686 when it was razed to the ground by the islanders who were extremely concerned that their traditional livelihood based on hunting, fishing, fowling and reed gathering would be threatened by the changing face of the Isle of Axholme. In order to complete his drainage scheme Vermuyden had to employ English workers and pay compensation to the fenmen for the loss of hunting and fishing rights.

Further riots erupted and Vermuyden did not hesitate to use force supported by the government in order to carry out his drainage schemes. The drainage of the Isle of Axholme was a formidable example of the use of royal authority to crush the peasantry.

In 1630 Vermuyden contracted to drain the Great Fen or Bedford Level, Cambridgeshire. When the project was completed in 1637, objections were made by other engineers who claimed the drainage system was inadequate. During the English Civil War in 1642 Parliament ordered the dikes to be breached and the land flooded in order to stop the advance of a Royalist army. In 1649 Vermuyden was commissioned to reclaim the Bedford Level and 40,000 acres were drained by 1652.

In 1653 Vermuyden, who had been knighted in the 1620s and became a British subject in 1633, headed an unsuccessful English mission to the United Provinces of the Netherlands in order to arrange a political union between the two nations.

In order to pay his workmen Vermuyden had to sell land which he had been given in part payment for his drainage undertakings. Eventually he had sold all his possessions. Nothing is known of his later life and it is believed that he may have escaped his creditors by living abroad for a time. Sir Cornelius Vermuyden died in London on 6 April 1683 and is buried in St Martin's in the Fields. He had married *circa* 1625 Katherine Lappe and they had a large family.

John WAKEFORD

When the news broke that the Archdeacon of Stow was to be tried by a Consistory Court for immorality the citizens of early twentieth century Lincoln were, to put it mildly, shocked. John Wakeford had been appointed Prebendary of Clifton in Lincoln Cathedral in 1910, Precentor in 1912, Archdeacon of Stow in 1913 and vicar of Kirkstead in 1914. He frequently lectured on Pastoral Theology at King's College London and at Durham University. Although his energy and excellent preaching made him popular with many of the cathedral community he was strong willed, tactless and egotistical. Almost from the commencement of his ecclesiastical career John Wakeford had made enemies. His forceful manner combined with his love of ritual and vestments coupled with his passion for taking religion to the people did not endear him to many of the clergy.

John Wakeford was born in Kentish Town, London in 1859. His father William was a policeman and his mother was devoutly low church. Five of their children devoted their lives to the Church of England. Surprisingly, it was a Devonport Rabbi who set John on the path to the priesthood. After matriculating in 1880 he began training for the ministry and after ordination in 1884 he was appointed curate of St Paul's, Devonport moving to West Alvington Devon in 1886. From 1886 until 1888 he was Missioner for the Diocese of Exeter and in October 1888 he was appointed to a similar post in the Diocese of Chichester. In 1893 he married Evelyn Worthington. His wife came from a family of parsons and, although her father liked Wakeford, her mother and brother did not. Shortly after his marriage Wakeford was appointed vicar of St Margaret's Anfield, Liverpool.

At Lincoln there were many opportunities for him to incur the displeasure of a number of influential clergymen. Charles Moore, Rector of Appleby Magna and squire of Kirkstead was one. Moore was very friendly with the Archdeacon Wakeford's brother-in-law and the two became determined to bring about Wakeford's downfall. Dean Fry, who appears to have been very unpopular, soon became Wakeford's enemy. Fry even arranged for Wakeford's chauffeur, who was the son of his own chauffeur, to report details of the journeys undertaken by the Archdeacon. Indeed it seems to have been Fry's habit to encourage workmen to report to him the activities of their supervisors.

The Consistory Court in 1921 centred on the fact that Wakeford had been seen in Peterborough Cathedral with a woman and it was alleged that he had committed adultery. Space does not permit a full account of the evidence produced at the hearing but this is recorded in detail in John Trehearne's book *Dangerous Precincts*. The Chancellor and his five assessors found '...the defendant guilty on each charge and this is the decision of us all, and I shall report to the Bishop in pursuance of statute. The Archdeacon has the right of appeal to the Provincial Court'.

Wakeford's appeal failed and his life was in ruins. In 1925 Wakeford published a slim volume entitled *Not Peace but a Sword* which contains a biography and a considerable number of letters which serve to prove his popularity. Archdeacon John Wakeford died in a lunatic asylum in 1930. Although Wakeford had acted rather unwisely at times after reading the evidence it seems very unlikely that he was guilty as charged.

John William Charles WAND

Bishop Wand was born at Grantham on 25 January 1885 and was educated at the Kings School, and St Edmund Hall Oxford. He was awarded a BA in 1907. He received his theological training at Bishop Jacob Hostel, Newcastle upon Tyne and after ordination a year later joined the staff of Benwell parish. This was the parish in which the Hostel was situated and had five churches with a population of 30,000 people most of whom were artisans or miners. In 1911 Wand became additional curate at Lancaster with a stipend of £200 a year. This time he found himself in a parish whose population covered a much wider spectrum - including the military, tradesmen and labourers employed at the local linoleum factory. He married on 11

October 1911 and although very happy in Lancaster he now had a wife and two children and he decided that he must find work with a higher salary. An interview at Salisbury Cathedral for a minor canonry was unsuccessful but he was successful in obtaining a lectureship at Salisbury Theological College. During the 1914-18 war, Wand was an army chaplain serving in the Far East before an attack of paratyphoid led to his evacuation to Malta and eventual return to England. After recovery he was sent to France and then into Germany after fighting ceased. In March 1919 he returned home and was offered the living of St Mark's Salisbury, which he accepted. He was also able to resume his teaching at the Theological College.

In 1925 Wand accepted the post of Dean of Oriel College, Oxford and he remained there until 1934 when he accepted the Archbishopric of Brisbane, Australia. In 1943 he returned to Britain on his appointment as Bishop of Bath and Wells and two years later he was appointed Bishop of London, a post he held until 1955.

Perhaps surprisingly Bishop Wand was then appointed a residentiary Canon of St Paul's Cathedral where he had had his *cathedra* (Bishop's throne) and he actually escorted his successor as bishop at the enthronement! Wand's final appointment says much for his character and popularity. He was a most diligent and conscientious canon.

Bishop Wand had written a number of books mainly on church history and after he retired from the bishopric of London he became an even more prolific writer producing numerous popular books commending the Christian faith. He also edited the *Church Quarterly Review*, wrote a weekly devotional column for the *Church Times,* and published a brief autobiography, *Changeful Page* in 1965.

He finally retired in January 1969 at the age of 84 and moved to the College of St Barnabas, Lichfield in 1975 where he died on 16 August 1977.

William WARRENER

William Warrener was the second son of a prosperous Lincoln coal merchant and was born in 1861. He studied at Lincoln School of Art under A. G. Webster and in 1881 won a *Mention Honorable* with *Un Aveu* which was later exhibited at the Royal Academy. In 1884 he received the Mayor of Lincoln's Gold Medal and a Queens Prize in the National Art Examinations at the Victoria and Albert Museum in South Kensington. In 1885 he won a scholarship to the Slade School and also studied in Paris at the Academie Julian under Gustave Boulanger and Jules Lefèbvre. Whilst in Paris he became friendly with William Rothenstein and Toulouse-Lautrec who painted Warrener's portrait. He was the model for Lautrec's famous poster *L'Anglais au Moulin Rouge* and figures in the poster *Jane Avril Dansant.* Rothenstein said that 'Warrener threw himself into the most advanced movements then prevalent in Paris in the 1880's and 1890's. He usually painted nude figures out of doors set against a background of the shrillest chrome yellow and viridian green the colour merchants provided'. Warrener's early work was rather academic but his time in Paris lead to a change to a more Impressionistic style.

When his brother John, who was a lieutenant Colonel in the Lincolnshire Volunteers, was killed in 1906 Warrener returned to Lincoln in order to take control of the family coal merchant's business. He never married and lived with his two sisters at St Margaret's Lodge, Upper Lindum Street in Lincoln. He gave up painting for exhibition but encouraged an interest in the arts in Lincoln. In 1906 he founded, and later became president, of the Lincolnshire Drawing Club, which later became the Lincolnshire Artists' Society. He also became a leading figure in the Lincoln Music Club and he was vice-president of the Lincoln Musical Society.

Unfortunately his sister, Maude, burned many of Warrener's paintings after his death in 1934. Apparently she feared that the paintings of nudes would damage his reputation in Lincoln! When she died in 1956 a room full of paintings that she had saved was auctioned at Lincoln Central Market. Thankfully fourteen of Warrener's oil paintings and a collection of his sketches and drawings can be seen in the Usher Gallery, Lincoln.

Frank WHITTLE

The brain child of Frank Whittle, the jet engine, was first used successfully to power an aircraft in flight on 15 May 1941 at RAF Cranwell. Lincolnshire can, therefore, claim the honour of hosting the first flight of a jet aircraft which was to have such a great impact on aviation history.

Frank Whittle was born at Earlsdon, Coventry on 1 June 1907. His father was a foreman in a machine tool factory and when Frank was four years of age he gave him a toy aeroplane with a clockwork propeller which he suspended from a gas mantle. This seems to have triggered Frank's life-long interest in aeroplanes. He was educated at Earlsdon and Milverton Council School and then won a scholarship to Leamington College. Frank spent many hours in the local library learning about steam and gas turbines and passed the entrance examination for RAF Halton as an aircraft apprentice. Unfortunately he failed the medical examination but he applied again using a different first name and was accepted by RAF Cranwell. In 1926 Frank Whittle passed a flying medical and was awarded a cadetship to the RAF College and qualified as a pilot. In 1926 he wrote a revolutionary thesis entitled *Future Developments in Aircraft Design.*

In 1928 he passed out and received the Andy Fellowes Memorial Prize for Aeronautical Sciences. After serving at Hornchurch and Wittering he became an instructor at Digby. In his spare time he developed the idea of burning fuel to force exhaust gases by compressed air which would move an aircraft at great speed through air which was too thin for propeller driven machines. The Air Ministry turned down his idea and Whittle became a test pilot. In 1934 he went up to Peterhouse College, Cambridge University and was awarded a First in Mechanical

Sciences. Two businessmen became interested in Whittle's jet engine and the Air Ministry agreed that he could work for six hours a week on the project.

Whittle's jet engine first ran on 12 April 1937 but it was not until June 1939 that the Air Ministry finally awarded a contract to him to build a lightweight jet engine. The first British jet aircraft, the Gloster Whittle E 28/39 'Pioneer' flew from RAF College Cranwell on 15 May 1941. As a result the Air Ministry ordered a twin-engined version and eight prototypes were built followed by an order for twenty operational machines which became known as the Gloster 'Meteor'.

In 1948 Air Commodore Frank Whittle retired through ill health and was awarded £100,000 by the Royal Commission on Awards to Inventors. He had been appointed CBE in 1944, CB in 1947 and he became a Knight of the British Empire in 1948. Whittle was made a Commander of the US Legion of Merit in 1946 and in 1986 he was appointed a member of the Order of Merit. He was a Fellow of the Royal Society and of the Royal Aeronautical Society. He settled in America in 1976 and was a member of the Faculty of the Naval Academy, Annapolis, Maryland. Sir Frank Whittle published *Jet* in 1953 and *Gas Turbine Aero-Thermodynamics* in 1981. He died on 9 August 1996.

Charles Frederick WORTH

Charles Frederick Worth was the son of William Worth, a well-to-do solicitor of Bourne. He was the youngest of five children and was born in 1825. William Worth became bankrupt in 1836 and deserted his family who went to live at Billingborough. Charles never forgave his father and he never saw him again. After leaving school he found work at a printers in Bourne but after a year he left for London and he was apprenticed to Swan & Edgar where he remained for seven years. At the age of nineteen he left to take up employment with Lewis and Allenby in Regent Street. He learned a great deal about French fashion and design and also took a keen interest in the arts becoming a frequent visitor to the National Gallery. In order to study fashion and design more closely he left the firm in 1846 and went to France. He arrived in Paris without any capital and knew no one but he was fortunate to find work with the firm of Gagelin. The firm was noted for its beautiful silks which were woven in the homes of the firm's employees.

At that time there was no fashion house in Paris which sold material and also produced finished garments as well. Young Worth realised the advantages of both operations taking place under one roof and he obtained permission from his employers to introduce this procedure and started in a small way by making cloaks. In 1855 he designed a train for a wedding dress for which he was awarded a medal. After twelve years with Gagelin's, Worth decided to go into partnership with Otto Bobergh, a Swede, and began making lovely and unusual cloaks. Materials were very exclusive and expensive and the House of Worth, at no. 7 rue de la Paix, soon dominated Paris fashion scene.

The firm quickly attracted clients who included the Queens of Portugal and Spain and the Empress of Russia. Worth's most regular client was Eugénie, Empress of the French, who was the centre of French society and set the fashion for the whole of France. Charles Worth's two sons, Gaston and Jean, assisted him in the business. By the time he retired Charles Worth was able to claim that he had been dressmaker for every Royal lady in the world with the exception of Queen Victoria. It is surprising that the famous designer from Lincolnshire should have failed to gain favour with the English sovereign.

Charles Worth died on 10 March 1895 at the age of 69 and was buried in Suresnes.

Patrick WYMARK

Patrick Carl Cheeseman was born in Cleethorpes, Lincolnshire, on 11 July 1926. He was the son of Thomas William Cheeseman who ran a small art supply shop. His mother, Agnes Maria Cheeseman, had always taken a keen interest in the theatre and was very active in amateur dramatics in Grimsby. It is not surprising that Patrick, as a boy, took part in many amateur productions. He was also prominent in drama at school and his first Shakespearian rôle was as Sir Toby Belch at the age of ten. Nearly twenty years later he played the same part in Stratford on Avon and at the Aldwych Theatre, London.

Patrick's early education was at Wintringham School in Grimsby and from there he went up to Edinburgh University to read History and Economics but, at the age of nineteen, he left to join the Navy. He became a sub-lieutenant and did minesweeping in the Mediterranean. After completing his National Service, Patrick went up to University College, London to read English with the vague intention of becoming a teacher. However, he spent most of his time with the Drama Society and he was advised to apply for an audition with the Old Vic School. He was accepted for a two year acting course.

Patrick adopted the surname 'Wymark' when he first appeared on the professional stage in 1951. He joined the Old Vic Company, with whom he toured South Africa in the following year. After a year at Stanford University in America as Artist in Residence he joined the Royal Shakespeare Company for four seasons. He then played with the 'Fifty-nine' Company at the Lyric, Hammersmith and appeared in several television plays, films and a revue *One to Another* with Beryl Reid in the West End. He then returned to Stratford and from there to a season at the Aldwych.

After a year working in television and films and an appearance as Bottom in *Midsummer Night's Dream* in Regent's Park, the opportunity came to appear in the television series the *Planemakers* for which he will be best remembered. This first series was followed by more film and television work including the voice of Churchill in *The Finest Hours*. As Sir John Wilder in the *Planemakers* Patrick Wymark portrayed a character seen as a power hungry, ruthlessly ambitious tycoon whose deepest conviction seemed to be that the aircraft industry, like marriage, existed for his personal advancement. Wymark allowed this stereotype to develop odd corners of sardonic humour and humanity as well as a suggestion that his centre, though unreachable, was quite soft.

It was natural that so forceful a TV characterisation should live again in a second series, *The Power Game*, to expand his industrial interests, flirt with politics and find an enemy as ruthless and ambitious as himself. Wymark's work in *The Power Game* brought him an *Actor of the Year* award.

Patrick Wymark died in his hotel in Melbourne, Australia on 20 October 1970 three days before he was due to appear in the leading rôle in *Sleuth* at the Playbox Theatre there. It was whilst he was at University College that he met and married his American wife Olwen and they had two sons and two daughters. He was aged 44.

James YORKE

James Yorke was the author of a book published in London in 1641 entitled *The Union of Honour containing the Arms, Matchers and Issues of the Kings, Dukes, Marquesses and Earles of England...inscribed to King Charles I and dedicated to Henry Frederick the son of Thomas Howard second Earl of Arundel.* The book contains dedicatory verses by a number of prominent people of the time including Richard Braithwaite, Or Elyot, Jo Prujean, Sir George Buc, T. Langford, Edward Bullingham, Percy Enderby and Thomas Heywood the actor.

Little is known of James Yorke except that he was a blacksmith. His name is inscribed above the altar in the Ringer's Chapel in Lincoln Cathedral as Master of the Cathedral Company of Ringers in 1633. His father, Henry Yorke, was one of the signatories to the 'Ordinaunces, Constitutions and Agreamentes' of the Company of Ringers of the Cathedral Church of the Blessed Virgin Mary of Lincoln dated 8 October 1612. Henry's name also appears above the altar as Master in 1618.

The Parliamentary Commissioners in a survey of former Chapter property dated 9 January 1649 named a James Yorke as tenant of Little Hill Close ('LAO Parliamentary Survey 1552829 CC27).

FURTHER READING : Further information about the bellringers at Lincoln Cathedral will be found in Ketteringham J, R. Lincoln Cathedral : *A History of the Bells, Bellringers and Bell ringing* (2000)

The title page of *The Union of Honour* (1641) with an engraved portrait of James Yorke

INDEX

This is primarily an Index to those who are featured in this book. These names are printed in **bold** type. I have also indexed Lincolnshire people and places together with a few people and places from outside the county where I have considered this information is of particular interest.

I have included in this Index all those people who were featured in *Lincolnshire People (LP)* and *Lincolnshire Women (LW)*. These names and page numbers are printed in ***bold italic***. Where these people are also featured in this book the page number is printed in regular type

A Racing Rubber	134
ADDISON, Christopher	***LP 11***
Adventures of Verdant Green	14
ALAN, Elizabeth	***LW 4***
ALDERTON, John	1
Alford	24, 33, 38, 41, 66, 110, 137, 141
Allington	98
ALLWOOD, Montagu	2
Alnwick, Bishop William	105
ANDERSON, Edmund	3
ANDREWS, Henry,	***LP 11***
ANGELL, Norman	4
ARUNDEL, James	5
As long as I know it'll be quite alright	101
Asher, Jane	91
ASKEW, Anne	***LP 11, LW 5***
Askey, Arthur	12
ASTON, Thomas de	6
Attlee, Clement	98
Austwick, John	99
Axholme, Isle of	131, 156
BAKER, F. T.	7
Baker, John	34
Ballard, Douglas	17
BANKS, Joseph,	***LP 12***
Baptists	94
Barker, Eric	127
BARLEY, Maurice W.	9
BARNARD, Charlotte Alington	***LW 20***
Barton, Maria	49
Barton-on-Humber	128
Basket, The	83
BASS, George,	***LP 13***
Baumber	44
Baxter, Raymond	53
Bed, The	54
Bedford Level	157
Belton Park	135
Bennett, Dr G.	12
Berthon, Peter	113
BERTIE, Peregrine	***LP 13***
BESANT, Annie	***LW 6***
Best Laid Schemes, The	55
Betjeman, Sir John	1, 22, 87
Bibliotheca Topographica Brittannica	88
BIGGADIKE, Priscilla	***LW 7***
Billingborough	161
Birds of Lincolnshire	138
Biscathorpe	119
Blackpool	35, 55, 100
Blankney Fen	122
Bloom, Alan	52
BLOOMER, Shirley	***LW 8***
BLYTON, Enid	***LW 10***
BOHEME, Revd George	11
BOLINGBROKE, Henry	***LP 14***, 7
BOLLE, Sir John	***LP 15***
BOOLE, George	***LP 16***
BOOTH, Webster	12
BOOTH, William	***LP 17***, 117
BOOTHROYD, Basil	***LP 18***
Boston	13, 25, 32, 66, 73, 86, 88, 93, 99, 103, 110, 140, 146, 149
BOTOLPH, Saint	13
Bottesford	81
Bourne	85, 112, 161
BRACKENBURY, Robert Carr	***LP 18***, 97
Bradford	4, 41, 72
BRADLEY, Edward	13
BRADSTREET, Anne	***LW 12***
BRANDON, Charles (Duke of Suffolk)	15
Bratoft Meadows	70
Brazen-nosed Society of Stamford	88
Breezie Langton	134
Britain and the British Seas	104
British Racing Motors (BRM)	113
Britten, Benjamin	152
Broadbent Theatre	17
Broadbent, Dee and Roy	17
BROADBENT, Jim	17
BROMHEAD, Gonville	***LP 19***

BROOKE, Frances	*LW 14*	Cook, Humphrey	113
Brotherhood of the Holy Redeemer	119	Cooke, Alistair	47
Brothers Together	147	**COOPER, Thomas**	*LP 27*
Brough, George	96	Corby Glen	62
Broughton	131	**CORR, Karen**	*LW 22*
Brown, Father	5	**COTTON, Revd John**	**32**
Brown, Gregory	127	Courtney, Tom	1
BROWN, Joe	**19**	Cowley, Stephen	35
BROWN, Peter	**21**	Cranwell	95, 141, 160
BULL, Deborah	*LW 16*	Cricket	42, 68
Burgh le Marsh	34, 36, 38, 60	Cromwell, Oliver	61
BUSBY, Richard	*LP 19*	Cromwell, Thomas	80
BUTLIN, Billy	*LP 20*	Crowland	64, 88
Byng, Hon. John	89	Croxby	2
BYRD, William	*LP 21*	**CULLEN, Professor Alex**	*LP 29*
Caistor	45, 145	**DADLEY, William**	**33**
CALEB, Theophilus	**22**	**DALDERBY, Bishop John de**	*LP 30*
CAMPBELL, Judy	*LW 18*	*Dam Busters*	154
Candle in the Wind	144	*Dangerous Precincts*	158
Candlesby	34	**DASHWOOD, Sir Francis**	*LP 31*
CAPES, Geoff	*LP 21*	DAVIDSON, Revd Harold F.	35
Carholme, Lincoln	45, 118	Dawson, Margaret Damer	136
Carlton	98	De Aston School, Market Rasen	7
CARNLEY, Sidney B.	**24**	**De ASTON, Thomas**	**6**
Carr, Colin	48	**DEXTER, Colin**	**36**
Cato Street Conspiracy	148	Diana, Princes	144
Cawkwell	93	**DICKINSON, Margaret**	**37**
CECIL, William	*LP 23*	**DICKSON, Barbara**	*LW 24*
Chaplin, Charles, M. P.	122	**DICKSON, Violet**	*LW 26*
CHAPLIN, Henry	*LP 23*	Digby	106, 160
CHARLESWORTH, E. P.	*LP 25*	*Dissertation on the Mint in Lincoln*	88
Charterhouse School	123, 144	**DIXON, Anne**	*LW 27*
Cheeseman, Patrick Carl	162	**DOBSON, Fred**	**39**
CHESHIRE, Leonard	*LP 25*	**DODD, Revd William**	*LP 32*
Child of Our Time	152	Donington on Bain	119
Childhood in Lincolnshire	86	**DREWRY, Arthur**	**40**
Choir School, Lincoln	12	Dwight, Reginald	145
Christ's Hospital School, Lincoln	2, 53, 70, 77	**DYER, H. J. H.**	**41**
CIBBER, Colley	*LP 27*, 46	**DYMOKE FAMILY, The**	*LP 33*
City School, Lincoln	7		
'CLARIBEL'	*LW 20*	**EAGLEN, Jane**	*LW 28*
Claxby	98	Edenham	62
Clayton & Shuttleworth	25	*Education of a Gardener*	123
CLAYTON, Nathaniel	**25**	**EDWARDES, George**	**44**
Cleethorpes	46, 55, 77, 141, 162	Ekberg, Charlie	48
COLEMAN, Ernest	**26**	'ELIOT, George'	*LW 30*
COLLIER, Brett	**29**	Elms, Keith	90
Collins, Pauline	1	**ELSEY, William E.**	**44**
Coningsby	45	Elsham	81

ELST, Violet van der	*LW 31*	Gibraltar Point	38
Emlyn, Thomas	11	**GIBSON, Guy**	**LP 40**, 155
English Racing Automobiles (ERA)	113	**GILBERT of Sempringham**	**LP 42**
Epstein, Jacob	128	Gill, Eric	128
Eresby	15	**GLEW, Montague F.**	**57**
EUSDEN, Laurence	**45**	Glossary of Lincolnshire Words, etc.	61
EVANS, Marian	**LW 30**	Gloster 'Meteor'	161
Evergreen	48	Gloster Whittle E 28/39 'Pioneer'	161
Ewerby	144	**GODFREY, Robert**	**59**
		GOE, Bishop Field Flowers	**LP 43**
FAIERS, Roy	**46**	Golden Sands Holiday Estate, Mablethorpe	71
Federation Internationale de Football Association (FIFA)	40	**GOOD, Jabez**	**60**
Fens and Floods of Mid-Lincolnshire	121	**GOODALL, Sir Reginald**	**LP 43**, 12
Figaro Here, Figaro There	139	**GOODRICH, Bishop Philip H. E.**	**61**
First Episode at Hainton	147	**GOOGE, Barnabe**	**LP 45**
FISHER, Brenda	**LW 33**	**GOULDING, Richard W.**	**63**
Fiskerton	39	Grainger, John	78
Flight of the Mew Gull	71	**GRAINGER, Percy**	**LP 46**
FLINDERS, Matthew	**LP 35**	Grantham	19, 26, 46, 125, 135, 156, 158
Flixborough	3	Graves, Frank	110
FLOWERS, Field	**49**	Gray, Thomas	46
FOALE, C. Michael	**50**	**GREEN, Diana**	**LW 38**
Foggin, Cyril	57	**GREY, Aggie**	**LW 40**
FOLKARD, Oliver G.	**51**	Grimsby	10, 38, 40, 72, 77, 93, 115, 141, 162
Folkingham	12, 51	Grimsthorpe	15
FOLLOWS, Denis	**LP 36**	**GROSSETESTE, Bishop Robert**	**LP 47**
Football League	40	**GRUNDY, John, Junior**	**LP 48**
FORBES, Rosita	**LW 34**	**GRUNDY, John, Senior**	**LP 47**
FORDYCE, Keith	**52**	**GUTCH, Eliza**	**LW 42**
FOSTER, C. W.	**LP 36**	**GUTHLAC, Saint**	**64**
FOWLER, James	**LP 37**		
FOXE, John	**LP 38**	**HADFIELD, Geoffrey**	**65**
FOXE, Richard	**LP 38**	**HAIGH, John George**	**LP 49**
FRANKLIN, Sir John	**LP 39**, 27	*Half-an-Hour at Lincoln Cathedral*	60
Freiston	149	**HAMMOND, Richard**	**66**
FRINTON, Freddie	**54**	Harburn, Ellen	136
Fry, Dean	158	**HARRISON, John**	**LP 50**
Fulletby	93	Harrowby, Earl of	149
		HASSALL, John	**67**
Gainsborough	1, 37, 66, 82, 93, 103, 121, 139, 143	Hatfield Chase	131, 156
GALITZINE, Yuri	**55**	**HAWKE, Lord Martin B.**	**68**
Gano, John	140	Hawley, Sir Joseph	134
Gardiner, Bishop of Lincoln	11	Haynes, Arthur	55, 125
Gate Burton Hall	1	Healey, Hilary	10
Gaunt, John of	7	**HEATH, Winifred**	**69**
George II	46, 60	Heath's Meadows	70
Geranium, Hardy 'Anne Folkard'	52	Hemingby	44
GIBBONS, Joan	**LW 36**	Henry IV	7, 104
		Henry VII	80, 15
		Henry VIII	15, 80, 144

HENSHAW, Alexander A.	70	JOHNSON, Maurice	88
HEYWOOD, Thomas	*LP 51*, 163	Johnston, Edward	127
Higgins, Fred	60	**JOLLAND, Wolley**	**89**
High Flight	106	*Jolly Fisherman, The*	67
Hill, Graham	113	**JOYCE, Eliza**	*LW 48*
HILL, Sir Francis	*LP 51*, 10		
HILTON, William	*LP 53*	Kemp, Eric	81
Hird, Thora	54	*KENDAL Madge*	*LW 49*
History and Antiquities of Boston	149	**KERRIGAN, Jonathan**	**90**
History of Lincolnshire Committee	8	**KEYWORTH, Leonard**	*LP 60*
HODGE, Patricia	*LW 44*	**KING, Bishop Edward**	*LP 61*, 84
Holbeach	4, 85, 88	King, Steve	101
Holden, Charles	128	Kirkby-on-Bain	134
HOLLES, Gervase	**72**	Kirton-in-Holland	88, 144
Holmes, Bill	62	Knaith	143
Holton-cum-Beckering	17	**KNOLLYS, Hansard**	**93**
Home Guard	39		
HONYWOOD, Michael	*LP 54*	*LAMBERT, Daniel*	*LP 62*
HOOLEY, Ernest Terah	**73**	*LANGTON, Bennet*	*LP 64*
Hooley's Confessions	73	*LANGTON, Archbishop Stephen*	*LP 64*
Horncastle	44, 57, 80, 101, 129, 140	*LATHAM, Robert*	*LP 65*
Housewive's Choice	52	*LAWRENCE, D. H.*	*LP 65*
Howells, Herbert	110	Lawrence, Sir Thomas	140
HUDSON, Charles	**76**	**LAWRENCE, Thomas E.**	**94**
HUGH of Avalon	*LP 54*	Lawsons, Nurserymen, Lincoln	39
HUGH, Little Saint	*LP 56*	**LEACH, Terence R.**	**96**
Humberstone	72, 93	*LEDWARD, Daphne*	*LW 52*
Hundleby, Allan	42	**LEE, Revd Austin**	**98**
HUNT, John	*LP 56*	*LEFFEY, Mary*	*LW 51*
HURT, John	77	Legsby	17
HUSSEY, John	**80**	Leverton, Herbert	85
HUTCHINSON, Annie	*LP 57, LW 46*, 33	*LIDGETT, Tommy*	*LP 66*
Huttoft	22, 71	*Life and Laughter in Lincolnshire*	40
		Lincoln, A dissertation on the Mint in	88
I Gotta Horse	119	Lincoln, Carholme	45, 118
Ikanhoe	13	Lincoln Castle	79, 114
Imp Youth Theatre	90	Lincoln Cathedral	7, 8, 12, 31, 59, 104, 108,
In Laudem Sancti Hugoniensis	111		110, 123, 133, 157, 163
INGELOW, Jean	*LP 58, LW 47*	Lincoln Cathedral Choir School	12
INGRAM, Herbert	*LP 58*	Lincoln Cathedral Company of Ringers	163
Isle of Axholme	131, 156	*Lincoln Cathedral, Half-an-Hour at*	60
		Lincoln Cathedral, Ringers Chapel	163
JACKLIN, Tony	**81**	Lincoln Christ's Hospital School	2, 53, 70, 77
JAMES, George W.	**82**	Lincoln, City School	7
James, Revd E. Bankes	84	Lincoln Civic Trust	9
JAMES, Revd Henry Law	**83**	Lincoln : Dernstall House	9
Jekyll, Gertrude	124	Lincoln : Ellis Mill	9
JENNINGS, Elizabeth	**86**	Lincoln Liberal Association	26
John, Elton	144	Lincoln Musical Society	111, 160
Johnson, Amy	70	Lincoln Prison	34, 114

Lincoln Record Society	72	**LUNN, Henry S.**	**101**
Lincoln Repertory Company	78	Mablethorpe	23, 43, 47, 70
Lincoln School	2, 9, 53, 70, 77	Mackay, Peter	117
Lincoln, Sincil Bank School	97	**MACKINDER, Halford J.**	**103**
Lincoln : St Mary's Guildhall	9	**MACKWORTH, Dean John**	**104**
LINCOLN, Tom a'	***LP 66***	**MAGEE, John G.**	**106**
Lincoln : Usher Gallery	8, 160	Maidenwell Manor	156
Lincolnshire Aero Club	70	***MAJOR, Ethel Lillie***	***LW 54***
Lincolnshire (Arthur Mee)	8	***MAJOR, Kathleen***	***LW 55***
Lincolnshire and the Fens	10	***MAKINS, Edward***	***LP 70***
Lincolnshire Artists' Society	160	**MALONEY, Michael**	**107**
Lincolnshire Church, A	22	Manby	51
Lincolnshire Church Notes	72	***MANNYNG, Robert***	***LP 71***
Lincolnshire Churches Revisited	151	Mareham on the Hill	23
Lincolnshire Drawing Club	160	Market Rasen	7, 17, 49, 57, 98, 120, 145
Lincolnshire Handicap	118	***MARRINER, Sir Neville***	***LP 71***
Lincolnshire, History of	8, 72	**MARSHALL, Dr Philip**	**110**
Lincolnshire History. & Archaeology, Society for	8, 45, 97, 135	***MARSHALL, William***	***LP 72***
Lincolnshire Houses	151	Marston	150
Lincolnshire Lawn Tennis Association	52	***MARWOOD, William,***	***LP 72***
Lincolnshire Life	40, 48	**MAYS, Raymond**	**112**
Lincolnshire Life Museum	7, 9, 40	**MERRYWEATHER, John**	**114**
Lincolnshire Local History Society	8, 97	***MILNER, Mary Ann***	***LW 57***
Lincolnshire Methodist History Society	97	**MITCHELL, Austin V. M. P.**	**115**
Lincolnshire Naturalist	138	**MONOLULU. Ras, Prince**	**117**
Lincolnshire Naturalists Trust	8, 70, 137	***MONSON, Sir William***	***LP 73***
Lincolnshire Naturalists Union	8, 64, 69, 138	Moore, Revd Charles	158
Lincolnshire Notes and Queries	97	*Morse, Inspector*	36
Lincolnshire Old Churches Trust	140, 151	***MORYSON, Fynes***	***LP 73***
Lincolnshire Portraits Survey	97	Mossman Monks	119
Lincolnshire Red Data Book	138	**MOSSMAN, Revd Thomas W.**	**119**
Lincolnshire Regiment	39, 148	***MURRAY, Flora***	***LW 58***
Lincolnshire Rising	15, 80	Museum of Lincolnshire Life	7, 9, 40
Lincolnshire Volunteers	159	Musson, Arthur	62
Lincolnshire Wildlife Trust	137		
Lincolnshire Yeomanry	40	Naturalists Union, Lincolnshire	64, 69, 138
Lindsey Loop	31	*Nature in Lincolnshire*	138
Lindsey Rural Players	17	*Nature Reserves in Lincolnshire*	138
LINLEY, Thomas, Jnr.	***LP 68***	Nettleham	69
Little Cotes	72	***NEWTON, Sir Isaac***	***LP 74***
Little Ponton	156	Normanby	34
Locksley Hall, North Somercotes	5	North Kesteven School	90
LOGSDAIL, William	***LP 68***	North Somercotes	6
London Underground Electric Railways	127	**NOTTINGHAM, Max**	**120**
Lost Lincolnshire Country Houses	73	O'Connor, Father (Father Brown)	5
Louth	22, 43, 51, 63, 80, 89, 93, 132, 156	Old Clee	44
Louth Naturalist, Antiquarian etc. Society	63	*Old Mother Riley*	99
LUCAN, Arthur	**99**	***OTTER, Tommy***	***LP 75***
Ludford Magna	2	***OWEN, Dr Dorothy***	***LW 60***

Owen, Sir Alfred	113
Owmby-by-Spital	144
PADLEY, James S.	**121**
PAGE, Russell	**123**
PAINE, Thomas	*LP 76*, 148
Panton	119
PARSONS, Nicholas	**125**
Pavilion Opera	139
PEACOCK Mabel	*LW 62*
PEASGOOD Julie	*LW 64*
PICCAVER, Alfred	*LP 77*
PICK, Frank	**127**
Piper, John	139
Piper, Peter	119
PITMAN, Sir Isaac	**128**
Plater, Alan	1
Plogsland Round Lincoln	31
PLOWRIGHT, Joan	*LW 66*
POLLARD, Su	*LW 68*
Potterhanworth	112
POUCHER, William A.	**129**
PROCTER, Norma	*LW 70*
PRYME, Abraham de la	**131**
RACE, Steve	*LP 77*
Radio Lincolnshire	22, 121
Raithby	97
Ranby	119
Rawding, Charles	85
Raymond Mays of Bourne	114
Richard II	7, 14, 134
Richard III	15
Richardson, Rupert	85
Richmond, Sir Ian	8
ROBERTS, Lucy	*LW 73*
ROBERTS, Nesta	**131**
ROBERTSON, Sir William	*LP 78*
ROBINSON, Frederick	*LP 80*
Roman Lincoln	10
Roman Lincoln	8
Roman Lincolnshire	8
Romance of Lincoln Cathedral, The	60
Ross, John Hume	95
Rowston Manor	147
Royal Navy in Lincolnshire	27
RUDKIN Ethel	*LW 75*
RUSTON, Joseph	*LP 80*
Ruston's Engineering Works	9
SARGENT, Sir Malcolm	*LP 8*, 12, 152
Saxilby	39
Scales, Prunella	90
Scarttho	94
Scopwick	106
Scotter	51
Scunthorpe	81, 121
Seaborne Observers	65
Sedgebrook	98
Seven Pillars of Wisdom	95
Shackleton, Sir Ernest	28
Shankland, Bill	81
Shaw, Thomas Edward	95
SHEPPEY, Dean John	**133**
Shodfriars Hall, Boston	99
Shorthand, Pitman's	128
Sibsey	99
SIBTHORP, Charles W.	*LP 82*
Sigh for a Merlin	71
Sincil Bank School, Lincoln	97
Skegness	21, 36, 67, 70, 122
Skegness and East Lincolnshire Aero Club	70
Skillington	76
SKINNER, Dr Joyce	*LW 77*
Skirbeck	32, 149
Sleaford	10, 19, 80, 96
Sloothby	34, 98
SMART, Hawley	**134**
SMITH, A. E. (Ted)	**137**
SMITH, Edith	**135**
SMITH, Captain John	*LP 83*
Society for Lincolnshire History and Archaeology	8, 45, 97, 135
South Kelsey	57
South Ormsby	62
Spalding	38, 88, 127
Spilsby	27, 34
Spiritual Railway, The	112
Spital Chantry Trust	7
Spital in the Street	7
Stamford	36, 62, 84, 88, 152
Stewart, Jackie	113
STOCKDALE, Freddie	**139**
STOKES Doris	*LW 79*
STUKELEY, Dr William	*LP 84*, 88
SULLY, Thomas	**140**
Surfleet	83
Sutton St Mary	51
SUTTON, Sir John D.	**141**
SUTTON, Thomas	**143**

Swarby	19, 145
SWIFT Sarah	*LP 85, LW 81*
SWYNFORD Katherine	*LP 86, LW 82*
Tathwell	45, 122
Tattershall Castle	15, 73, 89, 140
TAUPIN, Bernie	**144**
TAVERNER, John	*LP 87*
Taylor, Frank	127
Tealby	49, 147
Temple Belwood	73
Temple Bruer	122
Tennyson Research Centre	9
Tennyson Society	9, 97
TENNYSON, Alfred	*LP 87*, 6
THATCHER Margaret	*LP 89, LW 83*, 37
The Link	48
This England	48
THISTLEWOOD, Arthur	**148**
THOMPSON, Pishey	**149**
THORNDIKE, Sybil	*LP 90, LW 85*, 155
THOROLD, Revd Henry	**150**
Thorpe Tilney	139
TIPPETT, Sir Michael	**152**
TODD, Richard	**153**
Torrington, West and East	24, 119
Torry, Robinson	49
TOWLE, Arthur	**99**
TRITTON, Sir William	*LP 91*
Trusville Holiday Estate	70
Tupholme	122, 148
TURPIN, Dick	*LP 91*
TWIGG, John	*LP 92*
Ulceby	129
Ulceby Cross	34
Usher Gallery, Lincoln	8, 160
USHER, James W.	*LP 96*
VARAH, Rev Dr Chad	*LP 96*
VARLEY, Joan (Franklin)	*LW 86*
VERMUYDEN, Cornelius	**156**
Viking Way	31
Villiers, Amherst	113
Waddington	145
Wainfleet	93
WAKE, Hereward the	*LP 98*
WAKEFORD, Archdeacon John	**157**
Walcot	11, 52
WAND, Bishop John W. C.	**158**
WARRENER, William	**159**
WATKINS, William	*LP 98*
Watson, James	148
WAYNFLETE, Bishop William	*LP 99*
WEBSTER, Saint Augustine	*LP 99*
Well	24, 33
Wellingore	106
Welton	90, 97
WESLEY, Charles	*LP 100*
WESLEY, John	*LP 101*
WESLEY, Susanna	*LW 88*
West, Benjamin	140
West, Timothy	90
Whaplode Drove	51, 85
When I was Tealby Abbey	147
Whiteley, Richard	116
WHITGIFT, Bishop John	*LP 103*
WHITTLE, Sir Frank	**160**
Whitwell, Ben	8
Wickenby	17
Willingham	68
WILLIS, Dr Francis	*LP 103*
Willoughby	98, 137
WILLOUGHBY, Katherine	*LW 90*
WILSON, Catherine	*LW 92*
WILSON, Catherine Mary	*LW 94*
WILSON, Edward	*LP 105*
Wilson, Miss Florence	24
WINN, Henry	*LP 106*
WINT, Peter de	*LP 107*
Wintringham	162
WINTRINGHAM, Margaret	*LP108. LW 96*
Wood Enderby	93
Woodhall Spa	1
WORDSWORTH, Elizabeth	*LW 97*
WORTH, Charles F.	**161**
Wragby	39, 121, 149
Wyberton	93
WYMARK, Patrick	**162**
Yarborough, Earls of	4
Yates, Jack	22
YORKE, James	**163**
Ziegler, Anne	12

List of Subscribers

The Editor and Publisher of this book would like to thank those subscribers listed below, and also all those who did not with their names to be recorded, for supporting and encouraging the publication of this book.

Mrs Doreen Applewhite, Candlesby
Arthur Arbon, North Hykeham

Elizabeth Barrick, North Hykeham
Ifor Barton, Grasby
Maple Bedford, Louth
J. W. Belsham, Holbeach
Mrs Eleanor Bennett, Louth
Dean Bird, Lincoln
Sibthorpe Libry, Bishop Grossteste Coll, Lincoln
Penelope Bray, Southwold, Suffolk
D and O Brewster, Horncastle
Mrs Audrey Broome, Brigg
Margaret Brown, Lincoln
Peter Brown, Lincoln
Dave Burkitt, Nettleham

Rodney and Janet Callow, Lincoln
Mrs Audrey Clarke, Lincoln
Lieutenant E. C. Coleman, RN Bishop Norton
Major (retd) Brett Collier, Lincoln
Sir Patrick Cormack, FSA, MP
P. M. Criddle, Alford
Professor Alex Cullen, Hemel Hempstead

Mrs Jill Daniels, Waddington
Tim and Angela Devlin, Staplehurst, Kent
Colin Dexter, OBE, Oxford
Margaret Dickinson, Lincolnshire Author
Miss Margaret Diggle, Ringmer, Sussex
Jean Ducker, Langworth
Lt Col. J. L. M. Dymoke, MBE, DL.

Roy Faiers, Cheltenham
Peter Fairweather, Lincoln

Clixby Fitzwilliams, Healing
Air Cdre (rtd) Colin Foale, Cambridge
John Foster, Lincoln
David Freeman, Lincoln
John French, Barton-upon-Humber
Denis A. Frith, Grantham

Toy Gadd, Lincoln
Prince Yuri Galitzine, Stamford
Len Gaunt, Swinderby
Joan Goodrich, Lincoln

Gordon C. Hall, Grimsby
C. J. Hodgson, Lincoln
Mr and Mrs F. Holloway, Lincoln
John V. Hurt, Co. Kildare

K. D. Johnson, Lincoln

Jonathan Kerrigan, Bristol
Mike and Jean Kerrigan, Tathwell
Pat and Stan Kerrigan, Burton
Nigel and Sue Kirkman, Malmesbury
C. Bryan Kitson, Epworth.
Clifford and Eileen Knowles, Navenby

Mrs R. J. Learwood-Griffiths, Sutterton.
Horace Liberty, Lincoln
Lincolnshire County Library Service
Louth Naturalists', Antiquarian and Literary Society

Dr Philip Marshall, Potterhanworth
Anne and Michael Matsell, Grantham
M. G. Medcalf, Alford

Chris Medley, Newton-on-Trent
Austin Mitchell, MP, Grimsby
Miss F. A. R. Murray, O. B. E. Lincoln
Jim Murray, Tealby

Rex Needle, Bourne
Peter Noon, Scamblesby
Max Nottingham, Lincoln

Elizabeth O'Neill, Grimsby

E. R. Parker, Lincoln
Roger Parsons, New York, Lincoln
Professor M. E. Phipps, Brinkhill
David and Shervie Price, Harrington

Richard Ratcliffe, Clacton on Sea
Ken Redmore, Nettleham
Ellen and Michael Richardson, East Keal
David Robinson, OBE, Louth
Eileen Robson, Newark
Jill Rundle, Alford
Peter Rushton, Hemswell

Peter Sandberg, Ulceby
Mr and Mrs Philip Scorer, Lincoln

Scunthorpe Central Library
Mrs M Simpson, Alford
Joyce Skinner, CBE, Lincoln
Richard and Rachel Smith, Calne
Spalding Gentlemen's Society
Councillor W. J. Speechley CBE, Crowland
David Stocker, Oxford
Michael and Betty Stracey, Lincoln
Sir John and Lady A. F. Sutton, Stretton

Tony Taupin, Skegness
Michael Thomas, Aby near Alford
Frances Thompson, Scunthorpe
Gordon B. Thornton, Lincoln
Ruth Tinley, Lincoln
Richard Todd, Little Ponton
J. L. Tuxworth, Spilsby

Des Underwood, Swinderby
University of Nottingham Library

J. Ward, East Keal
Councillor Graham Wheat, Grantham
Pearl Wheatley, North Greetwell
Rt Hon Lady Willoughby de Eresby,
    Grimsthorpe Castle

"...Violence? I'll give 'em violence! I'll blow out Elton's candle if he steps in here!"
● See story on back page.

The above cartoon was published in the *Market Rasen Mail* dated 20 December 2000 and the article referred to was about a BBC documentary entitled *Saturday Night's All Right for Fighting*. This is the title of one of Bernie Taupin's songs based on his experiences growing up in Lincolnshire and the rivalry between the teenagers of Market Rasen and Caistor. The cartoon depicts the Aston Arms in Market Rasen as it was in the early 1970s.

I am grateful to the *Market Rasen Mail* and 'Runner's Eye' for permission to publish the cartoon.

See page 144.